Singing
the Vietnam
Blues

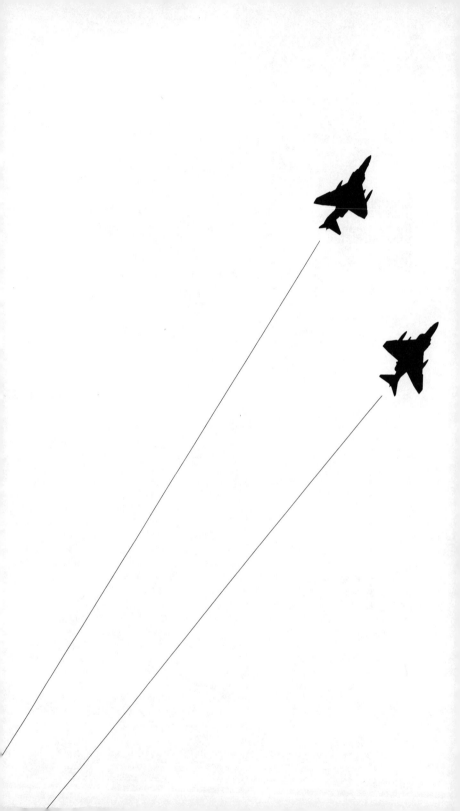

Singing the Vietnam Blues

SONGS
OF THE
AIR FORCE
IN
SOUTHEAST
ASIA

By Joseph F. Tuso

TEXAS A&M UNIVERSITY PRESS
COLLEGE STATION

Library of Congress Cataloging-in-Publication Data

Tuso, Joseph F.
      Singing the Vietnam blues : songs of the Air Force
in Southeast Asia / by Joseph F. Tuso. – 1st ed.
         p. cm. – (Texas A&M University military his-
tory series ; no. 19)
      Includes bibliographical references.
      ISBN 0-89096-383-5 (alk. paper)
      ISBN 0-89096-455-6 (pbk. : alk. paper)
      1. Vietnamese Conflict, 1961–1975–Poetry.   2. United
States. Air Force–Songs and music–Texts.   3. Air pilots,
Military–United States–Songs and music–Texts.   4. Air
pilots' writings, American–Vietnam.   5. Songs, English–
United States–Texts.   6. American poetry–20th century.
I. Title.   II. Series: Texas A&M University military history
series : 19.
PS595.V5T87 1990
782.42'164'1599–dc20   89-20529
                                                   CIP

Paperback cover art from a photo provided courtesy of
  Don Kilfoyle

To Neil Beer,
George Keegan,
and John Shaud,
who in war and peace
taught me
the music of flight

_____

Contents

Preface *page* xi

Overture 3

The Songs

Air Force Lament	21	B-52 Takeoff	54
Armed Recce	24	Bien Hoa Lullaby	54
The Ballad of Bernie		Blowing in the Wind	55
Fisher	26	Blue Four	56
The Ballad of Heinz E.		Bronco Song	59
Coordes	27	Brown Anchor	60
The Ballad of Jeb Stewart	29	The Bunker Song	62
The Ballad of Machete Two	33	Call Out the Reserves	63
The Ballad of Robin Olds	35	Charlie Went A-Running	64
The Ballad of the C-130	37	Chocolate-covered	
The Ballad of the Green		Napalm	65
Brassiere	38	Cloudy Night, No	
The Ballad of the PIO	39	Moonlight	67
Banana Valley	42	Come and Join the Air	
Bat Song	44	Force	68
Battle Hymn of the 85-mm		Cruising over Hanoi	70
Gunner	45	Dashing through the Sky	71
Battle Hymn of the Ranch		Dingbat	72
Hands	46	Don't Send Me to Hanoi	73
Battle Hymn of the Red		Down the Lazy Valley	74
River Rats	46	Downtown I	75
The Battle of Doumer		Downtown II	77
Bridge	48	Early Abort	78
The Battle of 18.23	50	Escorting a Spectre	80
Bear of the Sky	51	F-4 Serenade	81
Beside a Laotian Waterfall	52	Fighter Pilots	82

Fighter Pilot's Christmas 84
F-105 Alma Mater 85
GIB Named Richard 86
GIB's Lament 89
Hallelujah I 91
Hallelujah II 92
Hallelujah III 96
Hallelujah IV 97
Hello, Cam Ranh Tower 99
Here's to Old Bien Hoa 101
The Ho Chi Minh Trail 102
I 'Druther Be an F-4 Jock 103
I Fly the Line 104
If You Fly 106
I'm a Young Ranch Hand 107
In-Flight Refueling 108
The Inventory 109
I've Been Everywhere 111
I Wanted Wings 114
Joy to the World 117
Just Give Me Operations 117
King of the Trail 119
Let's Get Away with It All 120
Little Town Up North 122
MiG-19 123
The MiG-21 124
Mu Gia Pass 127
My Darling F-4 127
My Jolly Green 128
Napalm 129
Never Fly in the A Shau on Sunday 131
The New DCO 132
Night on the Town 133
Night Owls 134
Nimrod 135
Normandy's Sand 136
Northward Ho 137
Number One Clismas Song 137
Ode to a Great Fuckin' SAR Effort 139
Old 97, the O-1E 141
Old Smoky 143

Old Weird Harold 144
O Little Town of Ho Chi Minh 146
One Hundred Missions 147
One Hundred Sixty VC in the Open 148
On Top of Old Thud Ridge 149
On Top of the Pop Up 151
Our Leaders 152
The Panther Pack Is Prowling 154
Parties, Banquets, and Balls 155
The Phu Cat Alert Pad 156
Phu Cat Star 157
Pop Goes the Weasel 158
Puff 159
Puff, the Magic Dragon 160
Pull the Boom from the Gashole 162
Put Your Beeper on the Air 163
The Red River Valley 165
Republic's Ultra Hog 166
Saigon City 167
Sammy Hall 168
Shootin' Guns and Droppin' Bombs 170
Sittin' in the Cab of My Truck 171
Sixteen Tons 172
Skoshi Tiger 173
So Long, John 176
Song of the Wolf Pack 177
Son of Satan's Angels 179
Spray On, Spray on Harvest Rice 181
Spray the Town 182
Springtime on the Red River 182
Strafe the Town 183
Super Constellation 186
Tales That I Can Tell 189
Tay Ninh Mountain 190

Tchepone   191
The Thanh Hoa Bridge I   194
The Thanh Hoa Bridge II   197
The 388th   200
The 390th TFW Song   201
Thud Drivers in the Sky   202
The Thud Driver's Theme   203
Thud Pilot   204
Trees   205
Twelve Days in Ranch
    Hand   207
Twelve Days of Combat   208
Twelve Days of Tet   208
Uncle's Nephews   209
Up in That Valley   210
The VC Truck Driver's
    Blues   211
Waltzing Matilda   212
Wand'rin' Man   214

Way Down South in the
    Land of Rice   214
The Weasel Song   215
We've Been Working on
    the Railroad   218
Where Have All the
    Flowers Gone?   219
Where Have All the Old
    Heads Gone?   221
Whispering Death   222
Wild Weasel   224
Will the MiGs Come Out
    to Play?   226
Will There Be a Tomorrow?   227
Wingman's Lament   228
Wolf Pack's Houseboy   230
Yankee Air Pirate   233
The Yellow Rose of Hanoi   235
A ZPU Gunner   236

Final Movement   239
Glossary   243
Sources and References   267

Preface

The 148 songs in this volume were written or sung by American Air Force combat flyers during the war in Vietnam. These, of course, were not the only songs they sang, but I have generally limited the selections to those with subject matter directly related to that war. My own song, "Wand'rin' Man," was actually the first song in this collection, and I also include "Waltzing Matilda" out of respect for our allies the Australian fighter pilots, with whom I was stationed in Thailand in 1968.

I have edited the songs from wing and squadron songbooks, from songsheets, and from tapes, some of them made third and fourth hand. Thirty-three of the songs appeared in my Indiana University *Folklore Forum* monograph (1971), and others also appear in C. W. ("Bill") Getz's *The Wild Blue Yonder* (1981) where I could compare them with my own versions; a number of them appear in print here for the first time.

The authors are unknown, except for the 25 songs by Dick Jonas, who wrote many original lyrics and melodies, the three songs by Toby Hughes, and "Wand'rin' Man." Most of the songs apply original lyrics to already established melodies; for example, "Wild Weasel" is sung to the tune of "Sweet Betsy from Pike." These known melodies are given below the song titles. In those cases where no known melody appears, the song either has its own, proper melody, or I have been unable to ascertain it.

To aid the reader, I have included a glossary of more than 450 terms toward the end of the book for ready reference. I did not wish to overburden the songs with footnotes, and a number of the terms appear in several songs. The glossary contains much of the vocabulary of the U.S. air war in Vietnam and is, I hope, of some value and interest in itself. I would appreciate any comments from readers regarding any of the glossary entries.

Some of the songs contain profanity, and I pondered over deleting or disguising it when it appeared. I finally decided to be as faithful to the lyrics as possible—the included words and phrases were a natural part of the combat vocabulary, and such words spoken without malice by men who faced death cleanly every day seemed more a blessing than a curse. A reader who finds a song offensive may simply turn to another one.

I am grateful to John Carroll, Bill Craig, Lydia Fish, Hank Fordham, John Grathwol, Bud Hesterum, Alvin McLean, Paul Orf, Garry Peters, and others who provided me with songsheets, song-books, or tapes of Air Force songs from the war in Vietnam. My special thanks go to Dick Jonas, accomplished fighter pilot and songwriter, for the use of 25 of his songs as well as his valuable written comments on them. I appreciate the encouragement of C. W. ("Bill") Getz and the reference copy of his own excellent published collection *The Wild Blue Yonder*, the kindness of Bernard R. Marsh in lending me his rare reference copy of William Wallrich's *Air Force Airs: Songs and Ballads of the United States Air Force, World War I through Korea*, as well as Toby Hughes's permission to use his three fine songs. For suggestions as I prepared the glossary, I thank Dave Carson, Tony Dater, Jim Gaston, and John Pratt, former colleagues of mine at the U.S. Air Force Academy, all of whom flew combat in Vietnam; Gen. John Shaud; the U.S. Air Force Academy Cartographic Section of the Division of Geography; and the staff of the Academy library.

I owe a great deal to Brig. Gen. Jesse C. Gatlin, Jr., former head of the Department of English, U.S. Air Force Academy, and to Roy Troutt and Floyd Coppedge, president and academic vice-president, respectively, of the University of Science and Arts of Oklahoma (USAO), who encouraged me in this project and provided me much of the time needed to complete it. A USAO research grant enabled me to profit from the superb services of Joyce English in word processing and of Susan Griebel in proofing and correcting copy.

My wife Jean was loving and understanding, as always, during the many hours of separation as I labored in my study, and she was patient while I rambled on about the war in Vietnam as

I relived my part in it numerous times, my memory jogged as I read, reread, wrote, revised, and edited.

But most of all I must thank the American combat flyer—whether now home with his loved ones or missing or dead—for both inspiring and writing the songs in this collection.

Singing
the Vietnam
Blues

Overture

On a muggy day in May, 1968, I emerged from the womb of a laboring C-130 transport plane into the brilliance of sun-soaked Ubon Air Base, Thailand, home of the Wolf Pack, the U.S. Air Force's 8th Tactical Fighter Wing. A welcoming slap on the back by a friendly lieutenant colonel brought life to my cramped limbs. I had been preparing for this moment in one way or another for thirteen years. Very soon the Air Force would discover whether it would get its money's worth, and I would know whether I could "hack it." It was my first day in the combat zone.

Like a man sinking in murky waters, I relived my life as an Air Force officer and navigator in the brief moments it took to ride from the ramp to my new squadron, the 435th. Surrounded by sleek if droop-snooted F-4 Phantoms crouching in the seemingly endless revetments, I tingled with that same feeling of pride and awe I had felt ten years before, when, as a newly assigned navigator on the ramp at SAC's Davis-Monthan Air Force Base in Arizona, I had first passed in review before some forty critical B-47s.

I am of the Jack Armstrong generation, the latter days of the big bands, the time of Baby Snooks, the B-19, and corduroy pants in high school. I can remember ice trucks, an apolitical Shirley Temple, Wendell Willkie buttons, and muzzle flashes from the deck guns of Japanese submarines, viewed from the trembling rooftop of my home in a Los Angeles smaller and younger by more than 40 years.

In 1955 I left a Catholic seminary, forsaking my plans for the

Two F-105s are led on a bombing mission over North Vietnam by a radar-equipped F-100.
U.S. Air Force photograph

priesthood because of my desire for a wife and family. I had no thoughts then of "laughter-silvered wings." I had done well in a four-year college course geared to produce teacher-priests. I still wanted to be a teacher, so I chose an alternate but still idealistic career—the military. My hope was to teach English one day at the then-fledgling U.S. Air Force Academy.

Youthfully taking my drive and abilities for granted, I thought I needed but one thing to win an academy teaching slot—a commission as a Regular officer. After successfully passing the Aviation Cadet Qualification Tests, I was told I could be a pilot, but I would have to wait a year for entry into pilot training. If I wanted, however, I could leave for Lackland Air Force Base, Texas, and subsequent navigation training almost at once. I didn't know for certain what a navigator was, but I knew he was an officer. That was enough for me.

Upon graduating from the navigator-bombardier course at Mather Air Force Base in California, I had three choices: Strategic Air Command B-47 bombers or KC-97 tankers or Air Defense Command's Radar Observer School and F-89s. The prospect of flying in a fast fighter like the F-89 first excited me, but a senior navigator who had taken me under his wing told me, "Joe, if you can learn to navigate the B-47, you can navigate any bird in the Air Force." Since duty in the Strategic Air Command seemed also my best bet for an eventual Regular commission, I chose a B-47 assignment with the 303rd Bomb Wing at Tucson, Arizona.

In those days it took about two years for a SAC crew member to be accepted, to prove himself. Often I wondered whether I would ever make it. Many radar-simulated bomb drops and many navigation training missions later, it happened. I awoke one morning and realized I was a professional SAC navigator, one who could be counted on to pull long hours of alert, help his crew fulfill demanding training requirements, and help his wing successfully "grease through" Operational Readiness Inspections. SAC was my career's greenhouse. The hours were long, the flights rear-numbing, the pressures great, but I got the professional polish I needed. In SAC the navigator was a marketable commodity, for the spot promotions of entire crews and the fate of every bomber wing hinged on his ability to navigate and bomb. And so my decision to go to Tucson and B-47s had been a good one. My more than 1,000 hours of flying time in

SAC did help earn me a Regular commission, and in Tucson I also met and married my wonderful wife, Jean.

In 1962 I applied for duty at the U.S. Air Force Academy, and the Air Force apparently felt I was worth the investment of thousands of dollars more and two years of higher education, so I was selected to enter graduate school at the University of Arizona. After completing my master's degree in the summer of 1964, I reported for duty at the U.S. Air Force Academy.

I enjoyed teaching English and flying navigation training missions with the cadets even more than I had thought I would. Early in my first year there my department head, Col. Pete Moody, called me into his office and asked me if I would like to return to the University of Arizona in 1965–66 to finish my doctorate. I leapt at the chance. After completing my degree, then, I returned to the academy's English department in July, 1966, ready to settle in for three or four years of uninterrupted teaching. But that was not to be.

The superintendent who commands the U.S. Air Force Academy is usually a two- or three-star general. Directly under him are two one-star generals, the Dean of the Faculty and the Commandant of Cadets. Cadets spend most of their waking hours either with the dean's faculty members or under the supervision of military training officers, called Air Officers Commanding, or AOCs. One AOC is in charge of each cadet squadron. AOCs are selected for academy duty on the basis of their fine military records and potential, and most of them are pilots. They normally stayed at the academy for only two or three years, while faculty stayed for four or five. AOCs worked very long hours, often from 6:00 A.M. to 10 or 11 P.M. Faculty members were required to meet their classes, attend any necessary meetings, and perform certain other military duties but were not required to be in their offices from 7:30 to 4:30 like most Air Force personnel. If at home or in the library, they were expected to be grading papers, preparing classes, or perhaps doing some research. By comparison, the faculty seemed to have a rather "cushy" job, and the AOCs knew it. There was a good deal of rivalry and both good-natured and not so good-natured gibing between the two groups. In fact, the AOCs used to refer to us as faculty pukes.

When I returned to the academy from Arizona in 1966, I soon noticed that many of the AOCs were suddenly highly decorated with combat ribbons and other awards. Many had Air

Medals, Distinguished Flying Crosses, and Bronze Stars. They had served combat tours in Southeast Asia. Soon it became easier to distinguish AOCs from the faculty—the AOCs looked like be-medaled Hollywood generals, the faculty like city bus drivers in plain blue uniforms. Since faculty members had fixed tours of four or five years, some people began to regard faculty status as a hideout from the war.

Beginning in the early 1960s and increasingly through 1967, our country began to get more and more involved in Vietnam, but I had been oblivious to much of what was going on. My concentration had been on the poems of T. S. Eliot, Indo-European word roots, writing a doctoral dissertation, and other such fascinating subjects. I hardly knew there was a war on, much less that I would personally soon be playing a part in it.

Because of many factors, in the spring of 1967 the U.S. Air Force Academy Dean of Faculty had a serious meeting with all of his department heads. He told them of the need for the faculty to get involved in the war so they would be better role models for the cadets. He suggested that each department head should go back to his office, look over his roster of assigned personnel, and give him the names of as many "volunteers" as possible. Responding to what they took to be a directive, a number of heads simply identified faculty whose tours were up the following June. My department head, however, a West Point graduate and a real patriot, took the dean at his word and "volunteered" four or five of his faculty, most of whom still had three or four years remaining on their academy faculty tours. I was one of them.

When I got the news, I was flabbergasted. Here I had worked so very hard for so many years to become a good teacher, and now all this effort was being thrown aside to send me off to a silly war in some obscure country. And I had a wife and five young children, ages 18 months to 8 years. After I stopped feeling sorry for myself and the first shock of my predicament had begun to subside, I began to think of some larger issues. The wisdom of that war and its morality were being hotly debated, and national figures whom I admired were on both sides of the issue.

Up to that point there had been little protest within the Air Force about Vietnam. However, as more and more Air Force personnel were being sent to Southeast Asia, there were some signs of resistance. One Air Force Academy faculty officer, a pilot, refused to go on moral grounds. I also heard a rumor through the academy grapevine that one of our graduates, now an officer, had gotten into trouble at Hickam Air Force Base, Hawaii, for passing out antiwar leaflets during a function at the Officers' Club. Doubtless there had been more incidents, but I knew the Air Force had ways of keeping such things quiet. And then during a bull session at the academy Officers' Club one night, another officer whom I respected, a history professor, said that the war in Vietnam was primarily a nationalistic attempt at reunifying the country rather than a real Communist threat, and that, yes, we should be in it—but on Ho Chi Minh's side!

The more I heard, the more confused I got. Finally I asked another history professor friend to suggest some books I could read, and I soon began studying the history and politics in Vietnam from the 1920s through 1967. I also read every newspaper, *Time*, and *Newsweek* I could lay my hands on and spent hours in front of the TV watching important Americans debate the war. I knew I had only three choices: I could go, I could refuse to go, or I could leave the country as so many others were starting to do. But I didn't want to base my decision on cowardice—if I refused to go or took my family to Canada, I wanted it to be for moral reasons, not rationalizations. I was told to report to Fighter Weapons School at Nellis Air Force Base, Nevada, on January 17, 1968, to begin training in the F-4 Phantom.

As my reporting day grew nearer, I spent many sleepless nights, sometimes lying awake in bed, sometimes pacing the floor, and once or twice getting out my roadmaps and studying the best highways to Canada. All I had to do was take some Christmas leave, hitch up our travel trailer to our station wagon, load up my wife and kids, and head north. During this time my wife, Jean, and I shared our thoughts together, but both knew there were other, more horrible thoughts neither of us could share. I also prayed a lot.

In late November or early December I had read and thought enough, and I reached a decision. Despite my best efforts, I was unable to determine to my own satisfaction whether the war was moral or not. Nor could I determine whether the war and our policy in Southeast Asia were wise. What was *not* in doubt, however, was my duty to honor the oath I had taken as a commissioned officer to defend my country from all enemies, whether foreign or domestic. Also as part of that oath I had promised to obey the lawful orders of my superiors, and in this case, I was not convinced that the orders were unlawful. I thus reported as ordered to Nellis Air Force Base on January 17, 1968, determined to learn all I could about combat flying so I could fulfill my oath and return safely to Jean and my children. Five of us went through F-4 training at Nellis together from January through April 1968; two of the five—John Bush and Bill Justice—were later killed in the air war over Southeast Asia.

As the blue pickup pulled in front of Ubon's 435th Tactical Fighter Squadron, I felt like a young lieutenant again, despite the gold major's leaves on my shoulders. I was signed in, processed, hustled through ground school, and was off on my first combat mission. My aircraft commander, or AC, George Wooddy, was the quietest, most gentlemanly officer you'd ever hope to meet—on the ground. But in the air he yelled, cursed, and screamed me through two of my most memorable early combat missions over North Vietnam.

On that first mission we were going after 37-mm guns near Xuan Son, about 40 miles north of the DMZ. No sooner was the landing gear up after takeoff than I expected bullets to rip through the canopy. I was so green I didn't know that we had to cross the Mekong River before we were even eligible for combat pay. My throat was dry, my hands were sweating, and my mind was in a fog. Far away I heard a cacophony of radio calls—my headset went wild with disjointed voices. One of them was howling at me to switch our radio to tanker frequency, then later to Control.

We were cleared to hit our primary target, but I was still 15 minutes behind what was going on. Through the low, scattered clouds I saw North Vietnam for the first time, a bomb-cratered strip of brown, stretching from left to right in front of us with an incongruously beautiful blue gulf just beyond.

The AC yelled for me to call out his weapons settings. As I glanced down at my checklist, I saw a dozen chasms belching orange flames at us from the target area below. So those were 37-mm guns. "Damn it, finish the checklist!" the AC yelled. The next thing I knew, we were screaming down, down, in a 45-degree dive at 450 knots. I had done this maneuver on the gunnery range in the States, but somehow this was just not the same. I felt like

Maj. Joe Tuso, July, 1968

this was a bad dream, and the flak bursting all around us kept distracting me from the dream's main action in which I was supposed to be playing a part.

"Tuso, what the hell's our altitude?" The altimeter was spinning so wildly I could hardly keep track of it. My eyes darted from it to the airspeed indicator to the dive angle. I said something or other. Bombs away!

We made two more passes. Speed . . . blurred landscape . . . flak . . . dive . . . release . . . then the pressure of four or five Gs as we jinked precisely but violently left and right to spoil the gunners' tracking as we pulled off. I think we knocked out two guns on the last two passes. I don't remember. What I do remember is the voice of the AC screaming and pushing from takeoff to landing. After we landed, all George said was, "Pretty good mission."

My resentment of the first mission turned to anger, then to a desire to excel at my job in order to stop the AC's yelling. It worked. The better I performed, the more the AC let up on me. With his help I had learned to conquer the enemy in our cockpit—my own inexperience and fear—a prerequisite to coping with the hostile forces below. I was grateful throughout my combat tour, and still am, for what I learned from my first combat AC, George Wooddy, and for the emphatic way in which he taught me.

Many fighter pilots prefer to fly alone in a single-seat aircraft; others don't mind flying with another pilot; but some are hesitant about flying with a navigator, especially in combat, when one man's life often depends upon the actions of the other. When I arrived at Ubon, a question still hung in the air—would navigators "hack it" in the F-4's backseat? The navigators themselves never had any such question. Old pros like Bobby G. Smith and "Hesh" Altman blazed the way for those of us who came later. When I left Ubon in May of 1969, young navigators who would unquestionably hack it were pouring into Ubon with all the vigor and enthusiasm of the Oklahoma offense.

Some of the fighter pilots, however, had to be convinced before they put out the welcome mat. Spike was one of those. When I first flew with Spike, I had about 50 missions ritually marked on my red squadron baseball cap. Spike didn't have any, and as was customary with new pilots, he had to fly with an "old head" (someone with 15 or more missions) in his backseat for his first 15 rides.

Our target that day was a heavily defended highway and waterway complex in North Vietnam. For several days our squadron had worked that target, but we were dropping our special ordnance too high and were scattering it all over the countryside. Our squadron commander had decided that enough was enough, and he got the wing commander's permission to go in as low as necessary to get the job done.

At the briefing the squadron commander, who was leading the flight, showed us on a papier-mâché relief map how we could thread in trail around the peaks and up and down the valleys on our approach to the target. We would deliver our ordnance at about 300 feet above the ground with the aircraft straight and level for five or six seconds—an eternity when the "bad guys" are shooting at you. Throughout the briefing Spike was as pale as a ghost. The tactics would be tough for an old pro, so I could easily understand the apprehension of a man about to fly his first combat mission. The CO asked Spike if he thought he could hack it. What fighter pilot could say no?

When we got to the target area, there was a heavy undercast. There was a hole in the clouds we could descend through, but we were limited to one attack heading. The enemy gunners would be expecting us. Just before descent, I reminded Spike to set his weapon switches. The CO started down, and Spike and I followed in number two position, with Three and Four in trail behind us. Spike told me to keep calling off our altitude, first in 1,000-foot and then in 100-foot increments.

Ahead I could see Lead weaving left and right, up and down, amid the peaks. I glanced at the altimeter—700 feet. Spike cried, "Damn it, I lost him!" I told Spike to hold his heading and keep looking. We were now very close to the target. "Got him again, but hell, I can't see the target." I told Spike to keep his eyes glued on Lead and forget about the target.

I saw Lead level off and drop his bombs. We were directly in trail about three-quarters of a mile back. When we came abeam of the peak where I had seen Lead drop, I punched off our bombs. They were still coming off when I saw the orange streak of small automatic-weapon fire hosing up from the ground to meet us on our left. The bombs were off now—"Jink right!" I yelled. Spike pulled smartly up and right and began jinking, all the while calling out the enemy ground fire to Three and Four. They made their runs without incident. On the way home, Spike's voice sounded more relaxed.

Back at Ubon, after we climbed down the ladder, Spike said, "That was a hell of a mission!" "I thought you looked a bit worried during the briefing," I replied. "Hell, Joe," he said, "what had me worried was flying a mission like that with a *navigator* in my backseat!" He shook my hand, winked, and said, "I'm damned glad you were there."

From May, 1968, through April, 1969, I flew 169 combat missions over Southeast Asia, including 77 over North Vietnam. My two main interests were combat flying and letters to and from my family. I did have two other pursuits, however, that helped make being at war more bearable. I was able to teach two night English courses for the University of Maryland extension program, and I became very interested in Air Force songs of the Vietnam War era.

Occupational, social song, whether in the barracks or on the march, has long been a feature of military life, from the time of Caesar's legions to the present. The tradition has also figured prominently in the lives of American military flyers, partly because of the influence of the British Royal Air Force's strong song tradition during both world wars and the warm relationships between the two fighting forces. U.S. Air Force flyers have proven especially adept at parodying well-known melodies by adding their own creative lyrics. Folk-song melodies such as "Casey Jones," "Down in the Valley," "Strawberry Roan," and "Sweet Betsy from Pike" have all been used in Air Force songs, as have the 1868 hit "The Daring Young Man on the Flying Trapeze," "Rambling Wreck from Georgia Tech," and hillbilly music like "The Wabash Cannonball."

Air Force songs of the Vietnam era have also used a number of these melodies, as well as songs like "On Top of Old Smoky," "Jingle Bells," and "When Johnny Comes Marching Home." Many of the songs in this present volume also use melodies popular from the 1940s to the 1960s. Tunes of this era include the Andrews Sisters' "Along the Navajo Trail" (1945), the Peggy Lee hit "Mañana" (1948), Vaughn Monroe's "Ghost Riders in the Sky" (1949), and the antiwar song by Pete Seeger and Lee Hays, "Where Have All the Flowers Gone?" (1946), doubtless popular with combat flyers in Vietnam through the 1960s recording by Peter, Paul, and Mary. The most recent borrowed melodies include Petula Clark's 1965 hit "Downtown," Barry Sadler's 1966 "Ballad of the Green Berets," and "I've Been Everywhere," a song recorded by several pop and country performers in the 1960s and used in the Vietnam air war to list the many strange-sounding places a flyer has attacked.

I had sung and listened to Air Force songs since 1955 and during my 1968–69 combat tour, and I decided to collect as many songs as I could from the Vietnam War. The collection in this book represents only a number of the hundreds of songs composed at the many Air Force bases in Vietnam and Thailand. At some bases songs were doubtless composed and sung in the confines of a lonely room in the early morning hours after a mission—such songs were probably not meant for the public and, except for rare instances, will never be sung or seen again. But at other bases like Phu Cat and Cam Ranh Bay in South Vietnam, and Korat, Ubon, and Udorn in Thailand, songs locally composed and sung were often central to the flyers' social life and were sung, copied, and taped over and over again. In this latter case, each base or squadron usually had its own composer, men like Dave Wilson at Phu Cat, Dick Jonas of the 433rd Tactical Fighter Squadron at Ubon, the most prolific and probably the best Air Force songwriter of the war, or Jeff Wilkins, the minstrel of our own 435th.

Jeff was from the South, in his early twenties, and a bachelor. Southern folk ballads flowed through his veins, and many a night I heard him working on arrangements and lyrics through the paper-thin walls of our adjoining rooms. We had both arrived at Ubon at the same time, so I was able to observe Jeff's musical life move through several stages. At first he busied himself by listening to tapes of country performers. Next he plunked around and played American folk music on a guitar he brought with him from the States. Gradually home faded in his memory, and the war and his flying comrades began to occupy almost all of his waking thoughts. Jeff turned to practicing some of the songs in this collection and then performed them at squadron parties. Eventually he bought a Japanese twelve-string guitar and began composing songs of his own.

Jeff would start with a feeling, a mood, or a theme, and a melody from the past would seem to fit. He'd play and sing, composing orally, and either he would write out the lyrics when he finished, or another pilot would jot them down as Jeff composed. One night Em Roberts and I helped him write a song in this manner, but it was mainly Jeff's. He flew almost all his missions at night, the most dangerous kind of flying. As he wrote in one of his songs, "A man must have lust for the lure of the night."

Implicit in what I've said so far is the concept that a certain atmosphere, a certain kind of person, and sufficient leisure time were necessary for such songs to have been written. Dave Carson and Tony Dater, who were stationed at Da Nang in F-4s while I was at Ubon, told me that little or no original composition went on there. For the fighter pilot, Da Nang was considered an extremely grim base. Rocket attack was common, and when it was not actually happening, it was always feared. A man tended to avoid crowded rooms—he liked to know where the nearest shelter was. Things were quite different at other bases, and these bases seemed to produce more songs. At Ubon, for example, we lived a life very similar to that of the *comitatus*, or band of Anglo-Saxon warriors in the Old English heroic poem *Beowulf*. The center of our social life was our great hall, or Officers' Club. We ate all our meals there in an all-male, war-oriented, closed social group. Through our subchiefs, or flight commanders, we warriors were bound in loyalty to our tribe, or squadron, which was physically embodied in our lord, or squadron commander. His word was law—he punished misdeeds and dispensed rings of gold (Silver Stars and Distinguished Flying Crosses) for deeds of valor.

Once each day we would mount our valiant aircraft, which might be named "The Gunner" or, appropriately enough, "Thor's Hammer," and go on a mission. After the mission, we would invariably go to the great hall, join our comrades, and drink amid boasts of our exploits. Our hope of immortality was the promise that we could return home after completing 100 missions over North Vietnam or, after the bombing halt of November, 1968, upon completion of a calendar year of service. We were proud warriors; we rarely talked or thought of death—at least in public. No one ever criticized another's prowess except in jest, and our subchiefs and lord were the bravest, the most accomplished in battle, of us all. Both this dream of immortality and pride coexisted, however, under the looming presence of *wyrd*, or fate, for the "golden BB," that one artillery round or solitary missile destined from the beginning of time to shatter us from the sky, might be waiting for us on tomorrow's mission. In many ways it was not only an Anglo-Saxon but a very Hemingwayesque way of life. And although many of our comrades did die in battle, it was very often a rather antiseptic death—a dramatic fireball on a beautifully pastoral hillside, or sometimes a simple failure to return. Side by side with death existed another kind of immortality—almost every day new warriors arrived and old warriors left. Our number was always constant.

Every month my squadron, the Eagles, had a formal party. We lived and fought in our battle garb—our drab, green-gray flying suits—but once each month we put on very special, highly ornamented bright blue flying suits, richly polished black boots, and crimson scarves and gathered in the great hall at 8:00 P.M. For an hour or so we would stand and talk in small groups. Now and then I would catch a glimpse of our lord, chatting nobly with those around him. There was an aspect of great respect and deference in the faces of his followers, faces flushed with youth and the joy of life that filled the room. The drink was more a ritual than anything else—great amounts of it were consumed, but I rarely saw anyone drunk. The purpose of the feast was to promote fellowship and perpetuate the rebirth cycle by welcoming the newcomers and paying tribute to those who were leaving.

About 9:00 a feast was served by Thai women in native dress. The tables were sumptuously set. The lord and his staff sat at a table perhaps twenty feet long, with the lord at the center. At four tables aligned perpendicularly to the lord's table sat the warriors of the four flights, with those of highest rank sitting nearest the lord's table, and those of lower sitting farthest away. Expensive, choice wine was poured and repoured as we toasted the president, the king of Thailand, the Air Force chief of staff, the wing commander, and our own lord, the squadron commander. As we ate, occasionally a warrior would rise and jokingly toast another. The laughter and good spirits would resound. During the meal, a solitary singer or a group of singers would provide entertainment. On some occasions songsheets were provided, and we would all sing. Sometimes we sang ballads; sometimes, humorous songs that poked jests at the foibles of our fellows. The songs were often followed by a humorous dramatic sketch or comedy routine.

After the feast, we would sit and sip after-dinner drinks or smoke rich cigars while the new warriors were introduced by the operations officer. Each would say a few words as we sized him up. These were the untried men with whom we would soon be flying, fighting, and perhaps dying. Then those that were leaving would in turn mount the rostrum. Their talks were usually ten to fifteen mintues long, and thoughtfully, carefully prepared. After all, a man had a year to prepare this talk. Each wanted to sum up an indescribable year, to leave something of himself behind for his comrades before he was swept away to Valhalla by the Valkyrie-like C-130 transport that would leave the next morning, carrying only those who had the proper credentials. Finally the lord himself would speak, the wisdom of many battles behind him. He would welcome and encourage the newcomers and pay tribute to those who had successfully run the course. With this, the feast was over, but perhaps half the company would linger another hour or two, talking, drinking, and singing. On one occasion the great lord himself, the wing commander, stayed long after the feast, and we sang songs of our war and of his.

I hope that what I have said will help clarify the social context, the spirit, in which these songs were written and sung. Fellowship, love, hate, joy, loneliness, even despair—these are all found in the songs in this collection. I do not delude myself that these are great songs, but they are truthful songs, they are historic songs, and they deserve to be preserved. By some people, they will even be cherished.

The Songs

Air Force Lament

The U.S. Air Force that flew and fought over Vietnam became a separate service on September 18, 1947. Previously, its pilots, planes, and personnel were part of the U.S. Army. From humble if dangerous beginnings on August 1, 1907, when three airmen were assigned to form the Aeronautical Division of the U.S. Signal Corps, the flying arm was designated the Aviation Section, U.S. Signal Corps, on July 18, 1914, with a strength of 122 personnel. By the end of World War I in 1918, the Aviation Section's strength had grown to more than 195,000 men.

Another name change in 1918 lasted until 1926, at which time the strength of the Army Air Service (AAS) had declined from 195,000 to slightly over 9,500 men. The unit was renamed the Army Air Corps in 1926, and it continued to grow during the next 15 years to more than 150,000 personnel in June, 1941, when it was renamed the Army Air Forces (AAF). At the height of World War II in 1944, AAF strength was more than 2.3 million.

"Air Force Lament," earlier known as "The Air Corps Lament," or "Glory, Flying Regulations," was originally a late World War II song. Extremely popular and found in a number of songbooks, the earlier versions also highlight the speaker's clear frustration with the disparity between former wartime glory and the mundane regimentation of peacetime. After two introductory stanzas, stanzas 3 and 4 reflect Vietnam; 5 through 8, World War II; and 9, the Korean War. Gen. H. H. ("Hap") Arnold, especially praised in stanza 7, was the last commander of the Army Air Corps and commanded the new Army Air Forces throughout World War II, during which he was promoted to General of the

Army. Arnold was instrumental in getting the U.S. Air Force status as a separate service in 1947.

The song, set to the melody of the 1856 song "Battle Hymn of the Republic," a melody used in a number of Air Force songs, is a good example of lyric accretion. The stanzas on Korea and Vietnam were added to the World War II version, and in stanza 3, World War II "T-Bolts," or P-47s, are replaced by Vietnam-era "Nickels," or F-105s, and the earlier "Goering's" is replaced by "Hanoï's." (Field Marshall Hermann Goering commanded Hitler's air force, the Luftwaffe, in World War II.) With its martial melody and historical overview, the song has an epic ring to it. Whenever there are more wars, more stanzas will be added — but I hope that this is the last version.

Air Force Lament
Tune: "Battle Hymn of the Republic"

My eyes have seen the days of men who ruled the fighting sky,
With hearts that laughed at death, who lived for nothing but to fly,
But now those hearts are grounded and those days are long gone by;
The Force is shot to hell!

CHORUS (repeat after each verse except the last):
    Glory, flying regulations,
    Have them read at every station;
    Crucify the man that breaks them;
    The Force is shot to hell!

My bones have felt their pounding throb, a hundred thousand strong,
A mighty airborne legion sent to right the deadly wrong,
But now it's only memory; it only lives in song;
The Force is shot to hell!

I have seen them in their Nickels [orig., T-Bolts] when their eyes were
    dancing flame;
I've seen their screaming high speed dives that blasted Hanoï's [Goering's]
    name;
But now they just fly Sky Spots and hang their heads in shame;
The Force is shot to hell!

They flew their rugged Thunderchiefs [B-26s] through a living hell of
    flak,
And bloody, dying pilots gave their lives to bring them back,

But now they all play Ping-Pong in the Operations shack;
Their technique's gone to hell!

Yes, the lordly Boeing Fortress and the Liberator, too,
Once wrote the doom of Germany with contrails in the blue,
But now the skies are empty, and our planes are wet with dew,
And we can't fly for hell!

You've heard your pounding .50s blaze from wings of polished steel,
The purring of your Merlin was a song your heart could feel,
But now the L-5 charms you with its moanin', groanin' squeal,
And it won't climb for hell!

Hap Arnold built a fighting team that sang a fighting song
About the wild blue yonder in the days when men were strong,
But now we're closely supervised for fear we may do wrong;
The Force is shot to hell!

We were cocky, bold, and happy when we played the angel's game;
We split the blue with buzzing, and we rolled our way to fame,
But now that's all VERBOTEN, and we're all so goddamn tame;
Our spirit's shot to hell!

One day I buzzed an airfield with another reckless chap;
We flew a hot formation with his wingtip in my lap,
But there's a new directive, and we'll have no more of that,
Or we will burn in hell!

The Sabres in Korea drove the MiGs out of the sky;
The pilots then were fearless men and not afraid to die,
But now the regs are written, you can kiss your wings goodbye,
And you won't fly for hell!

Have you ever climbed a Thunderchief up to where the air is thin?
Have you stuck her long nose downward just to hear the screaming din?
Have you tried to do it lately? Better not, you'll auger in,
And then you'll sure catch hell!

My eyes get dim with tears when I recall the days of old,
When pilots took their choice of being old or "young and bold";
Alas, I have no choice, and I will live to be quite old;
The Force is shot to hell!

But smile awhile, my pilot, though your eyes may still be wet;
Someday we'll meet in heaven where the rules have not been set;

And God will show us how to buzz and roll and really let
The Air Force fly like hell!

FINAL CHORUS:
   Glory, no more regulations!
   Rip them down at every station!
   Ground the guy that tries to make one,
   And let us fly like hell!

Armed Recce

"Armed Recce" is one of three exceptionally fine songs in this collection written by Toby Hughes, who as a captain flew F-4 Phantoms out of Cam Ranh Bay with the 12th Tactical Fighter Wing from September, 1967, through August, 1968 (see also "One Hundred Sixty VC in the Open" and "Tchepone").

Some combat missions had specifically assigned targets, while others were armed reconnaissance or "recce" (pronounced "RECK-ee") missions during which the flight leader was free to strike "targets of opportunity"–whatever looked good and wasn't forbidden by the many and complex rules of engagement. Sometimes we would catch some supply barges in inland waterways, a missile transporter on a tree-obscured road, or as in this case, a truck convoy. When teamed up with a FAC (forward air controller) in a light spotter plane, fighter strikes on armed recce were sometimes spectacular in terms of munitions and supplies destroyed.

The speaker here is telling a neophyte flyer what a particular armed recce mission was like. He leads a flight of two to work the area just north of the DMZ. This song gives us both the excitement and fear of armed recce, with the speaker knowing at the end that while he has saved his life for one more day, he'll fly another such mission tomorrow.

Armed Recce
Tune: "The Fastest Gun Around"

In the skies of Southeast Asia,
Where the fighter pilots dwell,

There's a mission you'll fly a lot,
You'll get to know it well.

They call it armed reconnaissance,
And you fly it fast and low,
In the southern part of Package One
That's known as Tally Ho.

You're briefed on the defenses
All along the route you'll fly;
You're scared but still you gotta go,
And so you take the sky.

You get prestrike refueling and
You take the flight on down;
You cross the coast at Butterfly
And start to move around.

You head it north up Route 1-A,
The road looks clean and bare,
But a truck is mighty hard to see
From one mile in the air.

You know you've got to take it down,
Though your heart is in your mouth;
Now dead ahead's the ferry,
That's the point you'll turn her south.

And it's right there that your heart stops
As you see the thing you dread;
The triple-A is coming up,
It fills the sky ahead.

You fake a turn off to the left,
You break hard up and right;
Your wingman's in with CBU,
And it's a pretty sight.

And now you're heading south again
And really moving 'round,
To make a tougher target for
The gunners on the ground.

And now you see the convoy
Sitting still beside the road;

You arm up all the switches
And prepare to dump your load.

You touch off afterburner,
Popping up into the sun;
You keep the convoy in your sight
And start to make your run.

Then the gunners start to shoot again,
You see the flak ahead;
Then the bursts are all around you,
And the sky is filled with lead.

You can't go left, you can't go right,
The flak is all around,
So you keep the convoy in your sight
And keep on boring down.

You pickle off your bomb load;
You pull and trust to luck
That the triple-A will miss you,
And your bombs will hit the truck;

But the flak is coming closer
And your eyes are filled with tears;
Before you make the coastline
You have aged a hundred years

Then suddenly you're out of it,
The water's down below;
Breathe easy now but don't relax
'Cause sure as hell you know

That tomorrow is another day,
And once again you'll go
To the southern part of Package One
To recce Tally Ho.

Words by Toby Hughes, © 1968. Used with permission.

The Ballad of Bernie Fisher

Since the Air Force became a separate service in 1947, sixteen
of its members have earned the Congressional Medal of Honor,

the U.S. government's highest award for valor in combat: four during the Korean War, and twelve in Southeast Asia. Maj. Bernard M. ("Bernie") Fisher was one of the latter. Flying a small A-1E spotter plane with his call sign Hobo 51, Fisher was on a combat mission over the A Shau Valley, about 20 miles southeast of Hue in northern South Vietnam, on March 10, 1966. One of his fellows had been forced down, and despite heavy opposing fire, Fisher landed and picked him up. A fictionalized Bernie Fisher is the speaker in the song, which takes its melody from a well-known American folk song which was popularly revived in 1940 in a published version by A. P. Carter. The melody has been used in Air Force songs from World War II through Korea and in Vietnam.

The Ballad of Bernie Fisher

Tune: "The Wabash Cannonball"

Listen to the small arms, hear the twenty mike-mike roar;
The A-1Es are bouncing off the A Shau Valley floor;
Hear the mighty roar of engines, hear the lonesome Hobo call,
"I'll get you home to mother when the work's all done this fall."

"Listen, A Shau Tower, this is Hobo Fifty-One;
I want to use your runway although it is overrun;
A friend of mine is down there a-hiding in a ditch;
I want to make a passenger stop and save that son-of-a-bitch!"

(Repeat first chorus)

The Ballad of Heinz E. Coordes

Combat flyers sharing the cockpit of the same aircraft soon develop a very special relationship—one of mutual respect, friendship, and even a kind of love, for their lives depend on each other. In the song the "field grade and debonair" F-4 Phantom aircraft commander (AC), Leo Hicks, and his accomplished GIB ("guy in back"), Heinz E. Coordes, fly together all over the most dangerous part of North Vietnam—Route Package Six, the Hanoi area—as well as over Route Pack One, the area just above the Demilitarized Zone. A pilot himself (for some of the F-4 GIBs were navigators), Heinz later becomes an AC, while Leo goes on to become a forward air controller (FAC) at Fort Hood, near Killeen, Texas. In the last stanza Dick Jonas, also a pilot GIB, says that as much as Heinz admires Leo, he should tell Leo, if ever they meet again, that Heinz would rather be an AC flying on Leo's wing than a GIB in Leo's backseat. Dick's original melody is in some ways quite similar to the old barroom favorite "Ninety-Nine Bottles of Beer on the Wall."

This is the first of a number of songs in this collection with original words and music by Dick Jonas. Dick flew 125 combat missions in Southeast Asia with the 433rd Tactical Fighter Squadron of the 8th Tactical Fighter Wing at Ubon, Thailand.

The Ballad of Heinz E. Coordes

Once there was an F-4 jock by the name of Heinz E. Coordes,
Heinz was long and lank and mean and a man of very few words;
Heinz was a GIB that knew his trade in bomb and strafe and cap,
He could navigate his AC to any place that's on the map.

Heinz' AC was Leo Hicks, field grade and debonair,
But he wouldn't go to Route Pack Six unless old Heinz was there;
Leo said, "I got a shit-hot GIB that really knows his stuff,
If you play poker with Heinz E. Coordes don't never call his bluff!"

They rained bombs and CBUs all over North Vietnam,
Getting shot at with triple-A guns and Uncle Ho's MiGs and SAMs,
All the way from the Bridge to Kep to Bac Mai and Phuc Yen,
And all across the topside of Route Pack One, down the coast and back
*   again.*

Leo Hicks was the chief honcho of A Flight's valiant men,
And Heinz E. Coordes was Leo's GIB and he saved old Leo's skin;
He took Leo to Route Pack Six more times than he cares to say,
Heinz E. Coordes is the reason that Leo's alive and well today.

Well, the bear don't roam in the woods no more, he's a FAC down at Fort
*   Hood,*
And Heinz E. Coordes is a new AC and I'm sure he'll do quite good,
If there ever is a time in the years to come that Heinz and Leo meet,
Heinz, you can tell him, "I'll fly your wing, but never in your back seat!"

The Ballad of Jeb Stewart

Of "The Ballad of Jeb Stewart" Dick Jonas says:

> This song is a true story in almost every detail. It was told to
> me by Jeb's wingman. Jeb took a hit and ejected at Mu Gia
> Pass. He landed in the karst—craggy, sharp, extremely rough
> hills characteristic of that part of the world. Though his in-
> juries were so severe that he was conscious only part of the
> time, he directed the rescue forces which came to his aid,
> while hanging in his parachute in the rugged karst, using his
> survival radio. The PJs [parajumpers] were medics who para-
> chuted in to free him and care for his injuries so he could be
> hauled up by the Jolly Green helicopter.

This story, with a major difference, sounds like what happened
to "Hesh" Altman, a contemporary of Dick's in the 435th Tactical Fighter Squadron at Ubon. Let's hear Jeb's story first, and then
we'll hear Hesh's.

The Ballad of Jeb Stewart

On a steep and jagged hillside near Mu Gia Pass
Hanging in a parachute, this day is his last.
Just another fighter jock, they're mostly all the same,
But this one here was different, Jeb Stewart was his name.

Well, Jeb was feeling mighty poorly, both his legs were broke,
And I could see him hanging there between the puffs of smoke.
I told Jeb, "Now, drink some water, Sandy's on the way,
The Jolly Greens are coming in, we'll get you out today."

I could tell that he was hurt much worse than first I thought,
'Cause sometimes he just wouldn't answer then sometimes he'd talk.
"Ol' Jeb likely needs a doctor," I'd said to Crown,
And he came back with, "Jolly's got PJ's, they'll soon be down."

I held high and kept Jeb talking to me all the while,
When I told him here comes Sandy, I could see him smile.
Jeb said, "Listen babes, you have ol' Sandy watch his stuff,
They got ZPU and small arms, this one's gonna be tough."

Sandy flew right down the valley looking for the sites,
He pulled off with battle damage and turned around to fight,

Jeb called up and told him, "Sandy, bring it down again.
The guns are down behind the karst; now lay your napalm in."

Jeb worked Sandy like a FAC, "Hit twenty meters right,
Watch the small arms on the left," then all the guns went quiet.
Jeb was talking low and weaker, time was running out.
The guns were down and Jolly's here, but I began to doubt.

First the PJ's tried to reach him, but it took too long,
And I was Bingo minus seven, time to head for home;
All the way to Wolf Pack country not a word was said,
'Cause when the PJ's finally reached him, young Jeb Stewart was
*   dead.*

We rolled out and taxied in, and climbed out in the rain.
Hoot and Bill and all the boys, they met us at the plane.
I told Hoot Jeb didn't make it, they got him at the Pass,
And I came home because my bird was running out of gas.

Listen boys, and hear me good, I want you all to know,
That ol' Jeb died a hero's death, the way we all would go.

Hesh Altman's story is well told by Howard Sochurek in "Air
Rescue behind Enemy Lines," *National Geographic* 134, no. 3 (September, 1968): 357–64. Sochurek writes:

> One episode, which I found unforgettable, involved Capt.
> Herbert (Hesh) Altman of Boston. I heard about it when he
> dropped by Udorn to thank the PJ's who saved his life.
>   Hesh graduated from the Air Force Academy in 1962. At
> 29, lean and round-faced, he has the virile look that a bad scar
> on cheek and forehead gives a handsome man. He was on
> his fifteenth mission, flying as a navigator in the back seat of
> a McDonnell F-4D Phantom II, when he ejected, or "punched
> out."
>   "We were on a night mission to hit the supply route just
> south of the Mu Gia Pass," he said when I asked him the details. "You know the place. It's an area of volcanic crags and
> steep limestone cliffs. We rolled in over the trucks on a rocket
> pass, pickled two rockets against the trucks, and jinked."
>   Hesh used "pickled" for "fired"; by "jinked," he meant mak-

ing a sudden change in the plane's altitude and direction to keep radar-controlled weapons from scoring a hit.

"As we jinked, I saw tracers cross in an X right over our canopy, and I said, 'Judas, they almost got us,' to nobody in particular. But they *had* got us. We pulled up suddenly and then nosed over. We were down from 6,000 feet to 4,000 in 15 seconds.

"My pilot yelled, 'Get out, Hesh, get out, get out,' and I ejected. It was 7 o'clock and a pitch-black, moonless night.

"I saw the plane continue its dive after I got out. It buried itself in the steep slope of the cliff beneath me, doing 500 knots in a 30-degree dive, and when it exploded, parts of it hit me while I was still falling. I thought I was going to die right there.

"Then my chute popped, and I was in the air only five seconds before I hit. The chute caught in tree branches, slowing the fall before I slammed into a rock crevice so tightly that circulation was cut in both my legs. I noticed I had lost my watch, and the right side of my head was wet and sticky from a burn where I had been hit by the flying debris.

"I got out my radio and called the wingman who was circling overhead. I told him, 'I'm stuck in a crevice down here next to the burning airplane.'

"He answered, 'Have you spotted.'

"I looked down the mountain slope below me, about 1,000 feet straight down. On came North Vietnamese truck headlights along the Ho Chi Minh Trail. It looked like the Los Angeles freeway. I will never know why they couldn't see me hanging in that rock. In a period of about 20 minutes, I counted 40 trucks.

"Then my pilot, who was down somewhere near me, came in on his rescue radio, talking to the wingman in the air.

"He half whispered, 'They're coming down the hill with lanterns. There are bad guys all over the place. I don't think I'm going to make it. I'm signing off. Don't come in on beeper in the morning.'" [Hesh's pilot fears he may be captured that night, and his signal radio beeper used by the enemy to lure in friendly aircraft in the morning.]

Hesh wondered where his pilot was. He later learned that the pilot had buried himself in shrubs at the bottom of the slope near the road and had remained hidden the whole night as regular North Vietnamese soldiers searched for him with lanterns.

"After a long time," Hesh said, "the Sandys showed up and advised that rescue was not going to attempt a pickup that night. They told me to hang loose and they would be back at dawn."

All through that long night Hesh had visitors, small animals he could hear scrambling around him. He was illuminated at times by fires started by chunks of burning aircraft.

"About midnight," Hesh went on, "a chestnut-brown monkey came to see the burning wreckage and I said, 'Hi, monkey.' I petted her for about an hour, happy to have company. I scratched her under the chin and she really liked that. Seemed to me that she had been petted before. She crawled up and kept playing with my vest. I was trying to get my strobe light out in case I had a chance to signal. I had to take off my gloves to do it, and the monkey stole my gloves.

"I dozed off, but every time the wind blew, parts of the aircraft would fall out of the trees. I imagined noises behind me, even thought I heard bolt-action rifles being cocked.

"About daybreak I felt numb from the waist down and was hurting everywhere. It took two hands to use my radio. My batteries were loose and had to be held in place.

"About 0600 a Crown showed up and asked me for ten seconds of beep. I gave it to them.

"Then my pilot came on the air from down below and asked the Sandys to strafe the road. A work crew had appeared at dawn and was working 20 feet from his position.

"There was no firing other than their strafing, but over the hill a war was going on as Sandys hit AA gun positions.

"At 0745 I heard the choppers come in. I told them to get my aircraft commander first because he was down there with the bad guys. I had a bird's-eye view of the rescue with the chopper only 100 yards away.

"After they pulled the AC aboard, the same chopper came after me. Then we ran into problems. I was wedged in the rock and couldn't move. I asked to have the PJ come down to get me, but every time he got close he missed me. They just couldn't hover near enough because of the sheer cliff.

"The down draft whipped my parachute around my neck. Finally they swung the penetrator in like a pendulum and I grabbed it and pulled myself out of the crevice. I went up and down three times, messed up in chute, shroud lines, and branches. The third time up, they pulled me aboard, and I just lay on my back in the helicopter looking up at the PJ.

"I said, 'God, you look beautiful.'

"These Jolly Green boys are a breed all by their lonesome.

As happy as we were to get picked up, the Jolly Green were even happier to have done it."

Jeb Stewart and Hesh Altman—two different endings to similar stories. From a combat flyer's point of view, rescue missions were perhaps the most rewarding one could fly. When one of our people was hit and ejected, every possible human effort would be made to pick him up, and in the 8th Wing at Ubon we often used our F-4s to keep the bad guys away from our man until the Jolly Greens could go in and make the save. It certainly made it a lot easier to face hostile fire every day knowing everything possible would be done to get you out if you got hit. From June 5, 1968, to April 6, 1969, my 8th Tactical Fighter Wing lost 18 aircraft with 36 crew members aboard. Of this number, 11 were killed, 3 probably MIA, but 22, or about 61 percent, were picked up and brought back home, thanks to Crown, the Sandys, the Jolly Greens, and other supporting aircraft.

The Ballad of Machete Two

There's perhaps nothing a flyer fears more than running out of fuel. When the pilot or a navigator plans a mission, the minimum amount of fuel needed to return to base is checked and rechecked, and fuel use is carefully monitored in-flight. When a pilot calls out "Bingo," everyone knows it's time to head home. But in combat, fuel use is more difficult—often impossible—to control. Through a comedy of communication and judgment errors, two of my friends at Ubon had to eject from a perfectly good F-4D Phantom only two miles behind their third try to meet up with a refueling tanker.

"The Ballad of Machete Two" is the lyrical version of an incident that supposedly took place at Ubon. Since the story had a happy ending, the song is humorous and ironic.

The Ballad of Machete Two
Tune: "The Wabash Cannonball"

"Hello, Ubon Tower, this here's Machete Two,
It's rainin' on the runway, O Lord, what will I do?

My gas tank's gettin' empty, and I am puckered tight,
Tell me, Ubon Tower, why must we fly at night?"

"Hello there, Machete, do you see the runway's end?
'Cause if you don't then go around and we'll try once again";
"Machete Two is on the go, I need some JP-4,
Just let me hit the tanker, and then we'll try once more."

"Lion, I need vectors out to Green Anchor plane,
Please expedite the joinup, I'm flyin' in the rain,
I've got to hit the tanker, 'cause I sure need some gas,
If he ain't got no JP-4, then he can kiss my ass."

"Hello there, Machete, Lion here, you're three miles out,
I'll have you on Blue Anchor soon, of that there is no doubt,
OOPS, disregard the last word, you're fifty miles in trail;
If you will just be patient, this time I will not fail."

"Hello Lion, Machete, you can't mean fifty miles,
I'm reading seven hundred pounds here on my gas tank dials,
I'm headin' back to Ubon, I'll try it one more time,
The truth about my chances is that they ain't worth a dime."

My throttles back at idle, descending at max glide,
If we don't make it this time, we'll have to let it slide,
We've got it on the runway, pulled off and turned about,
Good Lord, look at those gauges, both engines just flamed out!

"Hello, Ubon Tower, this here's Machete Two,
I'm standing by my airplane, in mud up to my knees,
I don't know just what happened, I'd like to tell you how,
Won't you send the crew truck, I'd like to come in now."

"Hello there, Machete, this here is Ubon Tower,
Just make a left three-sixty, you'll be down within the hour,
We've got some TAC departures lined up on the other end,
Just let me get 'em airborne, and you can come on in."

"Ubon Tower, Machete, you just don't understand,
We are no longer flying, we're settin' in the sand,
Our airplane is inverted and lyin' on its back,
So come and take us home, I'm tired and wanna hit the sack."

"Machete, Ubon Tower, you say you're on the ground?
You know without a clearance that you can't set her down,
If you have violated regs you know you'll have to wait'
Machete, do you hear me?" "I hear you—FSH!"

The moral of my story is that if you're low on gas,
Just get it on the runway, and only make one pass;
On unprepared dirt runways—now listen carefully—
You know it is illegal to land the F-4D!

The Ballad of Robin Olds

Of his "Ballad of Robin Olds," Dick Jonas writes, "I remember the day Col. Robin Olds arrived at the home drome. He was the leader of the Wolf Pack. Robin told us, 'Gang, our mission is to fly and fight . . . and don't you forget it!' We flew Robin's wing across the Red River, down Thud Ridge so close to the ground you had to look up to see the treetops . . . and we were with him that day the Wolf Pack shot down seven bandits [North Vietnamese MiGs]. Yes sir, Robin Olds was the kind of fighter pilot the Phantom was built for."

Col. Robin Olds commanded the 8th Tactical Fighter Wing at Ubon Royal Thai Air Base, Thailand, from 1966 through early 1967. The 8th Wing was composed of the 433rd, 435th, 497th, and 555th tactical fighter squadrons flying F-4 Phantoms. The Wolf Pack, as it was known, shot down more enemy MiGs than any other U.S. Air Force unit did. I served under Olds's immediate successor, a Colonel Spencer, and later under Col. Charles C. ("Buck") Pattillo, who succeeded Spencer. Dick Jonas served in the 433rd while Olds was in command. The former wing CO's memory was still larger than life when I first arrived at Ubon, though Olds had departed some months earlier. A huge picture of his aircraft, F-4 tail number FP 680, hung over the main bar in our Officers' Club, despite Colonel Spencer's best efforts to have it removed. Spencer was often contrasted with Olds as an air leader and came off the worst for it, but again, who wouldn't? According to *Air Force Magazine* (May, 1986, p. 197), Olds is officially credited with 12 kills in World War II and 4 in Vietnam, including two MiG-17s and two MiG-21s. The disparity in Dick's second stanza crediting Olds with 22 kills when he arrived at Ubon is perhaps due to some unconfirmed kills Olds may have had in World War II.

Many Wolf Pack F-4 pilots loved Robin Olds and would have flown into the jaws of hell with him, as more than a few have told me. He was a superb flyer himself, an equally superb combat leader, and the quintessential free spirit who played hard as well as fought hard. Some time after his combat tour in Vietnam, Brig. Gen. Robin Olds was appointed Commandant of Cadets at the U.S. Air Force Academy while I was on the faculty there. He remained a colorful figure in peacetime, as he had been in war. He is retired now and living in Steamboat Springs, Colorado, and I can imagine him tearing skillfully down the ski slopes—still flying.

The Ballad of Robin Olds

We flew in the Wolf Pack with Robin Olds,
Some of us ain't coming back;
In a Foxtrot-four called the Phantom II
We flew with the Red River Rats.

Robin came over to Ubon,
An ace with twenty-two kills;
He led the 8th Wing to victory
In the skies over Hanoi's hills.

The 435th and the Nite Owls, too,
The Nickel and the 433rd,
Went with Robin through the jaws of hell,
Leading the Wolf Pack herd.

Smoking along to the firewall,
Twenty-five feet off the deck,
Move over, Hanoi Hanna,
Robin's gonna break your back!

Bandits! Bandits! Over Thud Ridge,
MiG Ridge and Haiphong, too;
No sweat, sir, Robin Olds is there,
And behind him is the Wolf Pack crew.

Words and music by Dick Jonas, from *FSH Volume I.* © 1969 by Enchantment Music Co. Used with permission.

The Ballad of the C-130

An Air Force fighter pilot honestly believes that he is the best pilot, flying the best aircraft, and serving in the best squadron in the Air Force. To maintain this image, he sometimes pokes fun at other flyers with less glamorous and less macho missions. The C-130 was a cargo-hauling workhorse of the Southeast Asian war. It brought new fighter crews to Ubon, Thailand, and to other places and was an especially welcome sight as it landed to take them home at tour's end. While a fighter pilot would secretly appreciate the C-130 and its crew, he puts them in their place in "The Ballad of the C-130." The humor is enhanced by his use of the serious, haunting melody by Stan Jones, which helped give Vaughn Monroe a hit in 1949. Since fighter planes often maneuver wildly enough so that five or six times the force of gravity is exerted on its crew (5–6 Gs), the 2-G pull by the C-130 to escape the fighters in stanza 2 adds additional sarcasm.

The Ballad of the C-130
Tune: "Ghost Riders in the Sky"

A trash hauler flew overhead one dark and windy day;
He passed over our runway as he flew upon his way,
When all at once our flight of four gave him an awful fright;
We flew within a hundred feet and pitched out on his right.

CHORUS (*repeat after each verse*):
Yippee aye aay, yippee aye o-oh,
Trash haulers in the sky!

We called out on the radio; he hit a power dive,
And prayed to God and Orville Wright that he'd remain alive;
He cut down through our pattern, and pulled about two Gs;
When he regained control again, he barely cleared the trees!

We told him on the radio, we said to him, "My son,"
We said, "My boy, if you want to live you'd damn well better run;
So push those frappin' throttles up and head across the sky,
And never venture near again where fighter pilots fly!"

The Ballad of the Green Brassiere

In "The Ballad of the Green Brassiere," a U.S. combat flyer pays sardonic tribute to a "friendly" Vietnamese girl ostensibly killed in a Viet Cong shelling. One could take the song straight, except for the nature of the only personal object remaining after the girl's explosive death. While the girl is blown to bits, her green brassiere is, miraculously, only "slightly tattered." A flyer's silver wings insignia left on her tombstone adds a certain touch. Barry Sadler was a highly decorated Army Green Beret, or Special Forces member, during the war, and his patriotic hit song of 1966 praising the heroism of that unit provides the melody for this particular song, which was probably written in South Vietnam in the late 1960s.

The Ballad of the Green Brassiere
Tune: "Ballad of the Green Berets"

Put silver wings upon her stone
To let her know she's not alone,
We love the maid who's buried here,
The girl who wore . . .
　　　The Green Brassiere.

Now let me tell you about this girl,
She's a true Vietnam pearl,
She wore a flower above her ear,
And on her chest . . .
　　　The Green Brassiere.

A VC shell came from above,
Only left one thing to remind us of
This little girl we loved so dear,
A slightly tattered . . .
　　　Green Brassiere.

Put silver wings upon her stone
To let her know she's not alone,
We love the maid who's buried here,
The girl who wore . . .
　　　The Green Brassiere.

The Ballad of the PIO

"The Ballad of the PIO," another song based on Barry Sadler's 1966 melody, chuckles at the mission of the public information officer (PIO), a military journalist who both wrote stories and carefully screened, on behalf of his commander, the information that would go to the civilian press. In South Vietnam he often flew with young lieutenants ("lueys"), pilots in U-H1 Bell helicopters, of Hueys, in search of news. In this parody the PIO dies and goes to heaven, but even there he is given another assignment.

The Ballad of the PIO
Tune: "Ballad of the Green Berets"

There he goes, the PIO,
Last to know, the first to go;
A hundred times he flies the Hueys
Flown by publicity-seeking lueys.

Out to battle he must go,
Sent by those in the know;
He may take a sniper's round,
And be left upon the ground.

Fighting men may pass him by,
And when they ask, "Who was that guy?"
"I dunno, it's hard to say;
What the hell, just let him lay."

And when he gets to the golden gate,
St. Peter says, "You've goofed up, mate!
So go to hell, in all your glory;
When you get back, you can do your story!"

To illustrate further, again humorously, the PIO's role in Southeast Asia, as well as to gain more insight into the fighter-pilot mystique, I here include "What the Captain Means Is . . . ," a classic dramatic sketch known to almost everyone who flew combat in Southeast Asia. The dialogue depicts a civilian news correspondent interviewing an unassuming Air Force Phantom jet fighter pilot somewhere in Southeast Asia in 1967. So the correspondent won't misconstrue the pilot's replies, the wing PIO is on hand as a monitor to ensure that the real Air Force story is told. The pilot was first asked his opinion of the F-4C Phantom.

> CAPTAIN: It's so fuckin' maneuverable you can fly up your own ass with it.
>
> PIO: What the captain means is that he has found the F-4C Phantom highly maneuverable at all altitudes, and he considers it an excellent aircraft for all missions assigned.
>
> CORRESPONDENT: I suppose, Captain, that you've flown a certain number of missions over North Vietnam. What do you think of the SAMs used by the North Vietnamese?
>
> CAPT.: Why, those bastards couldn't hit a bull in the ass with a bass fiddle. We fake the shit out of them. There's no sweat.
>
> PIO: What the captain means is that the surface-to-air missiles around Hanoi pose a serious problem to our air operations and that the pilots have a healthy respect for them.
>
> CORR.: I suppose, Captain, that you've flown missions to the South. What kind of ordnance do you use, and what kind of targets do you hit?
>
> CAPT.: Well, I'll tell you, mostly we aim at kicking the shit out of Vietnamese villages, and my favorite ordnance is napalm. Man, that stuff just sucks the air out of their friggin' lungs and makes a sonovabitchin' fire.
>
> PIO.: What the captain means is that air strikes in South Vietnam are often against Viet Cong structures, and all operations are always under the positive control of forward air controllers, or FACs. The ordnance employed is conventional 500- and 750-pound bombs and 20-mm cannon fire.
>
> CORR.: I suppose you spent an R and R |a Rest and Rehabilitation trip| in Hong Kong. What were your impressions of the Oriental girls?
>
> CAPT.: Yeah, I went to Hong Kong. As for those Oriental broads, well, I don't care which way the runway runs, east or west, north or south—a piece of ass is a piece of ass.
>
> PIO.: What the captain means is that he found the delicately featured Oriental girls fascinating, and he was very impressed with their fine manners and thinks their naïveté is most charming.
>
> CORR.: Tell me, Captain, have you flown any missions other than over North and South Vietnam?
>
> CAPT.: You bet your sweet ass I've flown other missions. We get scheduled nearly every day on the trail in Laos where those fuckers over there throw everything at you but the

friggin' kitchen sink. Even the goddamn kids got slingshots.

PIO.: What the captain means is that he has occasionally been scheduled to fly missions in the extreme western DMZ, and he has a healthy respect for the flak in that area.

CORR.: I understand that no one in your fighter wing has got a MiG yet. What seems to be the problem?

CAPT.: Why, you screwhead, if you knew anything about what you're talking about—the problem is MiGs. If we'd get scheduled by those peckerheads at Seventh for those missions in MiG Valley, you can bet your ass we'd get some of those mothers. Those glory hounds at Ubon get all those missions, while we settle for fightin' the friggin' war. Those mothers at Ubon are sitting on their fat asses killing MiGs, and we get stuck with bombing the goddamned cabbage patches.

PIO.: What the captain means is that each element in the Seventh Air Force is responsible for doing its assigned job in the air war. Some units are assigned the job of neutralizing enemy air strength by hunting out MiGs, and other elements are assigned bombing missions and interdiction of enemy supply routes.

CORR.: Of all the targets you've hit in Vietnam, which one was the most satisfying?

CAPT.: Well, shit, it was when we were scheduled for that suspected VC vegetable garden. I dropped napalm in the middle of the fuckin' cabbage, and my wingman splashed it real good with six of those 750-pound mothers and spread the fire all the way to the friggin' beets and carrots.

PIO.: What the captain means is that the great variety of tactical targets available throughout Vietnam makes the F-4C the perfect aircraft to provide flexible response.

CORR.: What do you consider the most difficult target you've struck in North Vietnam?

CAPT.: The friggin' bridges. I must have dropped 40 tons of bombs on those swayin' bamboo mothers, and I ain't hit one of the bastards yet.

PIO.: What the captain means is that interdicting bridges along enemy supply routes is very important and that bridges present quite a difficult target. The best way to accomplish this task is to crater the approaches to the bridge.

CORR.: I noticed in touring the base that you have aluminum matting on the taxiways. Would you care to comment on its effectiveness and usefulness in Vietnam?

CAPT.: You're fuckin' right, I'd like to make a comment. Most of us pilots are well hung, but shit, you don't know what hung is until you get hung up on one of the friggin' bumps on that goddamn stuff.

PIO.: What the captain means is that the aluminum matting is quite satisfactory as a temporary expedient but requires some finesse in taxiing and braking the aircraft.

CORR.: Did you have an opportunity to meet your wife on leave in Honolulu, and did you enjoy the visit with her?

CAPT.: Yeah, I met my wife in Honolulu, but I forgot to check the calendar, so the whole five days were friggin' well combat-proof—a completely dry run.

PIO.: What the captain means is that it was wonderful to get together with his wife and learn firsthand about the family and how things were at home.

CORR.: Thank you for your time, Captain.

CAPT.: Screw you—why don't you bastards print the real story, instead of all that crap?

PIO: What the captain means is that he enjoyed this opportunity to discuss his tour with you.

CORR.: One final question. Could you reduce your impression of the war into a simple phrase or statement, Captain?

CAPT.: You bet your ass I can. It's a fucked up war.

PIO: What the captain means is . . . it's a FUCKED UP WAR.

Whoever the anonymous author of "What the Captain Means Is . . . ," was, he well understood the nature of the fighter pilot, the slanting of news, and the use of humor to make a confusing, controversial war more bearable. His captain is profane, lusty, aggressive, and brutally frank, if a larger-than-life caricature. Fighter pilots also, at times, make fun of themselves.

Banana Valley

Of "Banana Valley," Dick Jonas says:

It don't take a Wolf Pack fighter pilot but a few missions to get used to the annoyance of flak and the stark terror of a SAM break before his fangs begin to get long, and he realizes the real reason for being over here—he's here to kill MiGs, and he's not going to rest easy till he gets his chance. Everybody wants to shoot down a MiG, but you can't go off half cocked.

It has worked out the other way around. When you go MiG
hunting, you've gotta be careful, especially if it's MiG-17s that
you find. They sneak off to Banana Valley and lay in the grass
like a snake, and just wait for somebody to make a slip.

The primal symbolism and undulating melody of this song work
quite effectively together.

Banana Valley

Just go on down to Banana Valley,
Go on down and meet your fate,
Just go on down to Banana Valley,
When you go down, down, down, you'd better learn to hate.

Well, I got friends in Banana Valley,
I got friends that learned too late,
I got friends in Banana Valley,
They went down, down, down, 'cause they did not hate.

There's snakes in the weeds in Banana Valley,
Them snakes in the weeds know how to hate;
Them snakes in the weeds in Banana Valley,
They go down, down, down, and there they wait.

Well, I heard all 'bout Banana Valley,
How fightin' them snakes could be so great,
It's so much fun in Banana Valley,
Gotta go down, down, down, and investigate.

Well, two weeks ago in Banana Valley,
Two of my friends killed one of them snakes,
Two weeks ago in Banana Valley,
They went down, down, down, to attend the wake.

So go on down to Banana Valley,
Go on down and meet your fate,
Just go on down to Banana Valley,
But when you go down, down, down, you'd better learn to hate.

Doodle-doody-doodle-doo.

Bat Song

The melody of "Sweet Betsy from Pike," sung from 1840 and earlier and first published in 1853, is another popular one often
used by Air Force songsters. The Bats, an Air National Guard Unit
from Sioux City, Iowa, flew F-100C Super Sabres out of Phu Cat
Air Base in South Vietnam from February, 1968, through late 1968
or early 1969. In the "Bat Song," the F-100s are directed to attack
an active enemy antiaircraft site by a rather timorous forward
air controller, who marks the target from a half a mile away. The
cloud cover is down to an exaggerated 200 feet, and things are
so hot that the Bats drop all of their bombs in one pass. As the
FAC assesses the damage from a humorous six miles away, the
Bats seem not to have accomplished much.

Bat Song
Tune: "Sweet Betsy from Pike"

Oh, do you remember the call sign of Bat,
In South Vietnam at a place called Phu Cat?
Where we lost Super Sabres by day and by night,
With wall-to-wall high drags we'd blast out of sight.

The FAC said, "Now, Bats, I am over Khe Sanh;
If you give me your lineup, I'll soon put you on;
The ceiling's two hundred, the run-in is tight,
But the target's a shit-hot, big triple-A site."

The Bats armed them up and then plugged in ABs;
They roared down the valley just over the trees;
The FAC lobbed his smoke from a half-mile away,
Saying, "Give 'em hell, Bats, I'll stay out of your way."

We rolled in on final amid the airbursts,
We pickled and pulled, till our hemorrhoids burst;
With shit in the cockpit and flak in the air,
The hell with four passes, we'll drop 'em in there.

The FAC started climbing to get BDA;
He used his field glasses from six miles away;
Said, "All bombs on target, what a hell of a show!
But Charlie's still shooting, now wouldn't you know?"

Sing good-bye to Sioux City, farewell to our kin,
When this war is over we'll come back again!

Battle Hymn of the 85-mm Gunner

The speaker in "Battle Hymn of the 85-mm Gunner" is a North Vietnamese soldier, probably in North Vietnam, who mans an 85-mm antiaircraft gun. He especially fears raids by F-105 Thunderchiefs and is finally killed in one. He goes to hell, but even there he is not safe from the F-105s. This song was probably written by pilots at an F-105 base in Thailand. The enemy here is not portrayed with any sensitivity or realism but seems more of a cartoon character. When flying over Hanoi, our air crews found the 85-mm gun a formidable weapon.

Battle Hymn of the 85-mm Gunner
Tune: "Battle Hymn of the Republic"

Mine eyes have seen the glory of the coming of the force,
And Uncle Ho has yelled and cussed and screamed till he is hoarse,
"Go out and man your guns, my boys, you have a job to do,"
The Thuds are coming in!

CHORUS *(repeat after each verse):*
　　Gory, gory, what a helluva way to die,
　　Gory, gory, what a helluva way to die,
　　Gory, gory, what a helluva way to die,
　　I don't want to fight no more!

Now as the Thuds are getting close, beside my gun I stand;
We all should feel quite proud to stand in defense of this land;
But getting my ass blown to bits is not what I call grand;
The Thuds are coming in!

There's 750s all around, the sky is full of shit,
And smoke and dust and arms and legs, don't like it one damn bit;
If they miss me this last time I think that I shall quit;
The Thuds are coming in!

We got hit and now are down below in Commie hell;
Each day they scare us pissless in a way we know so well;

Our Commie Satan he stands up, you hear that bastard yell,
"The Thuds are coming in!"

Battle Hymn of the Ranch Hands

One of our air strategies during the war in Southeast Asia was to spray the jungles with defoliating chemicals. This operation took place from 1965 to 1970 and was meant to clear large areas so that enemy troops could not concentrate. Crews who took part in this operation ironically called themselves Ranch Hands. One of the defoliants used was Agent Orange, the effects of which on friendly troops are still being debated today. (See also "Blowing in the Wind," "I'm a Young Ranch Hand," "Spray On, Spray on Harvest Rice," "Spray the Town," and "Twelve Days in Ranch Hand.") The spraying, to be effective, had to be done at relatively low altitudes, so the aircraft were quite likely to take hits from small-arms fire and .50-caliber automatic weapons. The United States was often criticized for this program by some in the world press, and the operation at its worst, when it infected civilians, helped increase antiwar activity within the United States.

Battle Hymn of the Ranch Hands
Tune: "Battle Hymn of the Republic"

My eyes have seen the Ranch Hands as they start a spray to pass,
Dropping to low altitude as .50s come through the grass;
They've got one hand on the throttle and the other on a bottle
Of Pabst Blue Ribbon Beer!

Glory, glory, what a hell of a way to spray,
Glory, glory, what a hell of a way to spray,
Glory, glory, what a hell of a way to spray,
And I hope to do it again another day!

Battle Hymn of the Red River Rats

Any U.S. flyer who flew across the Red River on combat missions into North Vietnam is eligible to be a member of the Red River Rats. Of his original song, Dick Jonas notes:

The thing I remember first about this song is that it was penned on a scrap of paper while airborne en route to Wichita, Kansas. McConnell AFB was Thud country in 1969. Those guys hosted the first RRVFPA (Red River Valley Fighter Pilots' Association) stateside practice reunion. There had been several practice Rats Reunions in Thailand in previous years, but this one in 1969 was the first in the States. Suffice it to say that Thud jocks are superb hosts. At that reunion, this song was adopted as the official song of the RRVFPA.

The reunions were called "practice" reunions because the members felt there could be no genuine reunion until the war was over and their POW comrades had come home. F-105 combat crew members had been trained for Vietnam at McConnell Air Force Base (see "F-105 Alma Mater").

Battle Hymn of the Red River Rats

The Red River Rats meet again,
Telling tales, remembering when
Battles joined in the skies,
Shed our blood, gave our lives;
The Red River Rats meet again.

War is never a beautiful thing,
But we fought for the right on the wing;
Dropping bombs, dodging flak,
Fighting MiGs, we'll be back,
Shout the Rats' battle cry, let it ring!

Look around, there's a few empty chairs,
Honored comrades should be sitting there;
Some are dead where they fell,
Some fight on from a cell,
Charge your glass, raise it high, drink to them.

I'll tell you a tale that will curl your hair,
I'll tell you the truth, 'cause I was there,
About what happened in Ho Chi Minh's backyard;
Gyrene, sailor, and Air Force type,
Black smoke pouring from a hot tailpipe,
Flyin' and fightin' and livin' a life that's hard.

Black smoke, flak smoke, red SAM fire,
Pressin' your luck right down to the wire,

Pickle 'em off and boot that mother for home,
But the battle ain't over till you've parked and chocked,
So if you fly and fight, keep your guns unlocked,
And don't try to fly and fight when you're all alone.

What's that telltale wisp I see?
That's a contrail pulled by a Fishbed-C;
The cards are stacked and it looks like time to deal.
Lead's got bandits twelve o'clock high,
Let's bend it around and scramble for the sky,
And arm your guns, this ain't no game, it's real.

We flew the Valley and the railroad lines,
From Dien Bien Phu to the Cam Pho mines,
But the price was high and measured in rich, red blood;
When tales are told in the halls of fame,
When warriors meet you'll hear these names:
"Skyhawk, Crusader, Intruder, Phantom, Thud."

The Red River Rats meet again,
Telling tales, remembering when
Battles joined in the skies,
Shed our blood, gave our lives;
The Red River Rats meet again.

Words and music by Dick Jonas, from *FSH Volume II, YGBSM.* © 1971 by Enchantment Music Co. Used with permission.

The Battle of Doumer Bridge

Located in the heart of Hanoi, the Doumer Bridge (pronounced DOUGH-mer), named after Paul Doumer (1857–1932), a former president of France, was an important target, both strategically and symbolically. More than a mile long, this highway and railroad bridge enabled vital war supplies to move from China to Hanoi, then on to South Vietnam via Thanh Hoa and the Ho Chi Minh Trail. U.S. president Lyndon Johnson planned a December, 1967, Christmas bombing truce in an attempt to get the North Vietnamese to begin working out a peace settlement, and the raid in "The Battle of Doumer Bridge" took place during the intensified bombing of the Hanoi area just prior to the truce. After this attack the bridge was repaired, and from then through February, 1969, at which time Johnson again halted all bombing in North Vietnam above the 19th Parallel, supplies continued to flow from the North to enemy troops in the South over this bridge without further interruption until President Nixon renewed the bombing of the Hanoi area in the early 1970s. The song's melody is taken from a traditional black American spiritual from around 1865 which was popularly revived through a new arrangement by Marshall Bartholomew in 1930.

The Battle of Doumer Bridge
Tune: "Joshua Fit de Battle of Jericho"

CHORUS (*repeat after each verse, twice after last verse*):
> *We fought the Battle of Doumer Bridge.*
> *Doumer Bridge, Doumer Bridge,*
> *We fought the Battle of Doumer Bridge,*
> *And the bridge went tumblin' down.*

Eighteen December, Sixty-Seven—
It seemed like a thunderclap;
We dropped Doumer Bridge on down
Into Ho Chi Minh's red lap!

Now you talk about your River Kwai Bridge
And the one at Thanh Hoa, too;
We got ten seconds over that bridge,
Then into the mountain dew.

Uncle Ho holds all the cards, boys,
And he plays them with great joy;
Wonder how he liked that game of bridge
Up at old Hanoi?

Now we lost some friends up yonder
Due to SAMs and MiGs and flak,
But if Ho puts that damn bridge up,
Well, we'll all be going back.

For those who've gone before us,
For those who've left our shore,
I know we're not forgetting them,
So let's sing it just once more!

The Battle of 18.23

The Jimmy Driftwood hit of 1959 provides the melody for this song, which tells the story of an F-105 raid on a bridge in North Vietnam. I've been unable to establish where 18.23 was, but as in the cases of the Doumer and Thanh Hoa bridges, this bridge too was probably repaired and reused by the dedicated enemy, despite the suggestion of final destruction in the song. But even here, the attackers know that there are still other bridges to hit. One of the greatest frustrations during the air war over Southeast Asia was the sure knowledge of combat flyers that every target, whether road, bridge, or river ford, would have to be hit over and over again. And even enemy trucks and supply barges seemed to multiply like rabbits. After President Johnson halted the bombing of all of North Vietnam on October 31, 1969, it was very frustrating to see reconnaissance photos of the Dong Hoi area full of supply vessels and stacked munitions that we were no longer permitted to hit. We in the 8th Fighter Wing had flown many missions over that area just 30 miles north of the DMZ prior to the bombing halt and had never seen such a bombing bonanza during months of combat missions. Although events might be moving toward a political solution, we well knew in November, 1969, that those vast supplies moving with impunity through Dong Hoi would kill many people down South before any truce was signed, and we could do nothing about it.

The Battle of 18.23

Tune: "The Battle of New Orleans"

To 18.23 we took a little flight,
On JCS direction we carried on the fight;
We took some "Baby Hueys"
And we took a Weasel, too,
And we bombed that bloody bridge
Until the pieces flew.

CHORUS *(repeat after each verse):*
    Oh, they fired their guns
    And the Fives kept a'coming,
    Though there wasn't nigh as many

As there was a while ago;
They fired their missiles
As the Fives began their run,
On that bloody fuckin' bridge
In the valley far below.

Oh, we lost four ships
And the men in them, too,
Before we dropped a span
In the muddy fuckin' goo;
We tried it twice by land,
And we tried it twice by sea,
The JCS were happy;
They giggled in their glee.

Now 18.23 will never more be used,
Once they decided how
The bombs should be fused;
There's no time for joy
And no time for sorrow;
The bastards have another
And it's fragged for tomorrow!

Bear of the Sky

The term "bear" was often affectionately used to refer to a co-pilot or navigator who flew in the backseat of the F-4 and some F-105s. If he was a pilot, this crew member was almost always eager to gain enough experience to move into the front seat and become the aircraft commander (AC). During my tour at Ubon, promising copilots were sometimes offered the option of returning to the States early and being retrained as aircraft commanders, *if* they were willing to return to Southeast Asia later for another complete one-year tour. Some took advantage of this option, and others refused, thinking that upgrading a pilot to AC should be based on merit alone, not on willingness to do double combat duty. Roger Miller's popular "King of the Road" (1965) praises the simple, carefree life of the American hobo, and in "Bear of the Sky" its melody thus provides ironic contrast to the plight of the poor Air Force backseater, whose sometimes menial role is highlighted. For a more positive view of the value of the bear, see the comments introducing "I've Been Everywhere."

Bear of the Sky
Tune: "King of the Road"

Back seat for sale or rent,
Radar sets, fifty cents,
He's got no landings yet,
No takeoff will he get.
Four hours on the boom in a
Cockpit with no damn room. He's a —
Man who flies, but don't fly,
Bear of the sky.

He knows every instrument, every dial,
He gets occasional stick time, once in a while,
And every week when the weather is clear,
The AC may let him lower the gear.

He rides in the rumble seat
And thinks it's quite a treat;
His AC will take care
While he rides through the air;
He takes up extra room, he rides
Through the sonic boom. He's a —
Man who flies, but don't fly,
Bear of the sky.

Beside a Laotian Waterfall

Perhaps a dozen Air Force songs have been based on the melody and theme of the old railroad song "The Dying Hogger," modified later to "The Dying Hobo." The original melody, dating from 1880–1910 or so, was used, for example, in World War I's "Beside a Belgian Water Tank," in World War II's "Beside a New Guinea Waterfall," and in Korea's "Beside a Korean Waterfall." The melody and its popular adaptations have become Air Force classics. This Southeast Asian version, like all of them, tells about a young pilot who finds consolation in his death by thinking about the better land to which he's going. The defiant coarseness of the last stanza serves to protect the singers—and the pilot in the song—from any charge of sentimentality. The death of the pilot is regrettable, of course, but fighter-pilot bravado must be maintained.

Even as late as World War II fighter planes were called pursuit planes and their pilots, pursuitors.

Beside a Laotian Waterfall

Tune: "The Dying Hobo"

Beside a Laotian waterfall
One bright and sunny day,
Beside his shattered Thunderchief
A young pursuitor lay.

His parachute hung from a nearby tree,
He was not yet quite dead,
So listen to the very last words
This young pursuitor said:

"I'm going to a better land
Where everything is right,
Where whiskey flows from telegraph poles,
There's poker every night.
There's not a fucking thing to do
But sit around and sing;
Where girls are really women,
Oh, death, where is thy sting?"

Oh, death, where is thy sting-a-ling-a-ling,
Oh, death, where is thy sting?
The bells of hell will ring-a-ling-a-ling
For you but not for me . . . so:

Ting-a-ling-a-ling, blow it out your ass,
Ting-a-ling-a-ling-ling, blow it out your ass,
Ting-a-ling-a-ling-ling, blow it out your ass,
Better days are coming by and by!

B-52 Takeoff

"B-52 Takeoff" may well have been written prior to the Vietnam War, but it was sung during that conflict. The Boeing Stratofortress (also sometimes called, like other big bombers, a Buff— "big, ugly, fat fellow), flying out of U-Tapao, Thailand, for example, would fly in large formations and demolish hundreds of acres of jungle in one giant arc-light mission. Other B-52s of the Strategic Air Command flew missions over North Vietnam and elsewhere in Southeast Asia from as far away as Guam, and their deadly missions ordered by President Nixon in the final months of the war helped drive Hanoi to a peace treaty. The song was perhaps written by a fighter pilot satirizing the B-52, by a B-52 pilot who would rather be in fighters, or even by a B-52 crewman affectionately poking fun at his own aircraft. Arc-light missions could destroy trees better than fighter planes could, but I often heard that just after the B-52s dropped their last bombs and departed, Viet Cong or North Vietnamese troops were right on the spot salvaging bomb fragments so they could reuse the metal against us.

B-52 Takeoff

Hand on the throttles,
All eight of them,
Release the brakes,
All sixteen of them,
Off we go into the
Wild blue yonder . . . CRASH!!!!!

Bien Hoa Lullaby

"Bien Hoa Lullaby" borrows its melody from a traditional Scottish song first popular in America about 1880. This melody, popular in other Air Force songs as well, and these lyrics were easily adapted to any U.S. Air Force base subject to enemy ground attack, especially in South Vietnam. In the Da Nang version of this song, for example, the last two lines of stanza 3 read: "The Gyrenes (Marines) are up even sooner / To recapture the ramp at Da Nang." The practice of sleeping within a protective ring of sandbags, referred to in stanza 4, could easily transfer to peace-time behavior. A friend of mine saved his life during an enemy mortar attack in South Vietnam by running into a sandbagged metal shower. He told me that when he returned home after the war, he at first felt quite uncomfortable showering at home with-out his sandbags.

Bien Hoa Lullaby
Tune: "My Bonnie Lies over the Ocean"

I went off to Southeast Asia
To fight my own war in the air;
I've spent half my tour in a bunker;
I don't think that it's really fair.

CHORUS (*repeat after each verse*):
   Roll in, roll in,
   My God, how the rockets roll in, roll in,
   Roll in, roll in,
   My God, how the rockets roll in!

Each day I go off to fly combat,
Then have a beer on the ground;
I usually finish the first one
Before we receive the first round.

Each morning we go off to combat,
At dawn in the clouds, fog, and damp;
The Army is up even sooner
To run the VC from the ramp.

And now my tour is all over,
I'll resume the life that I led;
My wife thinks that it's rather silly
To put sandbags all 'round our bed!

Blowing in the Wind

Among the most popular and powerful war-protest songs of the Vietnam era was "Blowin' in the Wind," a Bob Dylan composition performed by Peter, Paul, and Mary in 1963. Selling over two million copies, their recording was in the Top 10 of American popular songs and earned two Grammy Awards. Air Force Ranch Hands, flying chemical defoliation missions out of Da Nang, South Vietnam, had their own version of the song. Their mission received national criticism, and it would be easy for them to be self-conscious about it, especially if unforecasted winds blew their chemicals away from the target and over civilian villages. While there is no overt protest in the Air Force version, there does seem an undercurrent of quiet desperation, especially in the final two stanzas.

Blowing in the Wind
Tune: "Blowin' in the Wind"

How many hectares can a Ranch Hand spray
Before it's all blown away?
And how much rubber can a Ranch Hand kill,
Before Uncle Sam has to pay?

CHORUS (*repeat after each verse*):
   The answer, my friends, is blowing in the wind;
   The answer is blowing in the wind.

How many smokes can a Ranch Hand throw
Before the fighters can strike?
And how many hits can a Ranch Hand take,
Pretending it's something he likes?

How much Mateus can a Ranch Hand drink
At the Da Nang Ranch-IN?
And how many clubs can a Ranch Hand wreck,
On only a bottle of gin?

Blue Four

Of "Blue Four," Dick Jonas says, "In a flight of four fighters, Blue Flight, Blue Four is the youngest, least experienced, low man on the totem pole, fourth in command. For all these reasons in battle he is the most exposed, his position the most precarious, his life expectancy shortest of the four. I love him. He is my brother. When he went down, I wept unashamedly. The years can never heal the hurt nor dry the eye of any fighter pilot who returned home without his wingman." Dick's song, poignant yet patriotic, is in the tradition of the American fighter pilot since World War I.

Our losses in the 8th Tactical Fighter Wing were never easy to bear personally, but publicly we seemed almost to ignore them. Perhaps we had to in order to carry on. When I was assigned a room at Ubon the day of my arrival, I noticed my clothes locker was padlocked and there was a large, locked duffel bag on the floor in front of it. I asked the young pilot who served as housing officer about that. He looked away and replied, "Those are some things that need to be shipped out. The locker will be ready for your use tomorrow afternoon." I thought no more about it.

About one o'clock in the morning I was awakened by the door opening, and I looked up slightly. I knew that my new roommate, whom I had not yet met, had been on a night mission. Not expecting anyone else in the room, an exhausted looking major in a flight suit turned on the light and half flopped on his bed with his feet still on the floor. He closed his eyes.

"Hi," I said. I'll never forget the startled look in his eyes as he finally noticed me. His jaw fell, he paused and muttered, Hi," then reached up and flipped off the light. Nothing else was said, so I turned over and went back to sleep. The next afternoon when I returned to my room, I noticed my roommate's bed stripped, his locker open and empty. The duffel bag was gone, and my locker was now open and empty, too.

In a few minutes the young lieutenant came in to see how I was doing. "Where's Major Busch?" I asked. This time the housing officer looked right at me and said, "I forgot to tell him you'd be in here last night, and his other roommate had just been killed two days ago. Seeing you in his bed shook him up, so I've moved him elsewhere. He just can't stay in this room any more."

On June 5, 1968, I began to keep a list of our aircraft and crew losses. Other than people whom we recovered, the rest were:

> June 13, 1968: Aircraft exploded during a low-level night mission: Lieutenant Colonel Casey and Booth probably killed.
> July 24: 497th Squadron Nite Owls flight of two shot up: Pierce

and other recovered near Da Nang; Bush and Hackett lost over the water; Hackett's raft later found empty 25 miles offshore.

August 24: 497th bird lost; Reed and Ladewig killed near Xuan Son at night; F-4 hit the ground and blew up;

September 19: Roger Clemens and Pete Nash crash on landing at Ubon. Clemens killed; Nash ejects at near ground level, breaks both legs, injures spine, is shipped home.

January 29: 497th bird lost; Campbell and Calvert probably dead.

February 27: 497th bird lost during a rocket pass; Keller and Col. Meroney lost.

March 10: Lt. Col. Luna and Rutyna shot down over Laos. Rutyna recovered, Luna MIA or dead.

Maj. Jerry Rodell, our Ubon Catholic chaplain who later became an Air Force general, did lead some prayers at a mass for Lieutenant Colonel Casey in June 1968. I had seen Casey at mass regularly since my arrival on May 29. I don't, however, remember any memorial services for the others. At least not at Ubon. Col. Vergil K. Meroney III, our 8th Fighter Wing Deputy Commander for Operations, killed in February, 1969, is listed on panel 30W, line 6, on the Vietnam War Memorial in Washington, D.C. His son, Raphnell J., another fighter pilot who was lost before his father, is listed on panel 04E, line 112. I only flew once with Colonel Meroney but well remember our mission over North Vietnam, my sixty-eighth, in F-4D tail number 263 on October 13, 1968. Vergil Meroney was a gentle man, superb pilot, and sported an enviably glorious black mustache.

Blue Four

There's a fireball down there on the hillside,
And I think maybe we've lost a friend,
But we'll keep on flyin', and we'll keep on dyin',
For duty and honor never end.

There's an upended glass on the table,
Down in front of a lone empty chair;
Yesterday we were with him, today God be with him,
Wherever he is, in Your care.

They were four when they took off this mornin',
And their duty was there in the sky;
Only three ships returnin', Blue Four ain't returnin',
To Blue Four then hold your glasses high.

There's a fireball down there on the hillside,
And I think maybe we've lost a friend,
But we'll keep on flyin', and we'll keep on dyin',
For duty and honor never end.

Words and music by Dick Jonas, from *FSH Volume II, YGBSM.* © 1971 by Enchantment Music Co. Used with permission.

Bronco Song

Like "Blue Four," "Bronco Song" tells of death in the air, but more graphically and more immediately. An earlier version of the "Bronco Song" sung by James P. ("Bull") Durham in 1971 uses an O-2 rather than an OV-10 in stanza 1, and F-100s rather than F-4 Phantoms in stanza 4. Faster and more powerful than either the O-1 or O-2, the OV-10 Bronco had two turboprop engines. First flown in August, 1967, the Bronco was designed specifically for FAC operations and for limited quick reaction ground support— meaning "do the best you can with what you've got"—pending the arrival of tactical fighters. A total of 157 Broncos was delivered to the Air Force before Rockwell International ceased producing them in April, 1969.

I seem to remember seeing a Korean war version of this song somewhere. Sometimes appearing with the title "Dear Ma'am," the "Bronco Song" has a curiously lilting, playful melody that does not seem to suit the lyrics.

Bronco Song

Dear mom, your son is dead, he bought the farm today;
He crashed his OV-10 on Ho Chi Minh's Highway;
It was a rocket pass and he busted his ass.
Hmmm, Hmmm, Hmmm.

He went across the fence to see what he could see,
There it was as plain as it could be;
It was a truck on the road with a big, heavy load.
Hmmm, Hmmm, Hmmm.

He got right on the horn, and gave the DASC a call,
"Send me air, I've got a truck that's stalled."
The DASC said, "That's all right I'll send you Buick Flight."
Hmmm, Hmmm, Hmmm.

Those Phantoms checked right in, gunfighters two by two,
Low on gas and tanker overdue;
They asked the FAC to mark just where that truck was parked.
Hmmm, Hmmm, Hmmm.

That Bronco rode just in with his smoke
To exactly where that truck was parked;
Now the rest is in doubt, 'cause he never pulled out.
Hmmm, Hmmm, Hmmm.

Dear mom, your son is dead, he bought the farm today;
He crashed his OV-10 on Ho Chi Minh's Highway;
It was a rocket pass and he busted his ass.
Hmmm, Hmmm, Hmmm.

Brown Anchor

Sung to the melody of "Oh! Susannah," the Stephen Collins Foster song of 1848, which was used in a number of movies during the 1920s and 1940s, "Brown Anchor" gives us a rather disjointed story told by a less-than-delicate pilot. Pilots and aircraft assigned to "spare" duty took off only to replace a scheduled aircraft that developed mechanical or serious crew problems prior to takeoff. This spare pilot wants to take off so he can get another mission over North Vietnam, which will count toward the 100 he needs to go home (which he has completed in stanza 9), so he lies about Bear Four's fuel leak and takes off himself.

His flight refuels at Brown Anchor air refueling area en route to its target, and the chorus humorously explains what lengths a pilot might go to because of the problem of attempting to relieve oneself in the cramped confines of a modern fighter plane. Stanza 10 is cryptic. The last three stanzas explain how the pilot begins to count his sexual activities with his wife as he used to count combat missions in Vietnam. An Alpha frag, or counter, was a mission scheduled over North Vietnam that counted toward the 100; a Bravo frag was scheduled over South Vietnam, Laos, or elsewhere and did not count. It was called a freebie.

I knew a backseater at Ubon who finagled his way into every counter he could get. He'd been in combat only five months and had 80. He became so combat weary and burned out that our squadron commander sent him to Bangkok to relax and after his return let him fly only three or four counters a month.

Regarding the physical problems during combat missions, I remember once when I was flying with Lieutenant Colonel Sammons, our squadron commander. Our mission was a long one, and about an hour into it I started getting severe stomach cramps. I told Sammons, who was in the front seat, and he told me he would keep the mission short so we could get back as early as possible so I could relieve myself. Thirty minutes later my pain was excruciating, but I was still holding out. After fifteen minutes later, when the base was in sight, I could control myself no longer, and I told Sammons what had happened. He matter-of-factly called the tower at Ubon, and when we landed, a buddy of mine met us at the aircraft with some towels and a clean flying suit. He took me to a nearby washroom, and I cleaned up, changed, and rejoined the other three crew members at debriefing. Nothing was ever said to me by anyone about this incident, not even in jest. I expected some good-natured ribbing, but what would have been highly embarrassing in civilian life was treated professionally in combat. I appreciated that consideration, and had even more respect than ever for those with whom I flew and fought.

Brown Anchor
Tune: "Oh! Susannah"

The phone did ring at half past four, for briefing I weren't there,
"Get your ass here right away, you've been elected spare."

FIRST CHORUS (*repeat after next seven verses*):
   Oh, Brown Anchor, with my two-hour ass,
   A Fahnestock clip upon my dick,
   Oh, leader, go home fast!

I was setting by the runway, and feeling mighty low,
"Bear Four, you've got a hydraulic leak, I guess I'll have to go!"

I guess I told a little lie; it probably wasn't fair,
It was my only chance to say, "Bear Spare is in the air."

It was raining out when we took off, night weather we did fly;
We rendezvoused at nineteen thou'—my tanks were nearly dry.

As we climbed out I had to fart, my belly it did swell;
I had to put my mask back on, I couldn't stand the smell.

They're twelve o'clock at five miles, you're cleared refueling freq,
"Tally-ho!" our flight leader cried, and head-on we did meet.

We hung it out at fourteen thou'—the burner going strong,
The flak came flying by my bow, we can't hang out here long.

Oh, I pulled off the target and for BDA looked back;
I couldn't see the bomb burst for the son-of-a-bitchin' flak!

Finally got my hundred flown, to the States I'm flying back,
Six more hours on my ass, and then into the sack.

SECOND CHORUS *(repeat after next three verses, twice after last verse):*
    No more Brown Anchor for my two-hour ass,
    Get that clip right off my dick
    And jump in bed right fast!

I opened my hold baggage, my wife she sure did flip;
I hope that she will understand I just adopted "Nip."

I rolled over with a sigh, bed springs were sagging low;
Put a mark upon the wall, only ninety-nine to go.

Thought I had a Bravo frag as I jumped into bed,
It was a real tight target so I marked it up in red.

The Bunker Song

"The Bunker Song" takes its melody from an Irving Berlin hit first sung by Kate Smith on public radio on Armistice Day, 1938. During World War II, the song was again popularized by Smith in the movie *This Is the Army*, starring Ronald Reagan. The last two lines are probably a taunt at the enemy rocket firers that the speaker hurls from within the safety of his beloved bunker.

The Bunker Song
Tune: "God Bless America"

God bless our bunker,
Sand that we love;
Stand beside us, and protect us
From the rockets that fall from above;
From the island, from the river,
From Long Binh, to Saigon,
God bless our bunker,
The sand we love;
God bless our bunker,
The sand we love.
My father can play dominoes better than your father can play
*   dominoes.   A—men!*

Call Out the Reserves

Although some serve on active duty indefinitely, many Reserve personnel hold down civilian jobs and train a certain number of days a month. During emergencies they can be called to continuous active duty as needed. There has always been friendly rivalry between Reserve and active-duty personnel in the U.S. military. Air Force versions of "Call Out the Reserves" have been popular since Korea. This version, composed at Phu Cat Air Base in South Vietnam, makes fun of the F-4D fighter by calling it a "bomber" in stanza 3 and explains how even in their older F-100 Super Sabres, Reserve pilots can bomb more accurately than their F-4 counterparts.

Call Out the Reserves
Tune: "My Bonnie Lies over the Ocean"

In peacetime the Regulars are happy,
In peacetime they're happy to serve,
But just let them get into trouble,
They call out the goddamned Reserves!

CHORUS (repeat after each verse):
>   Call out, call out,
>   They call out the goddamned Reserves, Reserves,
>   Call out, call out,
>   They call out the goddamned Reserves!

> Now here's to the Regular Air Force,
> They have such a wonderful plan;
> They call out the goddamned Reservists,
> Whenever the shit hits the fan!

> Now here's to the great Fox-four bombers,
> They killed all the MiGs in the Packs;
> They carry a shit load of ordnance,
> But they can't hit a bull in the ass!

> Now here's to the Guard's Super Sabre,
> It couldn't survive an attack;
> But load up just four 750s,
> They put every one down the stack!

Charlie Went A-Running

An anonymous English folk song dating back several hundred years provides the melody for "Charlie Went A-Running." The Viet Cong, or VC, are the South Vietnamese Communist troops. In the U.S. Army's phonetic alphabet, VC is Victor Charlie, hence the name Charlie for any VC soldier. The first two stanzas describe the stealth of a mostly unseen enemy, while the last reflects a particularly effective strategy of both the VC and their allies, the North Vietnamese. Along the Ho Chi Minh Trail, enemy supply depots were even underground, and the North Vietnamese extensively used underground tunnels and factories during their successful war against the French.

Charlie Went A-Running
Tune: "Froggy Went A-Wooing"

> Charlie won't fight 'n' I don't care, un huh,
> Charlie won't fight 'n' I don't care, uh huh,

Charlie won't fight 'n' I don't care,
I think he's running off somewhere, uh huh, uh huh, uh huh.

He sneaked up to my front door, uh huh,
He sneaked up to my front door, uh huh,
He sneaked up to my front door,
He didn't knock, he left a claymore, uh huh, uh huh, uh huh.

Old Charlie's got some mortar shells, uh huh,
Old Charlie's got some mortar shells, uh huh,
Old Charlie's got some mortar shells,
I hope he blows himself to hell, uh huh, uh huh, uh huh.

Charlie's living underground, uh huh,
Charlie's living underground, uh huh,
Charlie's living underground,
When the monsoon comes I hope he drowns, uh huh, uh huh, uh huh.

Chocolate-covered Napalm

My study of Air Force song lyrics from World War I through World War II, Korea, and the war in Vietnam reveals increasing cynicism, black humor, and the use of profanity as Americans' view of war began to change. The next song, "Chocolate-covered Napalm," is ironic, sarcastic, and horrifying. Napalm (from *naphthene-palmi*tate) is a thickener used in jelling gasoline for use in incendiary air-to-ground bombs designed for use against enemy troops, trucks, and other light targets. The reference to Ho Chi Minh in the chorus tells us that the song was composed prior to Ho's death in September, 1969.

Stanza 2 is especially ironic. During World War II, American troops often gave Hershey bars to European youngsters as a sign of friendship. The allusion to Santa Claus in stanza 3 further relates napalm to children. The idea of the American chocolate industry vying to make napalm for war is black humor at its best—or worst. When dropped from a low-flying aircraft, napalm spreads flames and burning gel across a wide area, at the same time removing the oxygen. The results to human beings caught in a napalm strike are devastating. Those not killed outright find that they cannot remove the burning gel from the body without cutting the skin away. We never used napalm during our combat missions out of Thailand. I was told that the king would not permit it. It was used extensively, however, in South Vietnam and elsewhere.

As I was seeking a publisher for these songs, I first thought it would be especially appropriate if the U.S. Air Force itself would publish them, so I sent a sample manuscript to the Office of Air Force History after learning that they might be interested. On December 15, 1985, Richard H. Kohn, chief of the Office of Air Force History, wrote me the following: "After considerable discussion in the Office of Air Force History Publications Committee, we have decided that it will not be possible for us to publish "The Winged Muse." The nature of some of the songs, the considerable use of profanity, and the sardonic humor, all could be so easily misinterpreted that we believe it would not be appropriate for the Air Force to act as publisher of the volume."

I was surprised at this opening. I had thought that history was history, facts were facts, whatever their nature, no matter how profane or how sardonic. I read on. "For one thing, were we to publish the manuscript in its present form as an official Air Force publication, we would open our service to a variety of charges concerning the conduct of the air war in Southeast Asia. You and I know that we were not involved in a program of indiscriminate killing, but others may disagree after reading some of the songs."

Now I began to understand. I suppose the Air Force could not officially present a song like "Chocolate-covered Napalm" to the public.

Chocolate-covered Napalm
Tune: "Get Along Home, Cindy, Cindy"

Oh, chocolate-covered napalm is raining from the sky,
Chocolate-covered napalm is made for you and I;
It's so much fun to drop it, and here's the reason why,
When it finally hits the ground, it makes the people fry.

CHORUS (*repeat after each verse*):
   Git along home, Ho Chi Minh,
   Git along home, Ho Chi Minh,

> Git along home, Ho Chi Minh,
> We'll see you by and by.

Oh, Hershey made the first bid, with Nestlé close behind,
For chocolate-covered napalm, the brand was hard to find;
But Milky Way was chosen; they said it was the best;
The jelly-centered filling will handle all the rest.

The weather, it can't stop us, in rain or sleet or snow,
We must make our delivery to the land of Uncle Ho;
With four big loads of napalm, all tucked beneath our wings,
It makes you feel like Santa Claus and all the joy he brings.

Rockets, bombs, and mike-mike is all the normal load,
Pulling off at forty-five, then watch them all explode;
They really do the job now, except for one small thing,
Napalm does it better than any other thing.

When you punch it off the rails now, it tumbles and it rolls,
The flight path undetermined, because it falls so slow;
Though pinpoint bombs and accuracy is our main desire,
Napalm covers half the world, with smoke and fumes and fire.

Cloudy Night, No Moonlight

The next is one of several songs that use traditional Christmas
melodies, in this case the Franz Grüber and Joseph Mohr classic of 1818, to contrast starkly with war-weary and often despair-
filled lyrics. In stanza 1 our pilot is terribly afraid of a dangerous
mission to come in which nature, failing technology, and even
purpose all seem to conspire against him. His projected target
in stanza 2 is a heavily defended one he's worked before, and
he dreads the Russian Fishbed-D MiG Fighters of the enemy. The
last stanza puzzles me. I'd like to think the pilot is at midnight
chapel service in stanzas 1 through 3 and that he must leave to
fly his mission while the preacher is quoting from Matthew 7:26
over the chapel PA system. Breakfast could have been eaten just
prior to services so the flyer could make church, yet still take off
on time. At least I know the song works for me that way, for I
experienced the same things—praying to God before and after

deadly missions, with everything just seeming to get jumbled up with great irony, even the message of Christmas and the mess of war. We all knew in combat that our castles seemed built on dangerous, shifting sand.

"Cloudy Night, No Moonlight" came to me on a tape from Dr. Lydia Fish of Buffalo State College in New York, where she is director of the Vietnam Veterans Oral History and Folklore Project, an ongoing undertaking to collect, preserve, and promote the folk songs of the Vietnam War.

Cloudy Night, No Moonlight
Tune: "Silent Night"

Cloudy night, no moonlight,
God of Light, what a hell of a flight!
'Round my stomach a butterfly sails,
Sure as hell the radar will fail;
Could be we'll wipe out some trees,
Could be we'll wipe out some trees!

51-10, got it again,
We've had it before and we know the score;
Flak on the left and flak on the right,
Fishbeds-D and the old launch light;
I don't like odds of that sort,
To me it is cause for abort.

Pacing the floor, can't do much more,
Breakfast is done, now I wait for the fun;
Voice on the squawk box has words of our faith;
"Buildeth your castles . . ." I'm sorry it's late;
We shout, swear, and pound on the floor,
Then we slip out the back door.

Come and Join the Air Force

The earliest version of "Come and Join the Air Force" is found in *Songs of the Army Fliers*, published by the Order of Daedalians in 1937. Credit for the melody is given to E. H. Ford and Madeline Smith and for the lyrics, to Roland Birnn. This is another Air

Force classic, with versions popular in World War II and Korea, as well as in Vietnam. The first four stanzas give us a playful account of both the pleasures and terrors of a pilot's life. In this lyrical accretion, stanzas 1 and 3 are very similar to a 1942 World War II version, while stanzas 2 and 4 are very close to the 1937 original. Stanza 5, similar to a Korean War version, and stanza 6 directly relate this version to the war in Vietnam. The 1937 lyrics contain no profanity.

Come and Join the Air Force
Tune: "Come On and Join the Air Corps"

Come and join the Air Force; we're a happy band, they say;
We never do a lick of work, just fly around all day;
While others work and study, and soon grow old and blind,
We take to the air without a care, and you will never mind!

CHORUS *(repeat after each verse):*
     You'll never mind, you'll never mind;
     So come and join the Air Force,
     And you will never mind!

Come and get promoted as high as you desire;
You're riding on a gravy train if you're an Air Force flyer;
And when you get to general, you will surely find,
Your wings fall off, the dough rolls in, but you will never mind!

You take it up and spin it, and with an awful tear,
Your wings fall off, the ship spins in, but you will never care;
For in about two minutes more another pair you'll find;
You'll dance with Pete in an angel's suit, but you will never mind!

While flying the Pacific, you hear the engine spit;
You watch the tach come to a stop, the goddamn thing has quit;
The ship won't float and you can't swim, the shore is far behind;
Oh, what a dish for crabs and fish, but you will never mind!

While flying over Laos in a Thunderchief,
There's one thing to remember, and that's my firm belief,
I've only got one engine, Jack, and if that bastard quits,
It'll be up there all by itself, 'cause I will shit and git!

And if some wily MiG-21 should shoot you down in flames,
Don't sit around and bellyache and call the bastard names;

Just hit the silk, it's cream and milk, and pretty soon you'll find
There is no hell and all is well, and you will never mind!

Cruising over Hanoi

The next song, also called the "Fighter Pilot's Hymn" or "Save a Fighter Pilot's Ass," is another Air Force classic with numerous versions appearing during World War II and the Korean and Vietnam wars. The melody was probably originally from a song satirizing the Salvation Army, with the chorus lines, "Throw a nickel on the drum / Save another drunken bum." (see also "Hallelujah," I and II). Except for its chorus, this version is quite original and proper to the Vietnam War. The speaker was a junior pilot flying in the number four flight position, and although he tells us his story as a POW in the Hanoi Hilton, he seems in good spirits.

Cruising over Hanoi
Tune: "Throw a Nickel on the Drum"

We were cruising over Hanoi, doin' four-fifty per,
When I called to my flight leader, "Oh, won't you help me, sir?
The SAMs are hot and heavy, and MiGs are on our ass,
Take us home, flight leader, please don't make another pass!"

CHORUS *(repeat after each verse):*
  Hallelujah, Hallelujah, throw a nickel on the grass,
  Save a fighter pilot's ass;
  Hallelujah, Hallelujah, throw a nickel on the grass
  And you'll be saved!

I rolled into my bomb run, trying to set my pipper right,
When a SAM came off the launch pad and headed for our flight;
Then Number Two informed me, "Hey, Four, you'd better break!"
I racked the goddamn plane so hard, it made the whole thing shake.

I started my recovery; it seemed things were all right,
When I felt the dam-ned impact, saw a blinding flash of light;
We held the stick with all our might against the binding force,
Then Number Two screamed out at us, "Hey, Four, you've had the
  course!"

I screamed at my backseater, "We'd better punch on out—
Eject! Eject! you stupid shit!" in panic I did shout;
I didn't wait around to see if Joe had got the word,
I reached between my legs and pulled and took off like a bird.

As I descended in my chute, my thoughts were rather grim;
Rather than be a POW, I'd fight them to the end;
I hit the ground and staggered up and looked around to see,
And there in blazing neon, Hanoi Hilton welcomed me.

The moral of this story is, when you're in Package Six,
You'd better goddamn look around or you'll be in my fix;
I'm a guest at Hanoi Hilton, with luxury sublime;
The only thing that's not so great, I'll be here a long, long time.

Dashing through the Sky

Set to the rollicking melody of a tune J. S. Pierpont wrote in 1857, "Dashing through the Sky" was written prior to Ho Chi Minh's death in September, 1969. The F-105 pilots view their combat missions over the Democratic Republic of Vietnam (DRV), the euphemism for Communist North Vietnam, as if they were Santa Clauses. Despite the enemy's opposing surface-to-air missiles (SAMs) and MiG fighters, the jolly F-105 flyers deliver their gifts of cluster bombs (CBUs), 500- and 750-pound bombs, and Vulcan cannon fire. Such gifts give sardonic joy to the givers—if not to the receivers.

Dashing through the Sky
Tune: "Jingle Bells"

Dashing through the sky,
In a Foxtrot 105,
Through the flak we fly,
Trying to stay alive;
The SAMs destroy our calm,
The MiGs come up to play;
What fun it is to strafe and bomb
The D.R.V. today!

CHORUS (*repeat after second verse*):
    CBUs, Mark 82s, 750s too,
    Daddy Vulcan strikes again,
    Our Christmas gift to you!

Heads up, Ho Chi Minh;
The Fives are on their way!
Your luck it has gave in,
There's gonna be hell to pay!
Today it is our turn
To make you gawk and stare;
What fun it is to watch things burn
And blow up everywhere!!!

Dingbat

The pilot in "Dingbat" is flying a night mission over his assigned area of responsibility, a 20-mile stretch of highway running from the coastal city of Dong Hoi northwest to Ron, about 50 miles north of the DMZ in North Vietnam. Dingbat, the radio call sign of his support aircraft, both identifies targets and marks them with flares so our pilot can go after them. "Dingbat" is also slang for a rather dopey person. Dingbat sends the pilot on a wild-goose chase after a truck convoy near Phat Ban. The pilot flies so far looking for the invisible trucks that he apparently runs out of fuel and ejects from his aircraft, for the song ends with him swinging in his parachute. The melody is from the Jimmy Davis and Charles Mitchell song of 1940, which was popularly revived in 1962. Using the same melody, the Korean War version, from which this one is derived, was entitled "Moonshine."

Dingbat
Tune: "You Are My Sunshine"

You are my Dingbat, my only Dingbat,
You flare my targets, when skies are gray;
I chase your trucks from Ron to Dong Hoi,
Just to find they have all slipped away.

The other night, as I was flying,
I heard old Dingbat say,
"I've got a convoy down by Phat Ban,
Won't you head that way if you can?"

He said he had me in radar contact,
And I believed him like a dope;
I flew to Phat Ban, and still no convoy,
I had chased St. Elmo across his nose.

You were my Dingbat, my only Dingbat,
How could you let me down this way?
My chute was swinging; they heard me singing,
"Won't you take my Dingbat away?"

Don't Send Me to Hanoi

Just as fighter pilots often state their courage with bravado, they also sometimes proclaim their fear with gusto, especially in song. "Winchester Cathedral," a popular Geoff Stephen hit of 1966 performed by the New Vaudeville Band, provides the melody for "Don't Send Me to Hanoi." The persona speaking is an atypical fighter pilot—he doesn't want to fly into danger and is eager to say so. Long refueling missions in the Brown Anchor area followed by strikes over downtown Hanoi or Bac Giang hold no appeal for him. Nor does he enjoy flying support missions for B-52 bombers, or Buffs (from the first two syllables of "B-52," also an acronym for "big, ugly, fat fellows"), just north of the DMZ, even though it's closer to his home base. He just prefers milk runs, easy missions that pose no threat to himself or his aircraft, his bear—but didn't we all?

Don't Send Me to Hanoi
Tune: "Winchester Cathedral"

Don't send me to Hanoi,
Please, don't put my name down;
The shooting is bad there,
Don't send me Downtown.

The bridges at Bac Giang,
More milling around;
Another Brown Anchor,
I think I'll leave town.

Don't send me to Yen Bai,
I don't like that much flak;
It takes too much damn gas
To bring my ass back.

Don't send me to Dong Hoi,
I don't want to get none;
Those Buff support missions,
They make my ass numb.

Just send me on milk runs
Where there are no big guns;
I just want to fly where
It's easy on my bear!

Down the Lazy Valley

The Hoagy Carmichael, Sidney Arodin 1931 tune popularly revived in 1941 provides the lilting melody for "Down the Lazy Valley." A fighter pilot and his backseater are shot down by a SAM
just about over Hanoi. The exaggeration of pulling 12 G's to escape the SAM in stanza 3 is nicely balanced by the pilot's understated reaction at being shot down. The pilot fears that his flare
pen gun will jam and prevent his signaling his rescuers in their
HH-3E Jolly Green Giant helicopters (see "Jolly Green, My Jolly
Green"), but almost at once his rescuers are on the spot. The
penetrator is a relatively heavy, pointed metal object on the end
of the helicopter's rescue cable and is designed to plunge
through thick jungle foliage and carry the cable to a downed flyer,
who grasps it, secures himself to it, and is hoisted to safety. After rescue, our pilot's first flush of joy turns to gloom, however,
as he realizes that this was but the first of a hundred combat missions he must fly before he can return home, a popular kind of
ending for a number of these songs. No matter what the terror,
one must face it again and again.

Down the Lazy Valley

Tune: "Up a Lazy River"

Down the lazy valley where the ack-ack hides,
The lazy, lazy valley on the other side,
When you come around the ridge you get a big surprise,
Well, you better wake up, honey, better open your eyes.

Well, down the old Red River by old [Bac Mai],
With 85 millimeter on your left and your right,
Your gun is fired, you're jinkin', do you get a fright;
Well, I just take pictures, but I want to fight!

Well, I saw the SAM flash up, kind of gave me a chill,
Well, I just pulled 12 G's a'goin' over the hill,
Well, [my GIB's punched out] and my tail's shot off,
And I'd like to tell you, Colonel, kinda' pissed me off!

Well, I'm sittin' in a tree 'bout a half mile high,
I'm just swingin' left and right and lookin' up at the sky;
My G [suit's busted] and my flares are wet,
And I'd like to tell you, buddy, got a pocket full of shit!

Well, some Jolly Greens are coming over the hill,
I hope my pen gun works because I've had my fill;
Well, I see the Jolly Green comin' through those trees,
Well, he drops his penetrator and I'm swinging in the breeze.

Well, I'm sitting at the bar, getting wet,
Well, I find myself a'sweatin', 'cause I ain't done yet,
So pass the whiskey, brother, 'cause I'm feeling kind of low,
And I only got ninety-nine missions to go!

Downtown I

British singer Petula Clark was extremely popular with many of the Air Force personnel who flew combat missions in Southeast Asia in the late 1960s. In fact, she was so popular that I was able to buy five or six pirated record albums of hers even in Taiwan in late 1968 for 25 cents apiece. In plastic with colors like red licorice, chartreuse, and bright orange, these cheap records were good for only 15 or 20 plays, but they could be preserved beautifully on reel-to-reel tape. Many of us listened to Petula before we went to war, listened to her at war, and held onto her as someone we wanted to listen to after we got safely home.

Petula's 1965 hit "Downtown," written by Tony Hatch in 1964, gave both title and melody to two Air Force songs in Vietnam. "Downtown I," written in 1966–67, the earlier version, was a favorite with the 355th Tactical Fighter Wing at Takhli Royal Thai Air Base. These pilots flew F-105 Thunderchiefs, and while their version does depict the danger of missions over "Downtown," or Hanoi, it stresses the courage and dedication of the F-105 pilots. Dick Jonas's version, which I title "Downtown II," was popular at Ubon and provides a much greater sense of fear and danger, ending with a flight of U.S. aircraft feverishly attempting to evade two enemy SAM missiles over Hanoi. I've often wondered whether Petula or Tony Hatch have ever heard these versions of their hit, and if so, what they might think of them.

Downtown I
Tune: "Downtown"

When you got a belly full o' Bravos and Sky Spots
You can always go—Downtown.
When you been drinkin' and "cancel" you're thinking
You are sure to go—Downtown.
Listen to the music of the Fan Songs softly singing;
Look and see the contrails of the MiGs so swiftly winging;
Sweat out the booze;
The flak is much blacker there,
It shakes up the pilots; it shakes up the bears,
To go Downtown, tried flying fast and slow,
Downtown, tried flying high and low,
Downtown, everything's shooting at you.

Look and see the airfields with their runways so inviting,
See the interceptors coming up to join the fighting,
Get out of here;
The SAMs are much thicker here,
They come up in singles; they come up in pairs,
Downtown, everything's waiting for you.

Just when it seems one hundred come quickly
You can always go—Downtown.
Somehow the feeling in your stomach gets sickly
When you have to go—Downtown.
Crew chiefs launch their aircraft with a pride and care amazing,
Proudly watch the Thunderchiefs, their afterburners blazing,
They're going again;
Our buddies are jailed up there,
We still remember and we still all care;
So we go Downtown,
Till it is o'er and done,
Downtown, till it is through and won,
Downtown, everything's waiting for you.

Downtown II

Of referring to Hanoi as "Downtown," Dick Jonas says: "When you fly with the Wolf Pack you get to see a lot of countryside, and you get so you know each place by name. Some of those names are pretty hard to pronounce, but it doesn't take long to learn them. Then there are a few places that don't have names, so we name them to suit ourselves—Thud Ridge, Banana Valley, the Loop, the Railroad, both of them, MiG Ridge, the Island. But we don't name every place—some places don't need names. When you mention 'the bridge,' everybody knows what you're talking about. And for ever after, to the fighter pilots who flew in the Wolf Pack, there'll always be only one place that's called 'Downtown.'"

Downtown II

Tune: "Downtown"

When you get up at two o'clock in the morning
You can bet you'll go—Downtown;
Shaking in your boots, you're sweating heavy all over,
'Cause you've got to go—Downtown;
Smoke a pack of cigarettes before the briefing's over,
Wishing you weren't bombing, wishing you were flying cover,

It's safer that way—the flak is much thicker there—
You know you're biting your nails and you're pulling your hair;
You're going Downtown, where all the lights are bright,
Downtown, you'd rather switch than fight,
Downtown, hope you come home tonight,
Downtown, Downtown.

Planning the route you keep hoping that you
Won't have to go today—Downtown;
Checking the weather, and it's scattered to broken,
So you still don't know—Downtown;
Waiting for the guys in TOC to say you're canceled,
Hoping that the words they give will be what suits your fancy,
Don't make me go—I'd much rather RTB—
So you sit and you wait thinking, oh, FSH!
You're going Downtown, but you don't wanna go,
Downtown, that's why you're feeling low,
Downtown, going to see Uncle Ho,
Downtown, Downtown.

MISSILE FORCE, BURNERS NOW . . .
BARRACUDA HAS SWEEPING GUNS . . .
DISREGARD THE LAUNCH LIGHT. . . . NO THREAT. . . .

What do you mean, no threat?
There's a pair at two o'clock!
Take it down!
Downtown.

© 1987. Original lyrics by Dick Jonas. Used with permission.

Early Abort

In Air Force parlance, a flying mission is said to be aborted if it cannot be continued for mechanical or personnel reasons once the crew arrives at the aircraft. There can thus be aborts before, during, or after takeoff, as well as en route. "Early Abort" has been a popular Air Force song in its various forms from World War II through Vietnam, and as usual, the earlier versions are generally profanity-free. One reason for the song's popularity is that it can easily be adapted to fit any unit or aircraft. For example, insert the name "Olds" in the first line, add "8th Wing" to the chorus, delete the references to F-105s in stanza 4, and the song would work at Ubon.

In the Vietnam version the first stanza pokes fun at the unit's commander and the second at the pilots, who are trying to abort the mission before takeoff by claiming that their Inertial Navigation Systems (INS) are operating improperly. Stanzas 3 and 4 provide reasons for aborting en route, stanza 5 again laughs at the unit's leaders, and stanza 6 scoffs at the Air Force's leaders in general. The lively melody comes from a 1917 song by Shamus O'Connor. "MacNamara's Band," with lyrics by John J. Stamford, was featured in the 1950 musical film "I'll Get By."

Early Abort
Tune: "MacNamara's Band"

Oh, my name is Colonel _____, I'm the leader of the group;
Just step into my briefing room, I'll give you all the poop;
I'll tell you where the Commies fly, and where they like to roam,
I'll be the last one to take off, the first one to come home.

CHORUS (*repeat after each verse*):
    Early abort, avoid the rush,
    Early abort, avoid the rush,
    Early abort, avoid the rush,
    The _____ on parade!

I'm sure you've heard of nightmares and the things that they can do,
But if you'll come down to the line you'll see they're far from true;
The pilots, they are ready, but let their leader shout,
And all those bastards yell at once, "My INS won't check out!"

Oh, we fly those bloody F-4Ds a million miles an hour;
We can fly them in the rain and fog and in the bloody shower,
And if we fly so fast, it fills us with alarm;
Lose a bloody rivet and you've surely bought the farm!

Oh, we fly those bloody 105s at ninety thousand feet;
We fly them through the rain and fog and through the bloody sleet,
And when we're feeling bloody high, we're feeling awfully low;
Lose your cabin pressure and it'll be an awful blow!

And now I'm sure you know of all the leaders in the wing,
Any night in the O-Club you can hear how well they sing;

With words they fight a helluva war, they say they want to fly,
   too,
But you give them half a chance to fly, and here's what they will
   do:

Now when this war is over and we're back in the USA,
We'll fly the planes in all war games and do what the generals say.
But if we have another war and they send us overseas,
To hell with all the general staffs, to hell with those S.O.B.s.

Escorting a Spectre

A formidable weapon in the air war over Southeast Asia was the Lockheed AC-130 Hercules gunship, a specially adapted model of the C-130 turboprop transport. Armed with two 40-mm cannon, two 20-mm Vulcan cannon, and two 7.62-mm miniguns, a Spectre could be quite effective at night against enemy troops, trucks, and other targets, equipped as it was with special sensors and target-acquisition systems, including forward-looking infrared and low-light-level TV. The speaker in "Escorting a Spectre" is a fighter-escort pilot who both protects and works with the gunship on air-to-ground strikes. The flight comes under heavy ground fire from an accurate enemy gunner whose manhood the speaker praises in stanza 2. The Spectre soon locates the gunner's position, however, and after confirming it by a dangerous flyover pass, the fighter drops a 2,000-pound Mark 84 laser-guided bomb (LGB) on him. This earlier Irish melody about a dying soldier has been popular in the United States since 1860 under the earlier title "The Cowboy's Lament."

Escorting a Spectre
Tune: "The Streets of Laredo"

As I was escorting a Spectre one evening,
And we were in orbit 'round Delta One-One,
A non-Christian gomer who didn't speak English
Was shooting at us with a Communist gun.

His marksmanship showed he had his shit together,
He watered our eyes on the very first pass;

That non-Christian gomer who didn't speak English,
That son of a bitch had balls made out of brass!

The Spectre TV was locked on his location,
Their music was playing a symphony sweet;
The non-Christian gomer who didn't speak English
Was soon to receive a magnificent treat.

We trolled o'er the gun pit with lights bright and flashing,
He hosed at our ass as we jinked left and right;
The non-Christian gomer who didn't speak English
Was going to be sorry he fired that night.

We started our bomb pass from twenty-one thousand,
The sword locked up fast and the crosshairs were right;
We pickled our bombs and started our pulloff,
The Demon was loose to wreak havoc that night.
That non-Christian gomer who didn't speak English
Kept shooting at us till the LGB hit;
He won't shoot no more, bud, and that is for certain;
The MK-84 guided right into his pit!

F-4 Serenade

Although fighter pilots usually respect their colleagues who fly
other aircraft, sometimes they don't. In "F-4 Serenade," however,
the F-105 pilot's masterfully coarse sarcasm is directed not so
much at the Phantom's crew as it is at the aircraft itself. This is
probably a pre-1969 song, since most of the F-4s in Southeast
Asia after late 1968 were D-models rather than the C-models men-
tioned in the chorus. The F-4 had folding wings because it was
originally designed for carrier use by the U.S. Navy. And although
it didn't have an internally mounted gun, the F-4 could carry one
as needed. In fact, most of the criticisms of the F-4 in this song
are matters of opinion, although they are certainly forcefully and
uniquely expressed.

F-4 Serenade

I'd rather be a pimple on a syphilitic whore,
Than a backseat driver on an old F-4.

CHORUS (*repeat after each verse*):
>   Don't put me in an F-4C, 4C,
>   Don't put me in an F-4C.

I'd rather be a hair on a swollen womb,
Than be a pilot of an old Phan-tomb.

I'd rather be a pimple on a dirty cock,
Than to be an F-4 jock.

I'd rather be a bloody scab,
Than to fly a plane with a bent up slab.

I'd rather be a rotten bum,
Than to fly a plane without a gun.

I'd rather be a piss in a bottle,
Than to fly a plane with one more throttle.

I'd rather be a peckerless man,
Than to fly a bent up garbage can.

I'd rather be most anything,
Than to fly a plane with a folding wing.

I'd rather give up all my cheatin'
Than to fly a plane with a rotten beacon.

How much lower can you stoop
Than to want to fly a droop?

We don't know how they stay alive,
Flying something heavier than a 105.

Just remember, you Phantom flyer,
You have twice the chance for fire.

We got one engine, you got two,
As a word of parting, fuck you!

Fighter Pilots

The next song, also known as "Fighter Pilot's Lament" or "There Are No Fighter Pilots Down in Hell," has been very popular and frequently adapted since World War II. Its melody is from a traditional American Negro spiritual, "When the Chariot Comes," from about 1899, which has evolved into the familiar "She'll Be Coming 'round the Mountain." An almost equally used melody for these lyrics is the tavern song "Oh, It's Naughty, Naughty, Naughty, but It's Nice," which appears here in stanza 8. Although the song primarily contrasts the positive aspects of fighter pilots with the negative ones of bomber crews (an old theme of Air Force rivalry), I remember enjoying and singing this song in the late 1950s when I was a navigator flying in B-47 bombers in the Strategic Air Command. We bomber types really didn't take the criticisms seriously, and we respected the right of the fighter pilot to "strut his stuff," even at our expense. In the next-to-last stanza, the sedate 388th Wing crew members are a rival unit, while the ones who party and sing in the Officers' Club are F-105 fighter pilots of the 355th Tactical Fighter Wing, Takhli Royal Thai Air Force Base, Thailand. A famed member of the 355th was Lt. Col. Leo K. Thorsness, who was awarded the Congressional Medal of Honor for his heroic exploits in his F-105 over North Vietnam on April 19, 1967.

Fighter Pilots

Tune: "She'll Be Coming 'round the Mountain"

Oh, there are no fighter pilots down in hell,
Oh, there are no fighter pilots down in hell,
Oh, that place is full of queers, navigators, bombardiers,
But there are no fighter pilots down in hell.

Oh, there are no fighter pilots in the States,
Oh, there are no fighter pilots in the States,
They are off on foreign shores making mothers out of whores,
Oh, there are no fighter pilots in the States.

Oh, there are no fighter pilots in Japan,
Oh, there are no fighter pilots in Japan,
They are all across the bay getting shot at every day,
Oh, there are no fighter pilots in Japan.

Oh, there are no fighter pilots in the fray,
Oh, there are no fighter pilots in the fray,
They are all in USOs wearing ribbons, fancy clothes,
Oh, there are no fighter pilots in the fray.

Oh, the bomber pilot's life is just a farce,
Oh, the bomber pilot's life is just a farce,
The automatic pilot's on, reading novels in the john,
Oh, the bomber pilot's life is just a farce.

Oh, the bomber pilot never takes a dare,
Oh, the bomber pilot never takes a dare,
His gyros are uncaged, and his women overaged,
Oh, the bomber pilot never takes a dare.

Oh, there are no fighter pilots up in wing,
Oh, there are no fighter pilots up in wing,
The place is full of brass, sitting round on their fat ass,
Oh, there are no fighter pilots up in wing.

Oh, it's naughty, naughty, naughty, but it's nice,
If you ever do it once you'll do it twice,
It'll wreck your reputation but increase the population,
Oh, it's naughty, naughty, naughty, but it's nice.

Oh, look at the 388th in the club,
Oh, look at the 388th in the club,
They don't party, they won't sing, 355th does everything,
Oh, look at the 388th in the club.

When a bomber jockey walks into our club,
When a bomber jockey walks into our club,
He doesn't drink his share of suds, all he does is flub his dub,
OH, THERE ARE NO FIGHTER PILOTS DOWN IN HELL!

Fighter Pilot's Christmas

Being away from home at Christmas is a miserable experience
when you're at war. Dick Jonas says:

At some desperate point along the way to the elusive 100th
mission, each one of us stops and asks the profound question, "What am I doing here? Here I am with the finest education in the world, a half million dollars' worth of aviation skill,
and a citizen in the world's most progressive society. I must
be out of my mind to stake all that against the uncertainty of
one more mission." Well, it's the same question asked by other
fighter jocks in other wars, and it's the same answer, too. I'll

tell you the reason: Mom's apple pie, home, the Stars and Stripes, baseball, the girl back home, the Easter bunny, and Santa Claus. Yes sir, we believe in America and we love the old Red, White, and Blue, and we'll die before we disgrace either. But let's face it; fighter pilots are just human and patriotism gets a little watered down now and then, especially if it's Mother's Day or your wedding anniversary, or if it happens to be your little boy's first day at school and you're 12,000 miles away. And I guess about the toughest thing in any combat tour is not being home for Christmas.

Fighter Pilot's Christmas

Merry Christmas, Mom; Merry Christmas, Dad;
Merry Christmas to my love,
Merry Christmas to the sweetest little girls
That ever came from God above.

CHORUS:
> *Wish I could be home with ones I love,*
> *It's a long time since I've gone.*
> *Santa, take this heart of mine,*
> *And tie it up with bows and twine,*
> *And take it to the folks back home*

A turkey Mom will bake, and Dad will say a prayer,
And someone special thinks of me,
I'd give anything if I could be back home,
But it's so far across the sea.

CHORUS *(then repeat stanza 1, and chorus)*

Words and music by Dick Jonas, from *FSH Volume I*. © 1969 by Enchantment Music Co. Used with permission.

F-105 Alma Mater

McConnell Air Force Base near Wichita, Kansas, was a training base for Vietnam-bound F-105 pilots. When some of these pilots returned from Vietnam, they held a reunion at McConnell, and it was probably for this occasion that the "F-105 Alma Mater" was composed. (See the commentary on "The Ballad of the

Red River Rats.") The melody is taken from Cornell University's alma mater, which itself was adapted in 1872 from H. S. Thompson's "Annie Lisle" of about 1860. The first stanza is a humorous snapshot of the neophyte F-105 flyers training over Kansas, while the second is more ominous. The transition from humor to danger, like flying itself, is extremely rapid.

F-105 Alma Mater
Tune: "Far above Cayuga's Waters"

High above the Kansas flatlands
In their brand new toys,
Fly a bunch of frightened hamhands,
McConnell School for Boys.

Off to battle, led like cattle,
They are heard to sigh,
"To the port of embarkation
Follow me and die."

GIB Named Richard

The next unabashedly autobiographical Dick Jonas song employs the popular melody of the Kingston Trio hit also used in "Old 97, the O-1E." F-4D Phantom GIBs could be navigators or pilots. As a former B-47 navigator, I was already an experienced radar bombardier when I moved into F-4s. Most of the pilots were not so fortunate and had to learn to radar bomb from a back seat when they'd much rather be dive bombing from the front seat. To simplify things, pilots were told to turn up the gain knob to increase or "blossom" the target on the radar screen and then put their radar crosshairs on the dead center of the return until the bombs dropped. This would work well once the correct target was identified on the scope, but habitually using high gain would cause a number of returns to blossom, and one might grab one of them instead of the real target, especially if the radar operator lacked experience. Experienced navigator-bombardiers would keep the gain low so that radar returns would be small and sharp, and would keep adjusting the radar antenna tilt so as to keep the narrow radar beam exactly focused on the approaching target. They would also drop with the crosshairs centered, but on a much more clearly defined target, hence with better accuracy.

One of our tactics was to drop cluster bombs by radar at night from high altitude while flying straight and level so we could surprise Viet Cong or North Vietnamese repairing the roads. The day after such a mission over Mu Gia Pass, a pilot film scored my film in my presence and said I had missed my target by four miles or more (see stanza 4). I knew I had not missed, but before I could reply a senior navigator came over, looked at the film, and said: "Wrong. You think the target is that bright return just to the north. Major Tuso must be an old B-47 or B-52 navigator, 'cuz he's got his gain down and tilt set to pinpoint his target. I score it dead center." We didn't do many Commando Nails, or level radar bomb drops, at high altitude in the F-4D. I don't know that they were ineffective, or rather, whether the pilots in charge of the war, from the Wing Commander down to my particular aircraft commander, simply preferred to dive bomb. Dive bombing with the F-4D was a lot more accurate, so we left most Commando Nails to the B-52s, who carried so many bombs they would saturate an area—they could hardly miss. If a target wouldn't show up on radar, we'd aim at something nearby that would—an Offset Aiming Point (OAP)—and our computer would adjust so the bombs would really drop on the unseen target.

Colonel Meroney calls for Richard's flight commander, Compton, and his navigator mentor, Cox, and announces Dick's grounding only ten missions short of what he needs to go home. Dick finally gets a second chance at Hanoi's steel mills, a tough target, and at Hu Hung Ferry near the DMZ, a milk run, but must bomb Hu Yeng Ferry in the heart of Hanoi before he can ever see San Francisco Bay again. For more on Colonel Meroney, see my comments on "Blue Four."

GIB Named Richard
Tune: "The Man Who Never Returned"

Now, let me tell you the story
Of a GIB named Richard
And the way that he did fail;

He planned out the target,
Grabbed his trusty old hammer,
Went to fly a Commando Nail.

Did he ever return?
Yes, he surely returned
With his scope film in his hand;
When the DCO saw his documentation
He said: "I want to see that man!"

Richard's OAP was over on the coast
And the sun was at his back;
He stuck his head in the scope
And then he picked up the display,
Thinking "This time I've got a shack!"

Did he ever return?
Yes, he surely returned
Thinking he'd performed in style;
Unfortunately when the film was developed
He had missed by seven miles!

Well, Colonel Meroney
Picked himself off the ceiling
Screaming loudly "FSH!!!"
"Send me Compton and Cox,
Get 'em here in a hurry
To consider Richard's fate."

Did they ever return?
Did they ever return,
They were there post haste, you bet,
And the Colonel said
"Take Dick off the schedule,
He's the worst that I've seen yet."

Now, all day long
Richard sits around the squadron
Crying: "Who will fly with me?"
"All I need is only ten more counters
Until Frisco Bay I see!"

Did he ever come back?
Yes, he made a comeback,

They gave Dick one special good deal,
Said "You'll be back on status,
Just put five seven-fifties
Down the smokestacks of Ho's steel mills."

Will he ever return?
Will he ever return?
Will he learn to radar bomb?
If he ever comes back
Next it's [Hu Hung] Ferry,
Then we'll send poor Richard home!

Very early next morning
Then we found poor Richard
With his scope film in his hand;
He was all set to go
Bomb the mills at Thai Nguyen
Said "I'll show 'em I'm a radar man!"

GIB's Lament

"GIB's Lament" portrays the sometimes unglamorous life of the "Guy in Back," the copilot or navigator of an F-4D Phantom. I remember years ago singing a song called "The Best It's Ever Been," but now I can recall only the first two lines. The GIB's pilot in this song is not very good—he overshoots his tanker in stanza 2 and makes a bad landing in stanza 4—yet the GIB admits his own ineptness at bombing, or simply a lack of enthusiasm, in stanza 3. Wherever they appear, phrases like "the best it's ever been" are ironic and sarcastic. The repetition of "again" and "once again" enhances the monotony. Someone once defined military flying as "hours of sheer boredom interspersed with seconds of sheer terror." This song shows us the former aspect. Even a drink at the Officers' Club has become routine.

Our Officers' Club at Ubon had a main barroom about 30 feet wide and 60 feet long; a 25-foot bar ran along one of the walls. Five or six bartenders, usually Thai women, could serve at once, and beer was a dime, a mixed drink a quarter. Our jukebox played the same tunes for the year I was there. We fighter jockeys had two games we would sometimes play when things got too boring. Whenever someone would yell out "MiG Sweep!" six or eight flyers would join hands and go from one end of the room to the other dragging everything along with them—chairs, tables, and people. Another favorite was Carrier Landings. Five or six 5' x 5' tables would be placed in a line and then wet down with pitchers of beer. A flyer would then take a running start toward the lined-up tables, hit the first on his stomach, and slide—sometimes all the way to the end, where a person on each side would catch him. Most damage and injury occurred at the O-Club when only the serious drinkers were left. I had a personal rule of leaving the club whenever things started to get wild and there were fewer than 20 people in the bar. It was a good rule. (For a more positive view of the life of an F-4 GIB, see the commentary on "I've Been Everywhere.")

GIB's Lament
Tune: "The Best It's Ever Been"

Well, today I strapped my ass in once again,
In the back seat, where I've always been;
I've been riding "shot" so long
That my head is in a spin;
Well, today I strapped my ass in once again.

Well, today I locked on the tanker once again,
Had my head in the scope, where it's always been;
The joinup was cold, we overshot,
The best it's ever been;
Well, today I locked on the tanker once again.

Well, today I dialed the target in once again,
It was seven miles, the best it's ever been;
When the bombs came off, I think,
They hit very close to Vinh;
Well, today I dialed the target in once again.

Well, today I watched my AC land again;
He was long and hot, the best he's ever been;
When the gear held up and we rolled out
I unstrapped with a grin;
Well, today I watched my AC land again.

Well, today, I made the O-Club bar again;
Had a couple of drinks, must have been close to ten;
If I ever go home I'll denounce
This wicked life of sin;
Well, today I made the O-Club bar again.

Hallelujah I

"Hallelujah" I and II both are variations on the same melody used
for "Cruising over Hanoi." The World War II version was titled
"Fighter Pilot's Hymn," and the Korean, "Cruising down the Yalu."
All versions have the alternate title "Save a Fighter Pilot's Ass"
when that line appears in the chorus. The chorus and stanza 1
in "Hallelujah I" are from the World War II version, while stanzas
2, 5, and 6 are from the Korean. Stanzas 3 and 4, as well as the
last two lines of stanza 6, are generally new with Vietnam.

In "Hallelujah I" our narrator is a Republic F-105 pilot (he
flies a "Republic bomb" in stanza 4) who was rescued from a
drunkard's life by joining the Air Force. After getting battle damage while making attacks with bomb and cluster bomb units
(CBUs) too low over his target, he is chased south to the Mekong
River between Laos and Thailand by six enemy MiGs. He is almost out of fuel, and his call for help to his flight leader is somehow unheeded. He manages to make it back to a friendly base
to land but lands so low that he drives his landing gear up
through the floor of the aircraft. This story has two morals: (1) flying combat can be more dangerous than being a drunk, and
(2) if you fly too low and slow over your target, you're in for trouble. As we used to say in Southeast Asia, "Smart fighter pilots
don't get shot down."

Hallelujah I
Tune: "Throw a Nickel on the Drum"

CHORUS (*repeat after each verse*):
   Hallelujah, Hallelujah, throw a nickel on the grass,
   Save a fighter pilot's ass;
   Hallelujah, Hallelujah, throw a nickel on the grass
   And you'll be saved!

Lying in the gutter with a belly full of beer,
Pretzels in my whiskers, I knew the end was near,
Then came this glorious Air Force to save me from the hearse;
Everybody bust a gut and sing the second verse!

Cruising down the Mekong doing 650 per,
When I called my leader, "Oh, won't you save me, Sir?"
Two flak holes in my wing, my tanks ain't got no gas;
"Mayday, Mayday, Mayday, I got six MiGs on my ass!!!!"

I went into my bomb run, I went too goddamn low,
I punched the pickle button, let all those babies go,
I sucked the stick back in my gut and hit a high speed stall;
Now I won't see mother when the work's all done this fall!

I barrelled in for CBUs, I judged it far too slow,
The goddamn flak was all around, I heard a thump below;
I shoved the throttle to the wall, the fire light came on;
I cursed and swore, it helped no more, scratch one Republic bomb!

I flew my traffic pattern, to me it looked all right;
My airspeed read 180, my God, I racked it tight!
The airframe gave a shudder, the engine gave a wheeze,
"Mayday, Mayday, Mayday, Spin instructions please!!!!"

I flew my crosswind landing, my left wing hit the ground,
I heard a call from Mobile, "Pull up and go around,"
I yanked that fighter in the air a dozen feet or more,
The engine quit, I almost shit, the gear came through the floor!

Hallelujah II

Like "Cruising over Hanoi," "Hallelujah II" is far more original to Vietnam than is "Hallelujah I," and it's almost half as long. The chorus is now sung by a tanker crew who offer salvation to any fighter pilot with almost-dry fuel tanks, providing he can find the tanker. Our F-105 pilot here is flying quietly along, fantasizing about a young Thai girl (a "poo-ying") back in Takhli, when his aircraft is hit. He declares an emergency by calling "Mayday" and asks for a Ground Control Intercept (GCI) by radar to lead him to the tanker. The GCI controller, the lowest-ranking airman, tells the pilot he must first get approval from Seventh Air Force headquarters in Saigon before he can rendezvous him with a tanker, a sarcasm reflecting combat flyers' frustration at often being unable to make decisions in the field without permission from higher headquarters. Permission becomes a moot point, however, as a tanker pilot who has heard the conversation offers his help. He also reminds the F-105 pilot to disarm his 20-mm cannon before getting in refueling position behind the tanker. Just as our hero spots the tanker, he accidentally deploys his drogue chute, which is used to slow his aircraft while landing. Too slow now to catch the tanker and out of fuel, he can only eject from his aircraft.

On one of my F-4 combat missions out of Ubon, Thailand, I was flying in the lead aircraft with our 435th Squadron operations officer, whom I'll here call Lt. Col. "Snap" Swift. "Snap" prided himself on his skill in air refueling. In fact, during our premission briefing he told the other three aircraft commanders that he wanted them to do a perfect refueling job that day, and he pompously and at length told them exactly how to do it. As Lead, we would refuel first, with aircrafts Two, Three, and Four looking on.

"Snap" later eased right up behind the tanker's refueling boom, got its end latched into our receptacle, and we began taking on fuel—he was in perfect refueling position. After a while I began doing something in the cockpit and hit our speed brakes. Our F-4 suddenly lurched left and right and then fell off the boom. We were wallowing around a while before "Snap" figured out what had happened. I could almost hear the chuckles from the other three fighter cockpits. Once he had figured out what was wrong, "Snap" corrected the situation and then completed his refueling. Numbers Two, Three, and Four refueled beautifully after him. When we began our debriefing after the mission, the first thing "Snap" said was, "I hope you noticed how quickly I recovered after Tuso clumsily hit the speed brakes during refueling." The rest of us exchanged smiling glances. "Snap" was not well liked.

Some years later after the war we stopped at a base during an Air Force Academy cadet navigation training mission. In base operations the names of the local flying unit commanders were always posted conspicuously. I noticed that the commander of the local air-refueling outfit was a "Snap" Swift. "Serves him right," I thought. I've never quite been able to remember whether my hitting our speed brakes on that mission was an accident or not.

Hallelujah II

Tune: "Throw a Nickel on the Drum"

CHORUS (*repeat after each verse*):
> *Hallelujah! Hallelujah! Here's a tanker full of gas*
> *To save a fighter pilot's ass;*
> *Hallelujah! Hallelujah! Put your gas-hole on the boom*
> *And you'll be saved!*

> *I was cruising at six angels in my Foxtrot 105,*
> *Thinking 'bout the poo-ying back in the Takhli dive,*
> *When a sudden burst of ack-ack was all around the sky;*
> *"Mayday! Mayday! Mayday! My tanks are running dry!"*

> *So I squawked my parrot "Mayday" and called for GCI,*
> *Asking for a tanker to keep me in the sky;*
> *Well, the airman-third controller said, "Please don't go away;*
> *Let me call up Seventh to see if it's OK."*

> *Then a friendly tanker pilot called out, "Fighter jock, no sweat;*
> *I've got half a jug of coffee, so I'm not Bingo yet;*
> *If you get a vector to me I'll be glad to pass some gas;*
> *Turn your twenty mike-mike off, and don't shoot up my ass."*

> *It was really getting hairy as I sped my old Thud south;*
> *I could feel the cotton rising all inside my mouth;*
> *Then I saw the silver tanker and gave a happy shout;*
> *Then I saw my drogue behind and started punching out.*

Hallelujah III *and* IV

I include two more "Hallelujah" versions in this collection and am sure there must be several more, all of which use the melody from the WWII song derived from the original "Throw a Nickel on the Drum." Version III, from Korat Air Base in Thailand in 1968, describes not a particular mission, but rather emphasizes the pilots' respect and love for their F-105 Thunderchiefs. Probably from the 388th Fighter Wing, version III has unique stanzas in addition to the derived chorus, and is a good song in its own right. It is also straightforward and requires little comment.

"Hallelujah IV," however, is of special interest, for it is one of only two of my songs focusing on the F-111A fighter bomber, known affectionately as the "Aardvark." After an opening similar to that of "Put Your Beeper on the Air," we learn this song is about the "Switchblades," the aircraft commander seated on the left, and the WSO or weapons systems officers, either pilot (PWSO) or navigator (NWSO), seated on the right, in the 111's cockpit. "Switchblades" is an appropriate name for crew members flying an aircraft pioneering the concept of variable pitched wings. The aardvark is a South African mammal with a stocky body, long tapered snout, and powerful claws for burrowing. In fact, the aardvark does look a good deal like an F-111, and vice versa. The name is also appropriate since just as the aardvark burrows in deep after its prey, the F-111 flies automatically at low level with Terrain Following (TF) radar on its way to its target.

Flying very low and fast over rapidly changing terrain on automatic pilot can be extremely dangerous and forces the crew to have complete faith in the aircraft and its systems. Deliveries to the Air Force of the F-111 began in October, 1967, and its early use in Vietnam shortly thereafter was marred by more crashes than average, even for a new aircraft. Once all the bugs were out of it, however, the F-111A performed exceptionally well over North Vietnam in 1972–73 during those important closing months of the air war, and the "Aardvark" has continued to be an important weapon through 1990.

The F-111's less than fighter-like speed is humorously satirized in stanza 3, as is its early susceptibility to mechanical failure for the slightest of reasons, such as ingesting foreign matter from a passing seagull. The experimental nature of the F-111 comes through in stanza 4 when its bombs fail to release over the target. This patched up and glued together General Dynamics aircraft at least gets its crew back to base but loses both engines at that crucial moment just before landing. This song clearly reflects the early, trouble-ridden F-111 and its crew's distrust of and dislike for it, if in fact the song, like "Skoshi Tiger," was not actually written by critics of the aircraft and not its flyers. For a more serious, positive view of the F-111A, see "Whispering Death."

Hallelujah III

Tune: "Throw a Nickel on the Drum"

[Solo voice]   Oh, I'd like to tell a story
About the Thunder Thud,
The bad you heard about it
Is just a lot of crud.

It took a lot of us up north
And it brought us back again;
The man who speaks against it
Will hear our little hymn:

[Unison] HIM-M-M, HIM-M-M. FUCK HIM!

CHORUS *(repeat after each verse)*:
So hallelujah! Hallelujah!
Throw a nickel on the grass,
Save a fighter pilot's ass;
Hallelujah! Hallelujah!
Throw a nickel on the grass
And you'll be saved!

[Solo verses]   Oh, you say you fly up yonder,
That you're not afraid of flak;
You think you'll log a hundred,
You're a mighty scrappy chap;
You're shit hot and we know it
But the truth is this, my friend,
It's the 105 that'll take you there
And bring you back again!

Is it heavy? Yeah, it's heavy
And you'll curse it like a cob,
But it's not a dinky sports car,
It's built to do the job;
While the Air Force cried for Jollys
To come and pick them up,
It'll fly you safe and bring you back
To a cool one in the Club!

So don't you growl and grumble
Like a dog without a bone,

It's the one bird in this goddamn war
That's built to bring you home;
With your hand upon its throttle
You're in a separate class;
You're a fighter bomber pilot,
Let the others kiss your ass!

Hallelujah IV

Tune: "Throw a Nickel on the Drum"

It was midnight in Thailand,
All the air crews were in bed,
When up stepped Colonel Seaver,
And this is what he said:
"Pilots, gentle navs, fighter pilots all,
Switchblades, gentle Switchblades,"
And all the pilots shouted "Balls!"
When up stepped a young PWSO
With a voice as harsh as brass:
"You can take those goddamn Aardvark jets
And shove them up your ass!"

CHORUS (*repeat after each verse*):
    Oh, hallelujah! Hallelujah!
    Throw a nickel on the grass,
    Save a fighter pilot's ass;
    Hallelujah! Hallelujah!
    Throw a nickel on the grass
    And you'll be saved!

Up and down Mu Gia,
I know the route by rote,
The airplane's at two hundred feet,
My balls are in my throat;
The eighty-fives go flashing by,
They're bursting all around;
Don't make no fucking difference,
I'll probably hit the ground.

I crossed the ridge at Xuan Son,
My airspeed it was high;

I looked out of the window,
A seagull passed me by;
The seagull gave a grunt and shit,
The engine gave a wheeze;
"Mayday! Mayday! Mayday!
SOF's instructions, please!"

I flashed across the target,
My bombs they did not go;
I looked at my right seater,
He said, "Fuck, I don't know!"
I racked her hard up to the left
And straight ahead we flew;
I cursed General Dynamics
And fucking Elmer's Glue.

I flew my traffic pattern,
To me it looked all right;
My airspeed read one-fifty,
My God, I racked it tight;
The airframe gave a shudder,
The engines gave a wheeze,
"Mayday! Mayday! Mayday!
Spin instructions, please!"

I flew my crosswind landing,
My left wing hit the ground;
I heard a call from Mobile,
"Pull up and go around."
I yanked that Switchblade in the air
A dozen feet or more;
The engines quit, I almost shit,
The gear came through the floor.

We got the bird back to the ramp,
Or what was left of it;
The crew chief took one look at it,
My God, I thought he'd shit!
I'll never fly Switchblades again,
This flight will be my last;
I checked tomorrow's schedule,
I'm set to double blast!

Hello, Cam Ranh Tower

Although in some ways similar to "The Ballad of Machete Two," "Hello, Cam Ranh Tower" is a Vietnam original, although in the tradition of the Korean War's "Air Force 801" and "Itazuke Tower." In 1968–69 we flyers knew that the war was being protested at home and that congressional "hawks" were on our side, while the "doves" were against our being in Vietnam. For fighter pilots, it was generally as simple as that. The antiwar protest was not to reach its height until 1971–72, when actress Jane Fonda even made a sympathetic visit to Hanoi. But in 1968–69 we knew who Mike Mansfield (D-Wyo.) was, the Senate majority leader who outspokenly criticized U.S. policies and involvement in Vietnam.

In the song a crippled fighter plane, probably an F-4 Phantom, is trying to land at Cam Ranh Air Base on the coast of South Vietnam about 150 miles northeast of Saigon. But since Senator Mansfield, on a congressional junket, is also about to land, our stricken fighter is forced to wait and, just before it runs out of fuel, is told to divert and try to land at Tuy Hoa, about 70 miles north. Out of fuel, the crew ejects. The song is highly ironic, and its dialogue is beautifully done, with a bit of profanity only in stanza 5. (I remember a young GIB pilot who was especially adept at creative use of the fighter pilot's favorite F-word. It was he who probably coined the unforgettable adjectives "unfuckin'-believable" and "catafuckin'strophic," as well as a noun, the "F-fuckin'-4.")

During the time of this song, Cam Ranh Bay was a huge military installation with Navy and Marine personnel assigned, as well as Air Force. Civilian airliners landed frequently, and some of the fighter squadrons even had individual, not basewide, Officers' Clubs, with "hot and cold running stewardesses." We flyers in Thailand envied their clubs, possibly even their stewardesses, but not the occasional shelling they received from the Viet Cong. I don't know if Mike Mansfield ever visited Cam Ranh, but he could have. If he did, as in the song, his distant and almost symbolic interference with the war could easily have become literal interference with our flyers. In any event, this song captures the helplessness of the military when opposed by the power of Congress.

Hello, Cam Ranh Tower

Tune: "The Wabash Cannonball"

"Hello, Cam Ranh Tower, this is Hammer 41;
My BLC light's glowing, I've just lost PC-1,
The engine's running roughly, the EGT is high,
Please clear me for a straight-in, this bird's about to die!"

"Hammer 41, this is Cam Ranh Tower here;
We'd like to let you in right now, but a senator is near;
He's here to please constituents, his plane is close at hand,
So please divert to Tuy Hoa, we can't clear you to land."

"Hello, Cam Ranh Tower, this is Hammer 41;
I'm turning into final, hydraulic pressure's gone,
The generator's off the line, the RPM just fell,
Please send the senator around and tell him 'War is hell.'"

"Hammer 41, this is Cam Ranh Tower again;
You'll have to keep on circling, regardless of your plan;
I'm sorry 'bout your problem, but you will have to yield,
We must give the priority to Senator Mansfield."

"Now LISTEN, Cam Ranh Tower, I'll lay it on the line,
The situation's fuckin' tense, we're running out of time;
My fuel low level light is on, this bird's about to quit,
So tell that goddamn senator he doesn't count for shit!"

"Hammer 41, QSY to channel four;
You'll have to clear with Air Patch, I can't do any more."
"Roger, Cam Ranh Tower, I'm switching channels now,
I'm sure Air Patch will clear me to land this bird, somehow.

Air Patch, Air Patch, Air Patch, this is Hammer 41;
The tower made me check with you to see what could be done,
I know you'll understand my plight, I've confidence in you,
So clear me onto final, send the senator on through."

"Sorry 'bout that, 41, your story breaks our heart;
If this had happened yesterday we could have done our part;
You will divert to Tuy Hoa, consider this a must,
For Senator Mike Mansfield would dislike all this fuss."

"Roger, Roger, Air Patch, I get your message clear;
Situation understood; the VIP's too near;

We'll nurse this bird to Tuy Hoa, on this you can depend,
We'll keep this airplane flying, until the very end.

Mayday! Mayday! Crown, this is Hammer 41;
Our fate is up to you boys, now, the home drome let us down;
We can't make it to Tuy Hoa, we'll have to punch out here,
So please alert the Jolly Greens, we hope that help is near!"

BEEP
     BEEP
         BEEP
             BEEP
                 BEEP
                     BEEP
                         BEEP

Here's to Old Bien Hoa

The boredom and frustrations of war are featured in "Here's to Old Bien Hoa," the Vietnam version of Korea's "Here's to Old Kunsan." The reference to the Isle of Capri in the Bay of Naples in stanza 3 suggests that there might also be a World War II version of this song. Bien Hoa was a U.S. air base just north of Saigon, and the "roundeyes" in stanza 4 are the American wives and girlfriends—their Asian sisters have almond-shaped or slanted eyes, though I don't ever recall any of us in Thailand using those terms to describe Asian women. I also never heard the derogatory term "slopehead" used for Southeast Asians. This song might easily have been used at many U.S. bases in Southeast Asia simply by substituting "Ubon," "Korat," or "Cam Ranh" for "Bien Hoa."

Here's to Old Bien Hoa
Tune: "Sweet Betsy from Pike"

Here's to old Bien Hoa, a wonderful place;
The organization's an awful disgrace,
With majors and captains and lieutenants, too,
With their thumbs up their assholes and nothing to do.

It's up in the morning, they scream and they shout
Of plenty of things they know nothing about;

For the job that they're doing they say's number one;
They sit on their asses just having their fun.

It's out on the flight line, do that and do this,
And before very long, you really are pissed;
For the job that they're doing they might as well be
Shoveling shit on the Isle of Capri.

When this year is over, and time to go home,
It's back to our roundeyes to nevermore roam;
We'll think of old Bien Hoa and our misery,
We'll think of of Bien Hoa, the land of VD.

The Ho Chi Minh Trail

Named after the premier and military leader of the North Vietnamese, the Ho Chi Minh Trail was the major enemy supply route
from North to South Vietnam. More than 400 miles long, the trail
enabled supplies to move from Hanoi through Thanh Hoa to
Vinh in the North, into Laos through the Mu Gia Pass, and on
into the South near Kontum. A case of mortar shells might go
by railroad, truck, barge, and human backs till it could be opened
and used near Da Nang. The pilot in the next song flies the trail
probably looking for trucks to destroy with his 750-pound bombs.
When he reaches "Bingo" (low fuel), he heads 200 degrees on his
compass, or south-southeast, to get home. He'll fly the trail again
tomorrow, and he goes sufficiently far north to encounter surface-
to-air missiles (SAMs). The melody from the 1945 hit by Dick
Charles, Eddie DeLange, and Larry Marks was also used in an
Air Force Korean War song. In the Vietnam version the danger
of such flying is understated, the words and music providing a
rather relaxed mood.

The Ho Chi Minh Trail

Tune: "Along the Navaho Trail"

Every day along about sunrise,
When the skyline's beginning to pale,
I load six 750s,
And fly the Ho Chi Minh Trail.

I hate to see the flak a-burstin' 'round me,
I shiver when I think about its sting,
But over yonder hill the SAMs are rising,
They always seem to yank my pucker string.

Well, what do you know, it's Bingo already,
And two hundred's the course that I sail;
Tomorrow I'll load more 750s,
And fly the Ho Chi Minh Trail.

I 'Druther Be an F-4 Jock

As Dick Jonas says, "Any fighter pilot is torn between two possible career paths: to move smoothly up the rank ladder, broaden himself with an occasional desk job, and prepare for the responsibility and broader challenge of higher command, on the one hand; or, strap himself to the flying machine and flight line and fly constantly until he is old and gray. The two paths are obviously mutually exclusive except in extremely rare instances." This next song "expresses the gut-level desire of every fighter pilot, whether he flies the F-4 or some other fighter. By way of explanation, JP-4 is jet fuel which feeds the fighter's hungry engines; 1.65 Mach is more than one-and-one half times the speed of sound, which is part of the reason why we feel the way we do." Brig. Gen. Chuck Yeager knew this feeling well; Yeager always stayed in the cockpit, even flying unauthorized combat missions in Southeast Asia with his son. He made his choice and did not advance to the highest Air Force ranks.

I 'Druther Be an F-4 Jock

I 'druther be an F-4 jock
Than the governor of New York State;
Now, the governor's got a pretty good job,
And I suppose he thinks it's great;
But dropping nape and strafing trucks
Are two things he don't know,
And I couldn't fill the governor's shoes,
'Cause I couldn't spend all of that dough.

I 'druther be an F-4 jock
Than the owner of old Fort Knox,
And I like the smell of JP-4
Better than a rosewood box;
Hydraulic fluid and afterburner fumes
Just some kinda turn me on;
Feller, I'm happier flying F-4Ds
Than a hound dog gnawing a bone.

I 'druther be an F-4 jock
Than the Air Force chief of staff;
One good reason, I ain't got the rank
(Right here you're supposed to laugh);
It's a lot more fun just dropping bombs
And hassling two-on-two,
So I'll just stick to my gunnery range
And flying the Phantom II.

One of these days, I'll light my fire
And aim it straight at the sky,
And you'll hear me shout as I disappear
That a Phantom is the way to fly;
I'll do a high speed pass by the Pearly Gates,
About 1.65 Mach,
And I'll tell St. Peter, if he don't mind,
Just make me an F-4 jock.

Words and music by Dick Jonas, from *FSH Volume II, YGBSM.* © 1971 by
Enchantment Music Co. Used with permission.

I Fly the Line

Johnny Cash's 1956 hit "I Walk the Line" gives us the melody of
"I Fly the Line." The persona, a forward air controller, is assigned
to become so expert on a specific area in South Vietnam that
at 500 feet or so he can detect disturbed tree branches that perhaps hide enemy trucks. If the Air Force's mission is "to fly and
fight," that of the FAC is to "fly and find" (stanza 2, line 3). He feels
at home around An Khe in South Vietnam, but is less comfort-

able when tasked occasionally to spot targets in Laos or the area near the DMZ in North Vietnam. He isn't worried about small-arms or 37-mm cannon fire but gets nervous at such belt-fed automatic weapons as 50-caliber machine guns or 12.7-, or 14.5-, or 23-mm ZPU. This song was written prior to Ho Chi Minh's death on September 3, 1969. For more on FACs, see comments on "The Ballad of Jeb Stewart" and "Old 97, the O-1E."

I Fly the Line
Tune: "I Walk the Line"

I keep a close watch on these lands of mine,
I keep my eyes wide open all the time;
Directing air strikes is a specialty of mine;
This sector's mine, I fly the line.

Dawn patrol around An Khe is really great,
It's those out of country missions that I hate;
I'll fly and find it anywhere and any time,
Because they're mine, I fly the line.

Small arms and 37s I don't sweat,
.50 cal and ZPU is what I fret;
White puffs far away are an eager sign,
This sector's mine, I fly the line.

Armed with rockets and binoculars I go,
Out to see what I can see, and hope to know;
Where old Charlie runs and hides and spends his time,
This sector's mine, I fly the line.

I find Charlie on the ground, I call for air,
I roll in to mark when they get there;
"Hit my smoke and run in on the east-west line,"
This sector's mine, I fly the line.

The plane I fly is as old as Ho Chi Minh himself,
Sometimes I wish they'd never took it off the shelf,
Two hundred feet a minute rate of climb is fine,
This sector's mine, I fly the line!

(Repeat verse 1)

If You Fly

Also titled "Boom Today," "If You Fly" was originally a Korean War song using a popular melody of the 1890s. The references in stanzas 7 and 8 to the F-105 Thunderchief and the F-4 Phantom Two are Vietnam additions to the earlier song, while the last line of the chorus reflects the pilots' suspicions of the durability of General Electric (GE) engines. This song, popular in two wars, clearly—and playfully—reflects the pilot's love-hate relationship with his plane.

If You Fly
Tune: "Ta-Ra-Ra-Boom-De-Ay"

CHORUS (*repeat after each verse*):
> Did you go BOOM today?
> Did you go BOOM today?
> Two more blew up yesterday,
> GE ain't here to stay.

If you fly an Eighty-nine,
You must be deaf, dumb, and blind,
For your life ain't worth a dime,
What's your scheduled blowup time?

If you fly a Ninety-four,
You will never holler no more,
For your lot we do not pine,
It's better than an Eighty-nine!

If you fly an Eighty-six,
You will really get your kicks,
Bouncing those subsonic boys,
Playing with their radar toys.

If you fly a 101,
Tell yourself it's really fun;
One day it will pitch up with you,
And you will wish you never flew!

If you fly a 102,
Don't go up unless it's blue,

For if you feel one drop of rain,
You'll be in pieces, not a plane!

If you fly a 104,
The whole world flocks to your door;
Range is short, the wings don't last,
But golly, it sure does fly fast!

If you fly a Thunderchief,
You will soon shake like a leaf;
Flying it may make you sick,
It handles like a great big brick!

If you fly a Phantom Two,
Your flying days will soon be through;
It flies at twice the speed of sound,
If you can get it off the ground!

I'm a Young Ranch Hand

Sung to a popular melody, "I'm a Young Ranch Hand" features a flyer of defoliation missions who describes his work ironically ("I spray all the flowers"), yet calmly. He sprays deadly Agents Blue, Orange, and Purple all the way from the delta in southern South Vietnam to the town of Hoi An to the north, just south of Da Nang, to help the GI. In the original song from which this melody is taken, the "young" cowboy eventually dies, which makes the title of the Vietnam version ironic, as well. For a song showing the Ranch Hands' desperation more vividly, see "Blowing in the Wind."

I'm a Young Ranch Hand
Tune: "The Streets of Laredo"

I'm a young Ranch Hand, a rowdy young Ranch Hand,
I spray all the flowers until they do die;
I spray in the valley, I spray in the mountains,
I spray and I spray as long as I fly.

I spray up at Hoi An, I spray in the delta,
I spray the whole country to help the GI;

I spray it with blue and I spray it with orange;
Get my purple provider, as I say good-bye.

In-Flight Refueling

The next song tells the story of an F-105 pilot who heads out to Brown Anchor, a refueling area over the Gulf of Tonkin, and then runs out of fuel and lands in the sea. The story is one version of a pilot's worst nightmares but is told humorously. Two of my friends from the 435th Tactical Fighter Squadron at Ubon experienced the same events in January, 1969, but it was not humorous at all. The melody is from a popular American folk song of 1870–90, while the words are almost identical to an earlier Korean War Air Force song that has an F-100, rather than an F-105, lying out in the bay in the last stanza.

In-Flight Refueling
Tune: "Strawberry Roan"

Oh come, fighter pilots, both young and old,
And I'll tell you a story that'll make you turn cold,
A story of tankers, and a flight out to sea,
And I hate to tell you what they did to me.

Oh, we took off for Brown, oh, so early one morn,
The weather was balmy, but not really warm;
We soon left the coastline and headed to sea,
And for the last time, land did I see.

Oh, we flew on for hours, it seemed like more,
We flew and we flew till my butt it got sore,
And we finally got to that spot far from land,
Where there were supposed to be tankers at hand.

But yes, you have guessed it, no one was there,
Nothing around but ocean and air;
We called and we called, but it was in vain,
There was nobody out there to refuel my plane.

Oh, we circled and circled, and hollered for gas;
The pain was beginning to leave my poor ass;

'Twas beginning to pucker and turn a dull hue,
When finally a tanker came into view.

Well, bygones were bygones, and we didn't bitch,
We just latched onto that son of a bitch;
"Whoa," called the scanner, "it's under your wing,
If you don't hook up, you likely will ding!"

Well, I stabbed and I stabbed, and I stabbed some more,
But I couldn't hit that dirty old whore;
I looked at my gas gauge, and it was down low;
I backed off again, and tried it real slow.

So I tried it real slow, boys, but that didn't work;
I tried again fast—what a hell of a jerk,
The funnel it hit me one hell of a blow,
As I looked at the cold water down there below.

I looked at that water, so cold and so chilled,
And I thought to myself, "I'll soon be killed,
So I'd better hook up, and take on some fuel,
'Cause that water below looks uncomfortably cool."

So I finally did it; I hit that damn hose,
I hit that old funnel right square on the nose;
The engineer said, "Sir, you're taking on fuel,"
But the bastard was lying, the dirty old fool.

I called the damn scanner, said, "Turn on the gas,
I can't wait much longer, or I'll bust my ass."
He looked up from his Playboy and said with a grin,
"You know there are days, sir, when you just can't win."

That's the end of my story, I'm sorry to say,
That old F-105 lies out in the bay;
But I'll have my vengeance, you can bet your life,
'Cause there's one tanker pilot that I'm going to knife!

The Inventory

Air Force personnel often talk about "the inventory," or list of
official service equipment. The "best fighter in the inventory," for
example, might be the F-16, depending upon whom you're talk-

ing to. Unlike "If You Fly," which gives us a humorous inventory of Air Force planes of the past and present, "The Inventory" is a serious tribute to a number of the workhorses of the Air Force's air war over Southeast Asia. The F4-C, F-102, and F-104 were more common earlier in the war, and the melody is from 1966, so the song can perhaps best be dated 1967–68. "Bull" Durham says he first heard it at Da Nang.

The Super Spud of stanza 3 is the A-1E. In stanza 4 I'm not sure of Pony Express; perhaps it referred to the HH-43E Husky rescue helicopter. Stanza 5 gives tanker aircraft their proper respect, as does stanza 6 the B-52. Reconnaissance aircraft are featured in stanza 7, air-to-air birds like the F-102 and F-104 in 8 and 10; and 9 pokes delightful praise at the AC-47 (see "Puff" and "Puff, the Magic Dragon"). Missing from this otherwise excellent list are the O-1, O-2, F-5, OV-10, A-26, EB-66, EC-121R, FB-111, AC-130, probably a few others, and also U.S. Army and Navy aircraft, for after all, this is an Air Force song.

The Inventory

Tune: "Ballad of the Green Berets"

CHORUS:

> Silver wings that are no more,
> Camouflaged because of war,
> Men will die, but don't forget,
> They're all a part of our freedom threat!

The F-4C striking from the air,
It does a job beyond compare;
A funny bird to those who see,
Looks funny to everyone but me.

There's hardly a thing the Thud can't do,
All day long they're never through
Solving problems of this war's toil,
Like helping Hanoi with their excess oil!

The Super Spud in history lies,
Her pilots are courageous guys,
Making flights, flying low and mean,
Flying cover for our Jolly Green.

CHORUS

The Jolly Green and the Pony Express
Have rescued some of America's best,
Taking flak as in they go,
When they pull out with a "Ho! Ho! Ho!"

The One-Thirty-Five carries the aircraft fuel,
Some say this bird is just a tool,
The fighter-bombers are really the stars;
Without fuel, they can't go far.

The B-52 is a mighty bird,
It's gone to war, or so we've heard;
Dropping bombs on the jungle green
With casualties like we've never seen!

The RF-4 and the 101,
They don't come home till the job is done,
Taking film throughout the day,
Film that shows our Force the way!

The 104 looks like a toy,
Weapons she's got, and will deploy;
You know the MiGs don't get a thrill
Out of seeing that "toy" when it plays for real!

The Gooney Bird, that son of a gun,
I think they flew it in World War One!
A cargo bird that should be through,
Now the danged old thing is a fighter-bomber too!

Sirens blow and the pilots dash,
Seconds pass and the ABs flash;
They hit the air, what a job they do,
Flying interception, our 102!

CHORUS

I've Been Everywhere

As commander of the Seventh Air Force, headquartered in Saigon and supposedly directing the air war in Southeast Asia, Gen.

John D. LaVelle at times felt frustrated about political strictures limiting the targets he could tell his flyers to hit. The "rules of engagement" came mostly from Washington. LaVelle once said, "We have a saying we used in Vietnam, that we finally found out why there are two crew members in the F-4. One is to fly the aircraft and one is to carry the briefcase full of the rules of engagement." Dick Jonas provides another, less sarcastic reason for there being two F-4 crew members.

According to Jonas,

> We were a new generation of fighter pilots, and the Phantom was a new generation of aircraft, too much aircraft for one man, so they put two of us in it. The man who flies the front seat is the Aircraft Commander, the AC. The man who flies the back seat, well maybe I'd better tell you a little bit about him. You know how the Air Force is about abbreviations. Shortly after the Phantom came into the inventory, the guy in the back seat became known as the G.I.B., the GIB, the guy in the back seat. And there isn't a GIB in the 8th Fighter Wing that won't fight you if you call him a copilot, or a navigator, or some other dirty word. He's a GIB, and that's what you'd better call him. Just ask any AC that ever flew the Phantom and he'll tell you that some of the world's best fighter pilots fly the back seat of the Phantom. There's a lot of fighter pilots living today because they went up North to the badlands with a good GIB. I get the shakes just thinking about how it used to be breaking in a new AC in Route Pack Six [the Hanoi area]. There you were, an old head GIB with 50 or 60 missions under your belt, and you had to climb into the back seat with some guy that had been flying the front seat of the Phantom for all of six months, and that was back home in the States where they don't shoot at you. And before that he probably flew those little screaming training planes where the hairiest thing they do is a split-S. Yeah, I still get the shakes just thinking about it. But most of them had the sense to listen when the GIB talked, and those were the ones who turned out to be a pretty good FUF, that's F.U.F., the fellow up front.

Dick is kidding about the term "FUF," which wasn't really used, but his pride at being an F-4 GIB is clear enough. And some GIBs were neither pilots nor navigators. I especially admired Jim Graham and "Doc" Hudson of the 8th Fighter Wing, who both flew voluntarily during a shortage of GIBs and earned Distinguished Flying Crosses while flying with my squadron, the 435th. I had seen Jim around the squadron a lot in his flying suit and thought he was just another GIB. When I later reported to the hospital to get a prescription for some cold medicine and was ushered into Jim's office, I stared at him in amazement and said, "Why are you horsing around in here, Jim? Are you sick, too?" He smiled shyly and said, "No, Joe. I'm a flight surgeon."

The speaker in "I've Been Everywhere" is an F-4 backseater, a navigator or pilot, on a combat mission flying out of Ubon, Thailand. After his frontseater, the aircraft commander (AC), asks him if he's flown more than 10 missions over North Vietnam ("counters"), the 8th Tactical Fighter Wing GIB regales his AC with a tongue-twisting list of more than 35 places he's been in North and South Vietnam and in Laos. When new crew members first flew in the F-4 at Ubon, they would always fly with a partner in the other seat who had flown a minimum of at least 15 combat missions. The melody is from a country and western song of the same title popularized by Hank Snow in 1962, the fine lyrics by Dick Jonas.

I've Been Everywhere

Tune: "I've Been Everywhere"

Well, I took off from Ubon in a thick and heavy driving rain,
I toted my bombs out to Green Anchor tanker plane,
I had a brand new AC riding in the front seat,
A guy with six months' RTU, before that, a Tweat,
He asked me if my counters numbered much more than ten,
I said, "Listen Mac, there ain't no place up there I ain't been."

CHORUS *(repeat after each verse):*
    I've been everywhere, man, I've been everywhere,
    I've crossed the mountains bare, man,
    I've seen the flak-filled air,
    Of SAMs I've had my share, man, I've been everywhere!
Ha-ummmmm. . . .

I've been to
Hanoi, Haiphong, Phuc Yen, Yen Bai,
Lang Son, Hoa Lac, Phu Tho, Son Tay,
Hoa Binh, Nam Dinh, Thai Binh, Bac Ninh,

Thai Nguyen, Gia Lam, Viet Tri, Do Son,
Thud Ridge, MiG Ridge, Northeast Railroad,
Bac Mai, Ninh Giang, Bac Giang, Poo-Yeng.

I've been to
Sam Neua, Ban Ban, Quang Tri, Son La,
Bat Lake, Dong Hoi, Quang Khe, Than Hoa,
Red Route, Black Route, Blue Route, Purple Route,
Channel 97, and the Red and Black River Valley,
Land side, water side, down the slide, dang my hide,
In-town, crosstown, uptown, downtown.

© 1987. Original lyrics by Dick Jonas. Used with permission.

I Wanted Wings

This next song is another popular and classic Army Air Corps song originally written during World War II, with later versions from Korea and Vietnam. There is also a Navy version from World War II. The Vietnam version, almost twice as long as the earlier ones, borrows little from them other than the melody and the refrain "I Wanted Wings." The speaker, an F-105 pilot, has perhaps been to survival school at Stead Air Force Base near Reno, Nevada (no longer in existence), and laments that a flyer's life is not what he expected. He identifies closely in stanzas 7 and 8 with his fellows who are now POWs in Hanoi, and these somber thoughts lead him in stanza 10 to disavow his earlier gripes. In stanzas 11 and 12 he pays tribute to his fallen comrades who had truly earned their wings. The feelings in stanzas 7 through 12 are not expressed in the earlier versions. The reference to Ho Chi Minh in stanza 10 tells us that the song was composed prior to Ho's death in September, 1969.

I Wanted Wings
Tune: "I Wanted Wings"

I've been alive
Twenty years, plus four or five,
And I've tried many a pursuit;
I went to pilot school,

Learned the ropes and learned the rules,
And got my wings and my blue suit.

And then I went to get upgraded
And like a fool I made it;
Then they made me number four,
And then they sent me off to war, Buster;
I wanted wings
Till I got the goddamn things;
Now I don't want them anymore!

The Republic Thunderchief
Is just twenty tons of grief;
The dirty sons-of-bitches
Filled it with three hundred switches, Buster;
I wanted wings
Till I got the goddamn things;
Now I don't want them anymore!

To keep my body alive
They taught me to survive
At a place nestled in the hills;
They fed me porcupine,
And other goodies fine;
Pemmican to cure all my ills.

And in three weeks I had made it,
They said I'd graduated;
Well, buddy, if that's livin'
I think that I'll just give in, Buster;
I wanted wings
Till I got the goddamn things;
Now I don't want them anymore!

You can have your he-man training
In the snow, and when it's raining;
I'd rather be a weenie
With my tootie and martini, Buster;
I wanted wings
Till I got the goddamn things;
Now I don't want them anymore!

I don't want to stay,
But I cannot get away;

In Hanoi they all love parades;
Each day we take a walk
Through Hanoi Central Park,
Not dressed in style, I'm afraid.

Oh, those little yellow mamas,
Dressed up all in black pajamas;
Spectators, they just sit there,
Sometimes throw rocks, sometimes spit there, Buster;
I wanted wings
Till I got the goddamn things;
Now I don't want them anymore!

You can have your 105,
I'd much rather stay alive;
The lousy afterburner
Gets you north just that much sooner, Buster;
I wanted wings
Till I got the goddamn things;
Now I don't want them anymore!

These lines are in jest;
Thud drivers are the best,
At flying 'n chasing women, too;
The goods they deliver
Are sure to make Ho shiver,
And wish to hell this war was through!

And for some it is all over,
They lie down beneath the clover,
For they did go down in flames,
But we will not forget their names, Buster;
They wanted wings
And they've truly got their wings,
And they will wear them evermore!

For there are no regulations
For those heaven-bound formations,
If they don't like it, well,
They can split-S down to hell, Buster;
They wanted wings
And they've truly got their wings,
And they will wear them evermore!

Joy to the World

"Joy to the World" is one of a number of Air Force songs that combine beautiful Christmas melodies with brutal war lyrics. Songs of this type began with the Korean War and become more popular with Vietnam, perhaps reflecting the American flyer's cynicism that began to emerge after World War II. It somehow seems obscene to be dropping bombs on others on Christ's birthday, yet we did it in Vietnam. I remember a flight of four F-4s that had a spectacularly successful bombing mission on Christmas Day, 1968, and someone wanted to write up a report recommending that the flyers get Distinguished Flying Crosses. "If you do, better change the date on the report," someone else said, "or it wouldn't look good to the folks back home if they get wind of it." The date was changed, and the air crews got their DFCs. The popular Handel melody here was used in the 1719 Christmas hymn "Antioch," by Isaac Watts.

Joy to the World
Tune: "Joy to the World"

Joy to the world, the bombs will come,
Let's all go join the fun!
The bridges, dams, and power plants,
The schools, the kids, and even ants,
Will know the awesome sound
Of bombs hitting on the ground;
They'll shiver, they'll quiver—
Gee, war is fun!

Just Give Me Operations

Versions of "Just Give Me Operations" have been extremely popular from World War II through the Vietnam War. In each version, a fighter pilot is torn between his love of flying and his desire to play it safe by working in operations rather than flying combat missions. The chorus of the Vietnam version derives from the Pacific theater World War II version, with its reference to a "lonely atoll," or coral island. However, all the rest of the lyrics are original. Here our pilot gives various reasons for not wanting to fly over Laos ("Tiger Hound"), the Hanoi area ("Package Six"), or the extremes of South Vietnam ("Silver Dawn East" or "West") but finally decides, despite the danger and discomforts of flying combat, that he would rather fly the Phantom F-4D than work in operations after all. For a variation on this same theme about a forward air controller who's offered a desk job at headquarters near Saigon, see "Phu Cat Star."

Just Give Me Operations

Tune: "Just Give Me Operations"

Don't give me an old Phantom II,
That sports not one pilot, but two;
The guy in the back could just stay in the sack,
Don't give me an old Phantom II.

CHORUS *(repeat after each verse):*
　　Just give me operations
　　Way out on some lonely atoll,
　　For I'm too young to die,
　　I just want to grow old.

Don't frag me for old Tiger Hound,
Bad weather, high mountains abound;
They don't give you credit, so screw it, forget it,
Don't frag me for old Tiger Hound.

And don't frag me for old Package Six,
I'll be in one hell of a fix;
The MiGs all come on when my radar is gone,
Don't frag me for old Package Six.

And don't frag me for Silver Dawn West,
Your butt doesn't get any rest;
You think it won't last, your poor aching ass,
Don't frag me for Silver Dawn West.

And don't frag me for Silver Dawn East,
I hear it's one hell of a beast;
Both crew members reek, and you can't take a leak,
Don't frag me for Silver Dawn East.

Well, I'll take back that old Phantom II,
That sports not one pilot, but two;
The guy in the front seat might just sit on his rump,
I'll take back an old Phantom II.

King of the Trail

As in "Bear of the Sky," the Roger Miller pop tune of 1965 provides the melody for our next song. "King of the Trail" looks at
the enemy truck driver more humorously than does "The Panther Pack Is Prowling" or "Sittin' in the Cab of My Truck." We spent
many hours and lots of fuel and munitions chasing after trucks
that weren't there. In fact in almost a year of flying combat, very
often along the Ho Chi Minh Trail trying to halt valuable supplies,
I saw an enemy truck clearly only once in more than 160 missions. I also grew to wonder what these truck drivers were like.
In stanza 2, survival radios were all set on a common frequency
of 243.0, and the backseater hanging in the tree is an F-4 or F-105
GIB. Stanza 3 depicts the futility of American efforts to stop the
truck drivers, who were as cunning as they were tenacious.

King of the Trail
Tune: "King of the Road"

First six-ply, number three,
Destination DMZ,
Hand on the wheel and foot on the gas,
About three miles out of Mu Gia Pass
I keep a little extra rice,
And with a little bit of luck
Get a girl from a road crew
To sleep in my truck. I'm a—
Man of means, by no means,
King of the trail.

I know every bypass around Ban [Laboy],
Watching them waste bombs fills me with joy,
Every gunner in every town
That hoses off a few clips when Spectre's around;

I've seen truck parks for sale or rent,
Cave spaces, fifty cents,
Survival radios on 243.
So you can listen to the backseater hangin' in a tree.

Well, I'm a Ho Chi truck driver, number one,
Hauling my load and having my fun;
Old worn out tires and tubes,
From rolling over too many CBUs;
Well, I've been drivin' night owl all over these parts,
Putting up with Arc Lights and damn recce carts,
But thank God for them, they've saved my load,
Without the extra light I'd have run off the road!

I keep a little extra rice,
And with a little bit of luck
Get a girl from a road crew
To ride in my truck. I'm a—
Man of means, by no means,
King of the trail!

Let's Get Away with It All

Dick Jonas sings the next song on a tape provided by Lydia Fish. The melody comes from a Thomas Adair, Matt Dennis song from 1941, a time when Niagara Falls was still the place for newlyweds to go ("Let's take a trip to Niagara / This time we'll visit the Falls"). The rhythm is moderately fast, lilting, and playfully light, and the Dick Jonas lyrics give us a persona who is obviously in control of his subject, and himself.

Of this song, Dick Jonas asserts: "You can't make a fighter pilot believe that there's a better way than his of getting a job done. It's not that he's bullheaded or obstinate or anything like that. He just believes in himself, and that's the way he feels about every subject, from the best way to mix a drink to how to run the war. I can hear it now along the bar at the O-Club at good old Ubon Ratchathani." And then Dick picks up his guitar and sings. . . .

Let's Get Away with It All

Tune: "Let's Get Away from It All"

Let's take a trip to the Package,
We've got plenty of gall;
Let's kill a SAM site,
Let's keep it uptight,
Let's get away with it all!

Let's bomb the heart of Hanoi,
Let's strafe Embassy Row,
Let's drop some napalm
All over Gia Lam,
Let's have a really big show!

We'll travel around from town to town,
We'll clobber every place:
We'll drop bombs and CBUs
On every MiG air base!

Let's strafe the ships in the harbor,
Let's bomb the dikes above all;
Let's cross the ridges
And let's bomb the bridges,
Let's get away with it all!

© 1987. Words by Dick Jonas. Used with permission.

Once the flyer destroys the SAM site, he can attack Hanoi safely from its very heart, through the Embassy Row of foreign nations critical of the United States, and on to nearby MiG airfields. The fifth line of stanza 2 hearkens back to a famous line often used by TV celebrity Ed Sullivan in introducing his classic Sunday "Show of Shows" in the 1950s, as with great enthusiasm he would announce acts and promise viewers, a "r-r-really big *shew.*"

Our singing pilot really warms up to his fantasy in stanza 4 and suggests attacking the ships in Haiphong Harbor, as did Sen. Barry Goldwater, and even destroying dikes which would flood the Hanoi area, another no-no according to U.S. strategic targeting policy. Hitting forbidden targets that really counted was an almost universal yearning among U.S. flyers, and a central theme of Stephen Coonts's fine novel, *Flight of the Intruder* (1986). Our pilot knows his target choice is limited, but delights in the idea of "getting away with" hitting those targets *he* thinks will help end the war.

Little Town Up North

Dick Jonas's 1969 song "Little Town Up North" is a study in indirect references. The town itself is Hanoi, located on the south bank of the Red River; the pilot's "pals" are his fellow combat flyers; and the "little old man" of stanza 3 is Ho Chi Minh, leader of Communist North Vietnam.

Little Town Up North

There's a little town up north setting on the banks of the river;
Seems like the people up there just don't like me and my pals,
'Cause every time we go to the town on the banks of the river,
They start shooting at us with everything the law allows.

We went up there last week to the town on the banks of the river,
With a little token of our generosity hung onboard,
Dropped our gift on the bridge in the town on the banks of the river,
But I don't think they like any gift that we can afford.

There's a little old man who lives in the town on the banks of the river,
With little beady eyes and a scarcity of hair on the top of his head;
If the little guy who lives in the town on the banks of the river
Had his way, all of me and my pals would all be dead.

Every time we go to the town on the banks of the river,
All of the people up there unlimber their guns at us;
They're kinda weird up there in the town on the banks of the river;
Just don't understand why they gotta make all of that fuss.

We've paid quite a few calls on the town by the banks of the river,
But we ain't had an opportunity to entertain them down here;
They better hurry up and return our call on the town by the river,
'Cause we gotta go back home across the ocean at the end of the year.

Seems like the folks up north in the town on the banks of the river,
Shooting at me and my pals is doggone mean and sore;
If that's the way they feel in the town on the banks of the river,
It don't hurt me not a bit 'cause I ain't going back no more.

Words and music by Dick Jonas, from *FSH Volume I.* © 1969 by Enchantment Music Co. Used with permission.

MiG-19

A popular movie cartoon from the 1950s on featured Sylvester
the cat, who was always trying to sneak up and catch Tweetie-
Bird the canary so he could eat him. "MiG-19" casts a U.S. F-4D
Phantom in the Tweetie-Bird role, with the Soviet MiG-19, Ivan,
playing Sylvester. In an earlier Korean War version, a U.S. F-84
fighter plane was Tweetie, and a MiG-15 was Sylvester. Both
versions take their melody from the 1950 Tweetie-Bird song by
Allan W. Livingston and Warren Foster.

North Vietnamese pilots flying MiG-17s, -19s, and -21s were
a formidable threat to American flyers during the air war over
North Vietnam. Some of the missions I flew in the F-4D were in
support of Royal Laotian troops fighting the Communist Pathet
Lao near Sam Neua in northeasternmost Laos. This area was only
about 100 miles, or 15 minutes, from Hanoi and its nearby MiG
bases.

Sometimes the North Vietnamese would wait until a flight
of our F-4s had finished dropping its bombs or other ordnance,
and as we left the target area with just enough fuel remaining
to get to our tankers and then home, they would launch a flight
of MiGs from the Hanoi area to come down and pretend to chase
us away. I often imagined the Pathet Lao troops on the ground
yelling and cheering as they saw their courageous allies fly in
and frighten away a cowardly bunch of U.S. "Yankee Air Pirates."

After this happened a few times, we decided to use this
trick to our advantage. We sent a flight of four Phantoms in to
work Sam Neua one day and dispatched another flight of "clean"
F-4Ds (aircraft with missiles but no heavy bombs) to arrive at
low altitude below enemy radar just when our earlier flight had
to leave. I was in one of the low-flying, fully fueled birds; my air-

craft commander had on his white silk scarf that day and was eager to get himself a MiG. As our buddies left, we picked up on radar a flight of MiGs heading toward us from the northeast. We immediately climbed to 10,000 feet and were soon heading directly at the unaware incoming MiGs. When we were about 30 miles, or two minutes, away, the MiGs must have spotted us, for they suddenly turned 180 degrees and hightailed it back toward Hanoi. We weren't allowed to follow them, so we turned southwest and headed home too. My aircraft commander was quite disappointed that our ambush had not worked out, but I felt relieved. And yet, a part of me was disappointed too.

MiG-19

Tune: "I T'aught I Taw a Puddytat"

I t'aught I taw a MiG-19
A 'tweeping up on me;
I did, I did, I taw him,
As big as he could be!

I am that great big MiG-19,
Ivan is my name,
And if I catch that F-4D
I'll shoot him down in flames!

The MiG-21

Dick Jonas's "The MiG-21" well captures the excitement of air-to-air fighter combat. Respect for one's aerial adversary and his flying machine goes back to World War I, and in stanza 3 our U.S. pilot gives most of the credit for his success to his aircraft, the Phantom. In stanza 5 the pilot is proud of the fact that his flight of four F-4s knocked down a flight of two MiG-21s. Though the odds do favor the Phantoms (in Fighter Weapons School my instructor pilot told me that the best fighter tactic of all is to outnumber the enemy), our pilot here can be justifiably proud, for his flight of four, working as a unit, destroyed another flight of two, and with no friendly losses. Of this song, Dick Jonas says: "The MiG-21, man, what an airplane! Beautiful, graceful, and fast.

And the guys who fly them are fighter pilots, too. That ought to tell you something right away. The Wolf Pack's got a lot of respect for MiG-21s."

In an *Air Force Magazine* interview published in April, 1987, Brig. Gen. Robin Olds called the F-4 "a bird for its time," noting that the Phantom II had "speed, range, power, work load . . . and was surprisingly maneuverable." It could and did "outduel the MiG-21 at low altitude. . . . What a machine!" In 1967, when he was asked to tell about his first aerial victory in Vietnam, then-Colonel Olds is quoted as saying, "To make a long story short, the MiG lost."

The MiG-21

Now a MiG-21 is a great airplane,
So the Phantom pilots say,
And I don't think we can doubt their word,
They go up there every day;
Long and sleek and fast and high—
It's a dang mighty fine machine,
You can take the word of an F-4 jock,
A MiG-21 is mean.
But so is a Phantom—ugly—but big and powerful,
And faster than greased lightnin'.

Now, there's a lot to be said
For the guys who fly the MiG-21 up north;
I don't reckon they make very much
But every dime they're paid, they're worth;
I mean, how much guts does it take
To jump a force of twenty-four Thuds
That's covered by a cap of F-4Ds
And eight MiG-hungry studs?
Yep, those MiG drivers are pretty sharp,
But not very smart; in fact,
They gotta be outa their ever-lovin' minds
To tangle with a Phantom.

Now, take it from a guy who's been up north
And had at a MiG or two,
That's a good way to end your tour right now,

I'm here, and I'm tellin' you;
He's at ten o'clock high and goin' to eight
And next at your deep six,
And your eyeballs are goin' like mad,
Little man, you're in a fix!
But no sweat, GI—that Phantom will reach up,
Grab ahold of you, spin around, and swat that MiG
Between the eyes—and bring you home a hero.

If you wanna know how to fight a MiG-21
Here's what you can do,
Talk to the guys that've been up there,
They'll tell you a thing or two;
Guys like Olds and Barrios,
Bogolofski and Kirk—
They'll tell you that in a minute and a half
You can do a whole day's work;
They fly the Phantom—or rather it flies them,
It all depends on how you look at it.

I had my chance not long ago when the MiGs came out to play,
And I was just one of eight good men that went up there that day;
Throttles wide open and climb and dive and pirouettes and dips,
Just take my word about MiG-21s, those dudes are mighty fine ships.
It was four Phantoms and two MiGs when we got started—
When we got done, it was just four Phantoms.

Yeah, a MiG-21 is a mighty fine ship,
All the Phantom pilots say,
And that little game is all for keeps
When the MiGs come out to play.
We've been up there, and we'll go up there
Till this clambake is done,
And there's been fights, and there'll be fights
Between the Phantom and the MiG-21—

But just have a look at the scoreboard, friend—
It's all in favor of the Phantom.

Words and music by Dick Jonas, from *FSH Volume I.* © 1969 by Enchantment Music Co. Used with permission.

Mu Gia Pass

Mu Gia Pass is about 60 miles northwest of Dong Hoi, where the Ho Chi Minh Trail enters southern North Vietnam from Laos. We bombed the pass frequently, hoping to slow up the supplies moving from North to South Vietnam. The pass was a good place to find enemy supply trucks in the open, but our fighters were also exposed to enemy groundfire as we came in low on limited angles of attack attempting to hit trucks on the narrow, winding roads. The "wampum" in the next song probably refers to cluster bomb units (CBUs), which were especially effective against trucks and troops. In addition to dive-bombing with CBUs, for a time we also dropped CBUs from high altitude at night by radar on Mu Gia Pass, but I never had any evidence that the latter tactic was very effective.

Mu Gia Pass

There's a road that's up in Laos and it's called Mu Gia Pass,
And the flak bursts up there form an undercast;
On the days when Charlie's shooting you don't need to navigate;
You can find the target by the ack-ack blast.

Well, 'twas in the dark of evening when the sun was going down,
And the haze had cut the viz to fifty feet;
We were headed for Mu Gia Pass with wampum on our wings,
Just to lay them golfballs down that one-way street.

So keep your hand upon the throttle, keep your light upon the star,
Never ask the Lead for more than two percent;
For if you're flyin' low enough your ass can take a hit,
So just shut your mouth and keep your throttle bent.

My Darling F-4

Sung to the melody of "My Darling Clementine," the title of "My Darling F-4" proves ironic, for in the song the pilot refers to his craft as a whore and a sacred cow. His Phantom has developed serious engine trouble, and he is forced to eject over water, probably over the Gulf of Tonkin. This type of incident could certainly cause one to become disenchanted both with his aircraft and with the government officials (stanza 3) who authorized its purchase. Written by Percy Montrose in 1884, "My Darling Clementine" was popularly revived in the 1960s during the Vietnam War. Though not often used in Air Force songs of this era, the melody seems to work especially well in this case.

My Darling F-4

Tune: "My Darling Clementine"

In the cockpit of the F-4
Trying hard to reach the shore,
But alas my engine faltered,
Fare thee well, my F-4.

CHORUS (*repeat after each verse*):
Oh my darling, oh my darling,
Oh my darling F-4,
You are lost and gone forever,
Fare thee well, my little whore.

When you're spinning very flatly
And you've got a furrowed brow,
That's all brother, hit the jumpsack,
Bid farewell to your sacred cow.

All the brass hats in our Congress,
They each signed for this here whore;
They are lucky they just bought it,
They don't fly the ole F-4!

My Jolly Green

The Jolly Green Giant, an HH3-E helicopter, was always a beautiful sight to a downed American flyer awaiting rescue. In fact, thousands of Americans were rescued by helicopter from enemy hands, and the Jolly Green soon became the beloved symbol of those rescues. This helicopter appears in many songs but also has and deserves one of its own, which seems to have been known and sung throughout Southeast Asia. After his aircraft is hit, our flyer pulls his ejection handles and is soon safe on the ground, dreading the probable presence of the Viet Cong, or Charlie. Almost at once the Jolly Green arrives to pick him up, its PJ, or parajumper, lowering his cable to hoist the flyer to safety. The music is from the country and western hit of the sixties by George Hamilton IV. The song is simple, its words matching the melody flawlessly.

My Jolly Green
Tune: "Abilene"

CHORUS (*repeat after each verse*):
> *Jolly Green, Jolly Green,*
> *It's all painted brown and green,*
> *Well, the prettiest sight that I've ever seen,*
> *Is Jolly Green, my Jolly Green!*

Got shot down late last night,
Flak and the missiles were hittin' just right,
Well, I reached for the handles and with all of my might
Yelled: "Jolly Green, my Jolly Green!"

I sit alone in a tree,
I'm scared of Charlie as I can be;
Well, I hope that I will soon be seen
By Jolly Green, my Jolly Green.

Sound of rotors now I've heard,
Here comes that great big whirlybird,
PJ's cable now I've seen,
On Jolly Green, my Jolly Green!

Napalm

According to the famed American poet Carl Sandburg in his *American Songbook* (1927), "The Good Ship *Titanic*" was perhaps adapted from an earlier song, "De Titanic," sung by American black troops aboard transport ships during World War I. An earlier Korean War song uses this poplar melody, as does the Vietnam War version of "Napalm."

In "Napalm" a U.S. pilot first drops napalm near Hanoi and then shoots some rockets at Dong Hoi, just north of the DMZ. However, on what is most likely a third mission, he gets his come-uppance over Thai Nguyen, an enemy airfield near Hanoi, and is forced to eject, or "hit the silk," after his aircraft is crippled by groundfire. While this song lacks the black humor of "Chocolate-covered Napalm," it understatedly jabs at the pilot's full aware-ness of the insignificance of his first two targets. This song is sung humorously, using a high, squeaking falsetto for the line "Itty bitty children lost their lives!" in stanzas 2 and 6.

Napalm
Tune: "The Good Ship *Titanic*"

It was up by Hanoi where the Red meets the sea,
I was out on a recce to see what I could see,
When I spied a farmer with his pitchfork in his hand;
It was sad when my napalm went down!

It was sad, oh, it was sad,
It was sad when my napalm went down
(hit the farmer);
There were husbands and wives,
Itty bitty children lost their lives!
It was sad when the napalm went down!

It was up at Dong Hoi where I won my DFC,
I was out on a recce to see what I could see,
When I spied a church below and I let my rockets go;
It was sad when those rockets went down!

It was sad, oh, it was sad,
It was sad when those rockets went down
(hit the steeple);
All the people ran like hell,
When those rockets hit the bell,
It was sad when those rockets went down!

It was up by Thai Nguyen when I knew I was through,
The 37s and 57s had shot my turbine through,
It was when I hit the silk, O my God, I strained my milk!
It was sad when that pilot went down!

It was sad, oh, it was sad,
It was sad when that pilot went down
(hit the bottom);
There were husbands and wives,
Itty bitty children lost their lives!
It was sad when that pilot went down!

Never Fly in the A Shau on Sunday

Like "The Bat Song," this next song was composed at Phu Cat Air Base in South Vietnam. The title humorously alludes to *Never on Sunday*, a popular motion picture in which the main character, a prostitute with a heart of gold and eyes full of the fire of life, never plies her trade on Sundays—well, almost never. The first three stanzas set up the situation and ask the question, Why is flying over the A Shau particularly dangerous on Sundays? The answer in stanza 4 reflects the F-100 pilot's pride in his status as a member of the Air Force Reserve. The last two words of the song form a common phrase signifying the highest praise a fighter pilot can bestow. It might be loosely translated, "eminently superior."

Never Fly in the A Shau on Sunday

Never fly in the A Shau on Sunday,
That fills our hearts with dread,
For Charlie selects his best gunners
To fill the sky with lead.

Many a hot fighter pilot
Had pulled off a dive-bomb pass
With both 750s on target, friends,
And Charlie still hosing his ass.

Now why is it always on Sundays
That Charlie is hosing us down,
But he never can zap us on weekdays,
When he mans his guns with clowns?

The answer, my friend, is apparent,
Those gunners are the best that he's got;

For Reservists all train on the weekends,
And Reservists are always shit hot!

The New DCO

"The New DCO," another Phu Cat song, uses the melody from "Jimmy Crack Corn," written in 1846 by Daniel Emmett and made popular in the 1950s by the American folk singer Burl Ives. The composer Daniel Emmett is best known for his song "Dixie."

The pilots in this Vietnam version always had good bomb damage assessment (BDA) until their new DCO (deputy commander for operations) arrived. The DCO supervises all flying in a fighter wing, and fighter pilots always dislike it when a new DCO comes in and starts changing things when he doesn't know what he's doing. In this case, the pilot consoles himself in the chorus by knowing his tour will soon be over and he'll be leaving a bad situation.

The New DCO
Tune: "Jimmy Crack Corn"

In Vietnam six months ago,
We still were free to run our show;
Our BDA was always high,
Cause the old heads showed us how to fly.

CHORUS (*repeat after each verse*):
　　Phu Cat sucks, that's plain to see;
　　This chicken shit sure gets to me,
　　But in a few more months I'll be free,
　　And they can shove it up their ass!

The guys who showed us were the best,
They killed the Cong with all the rest;
They showed us how to stay alive,
When flak bursts filled the northern skies.

Well, the war has ended once again,
And a new DCO has just stepped in;
He's never been in Vietnam,
But he tells us how to drop our bombs!

Night on the Town

"Night on the Town" uses a melody rare to Air Force songs, Little Red Riding Hood's song from a cartoon movie. The title is ironic, for a "night on the town" for these F-105 Wild Weasel pilots is a raid on Bullseye, or Hanoi. Weasels were specially modified F-105s whose mission was to detect enemy SAM sites and then dive in and destroy them. Their weapon was the formidable Shrike, or AGM-45, an airborne missile ten feet long propelled by a solid-fuel rocket motor, carrying a 145-pound high-explosive fragmentation warhead, with a range of more than three miles. Weasels would usually accompany other flights of fighter-bombers and provide protection when there was an enemy missile threat en route to or at the target area. The Shrike was used in Vietnam from 1965 on, and this song was composed some time after that, but before February, 1968.

The Weasels would "green up," or prepare their Shrikes for launch, and warm up their ECM (electronic countermeasure) pods, which jam enemy radar. A Weasel had a dangerous job, but as the last three lines reveal, often a highly rewarding one as well.

Night on the Town
Tune: "Over the River and through the Woods"

Over the river, across the fence,
To gomer's house we go;
The Thud knows the way,
It's Bullseye today
To visit Uncle Ho, OH!
We're Weasels, you know, so look out below,
'Cause we've got our shit together;
Chasing down SAMs and Firecans
And always in dogshit weather.

Green up the missiles and warm up the pods,
Their GCI's got us now;
Tune up the scope,
They'll launch one, we hope;
Get ready to take it down;
Then just for spite we'll punch off a Shrike,

Sweet Jesus! What a shit-hot day!
Dropping their socks and cleaning their clocks
And blowing their shit away!

Night Owls

"Bye Bye Blackbird" (1926), with melody by Ray Henderson, was very popular at piano bars across the country in the mid-1950s. The Night Owls were members of the 497th Tactical Fighter Squadron, 8th Wing, at Ubon, Thailand. They wore black rather than the usual green-gray flying suits and flew almost completely at night. For a time the U.S. government would not admit that we were flying combat missions over Laos, though the press was full of it. A Night Owl flyer returning from leave in the States brought us a copy of *Time* magazine that featured the 497th and its night missions over Laos, which gave us quite a chuckle.

Making dive-bombing runs over Laos and Vietnam at night was extremely dangerous, and the 497th had more than its share of losses. It also had a good deal of justifiable pride and high morale. On a rare night when the Owls would "stand down," or not fly at night because of bad weather, those of us in other squadrons enjoyed hearing their exploits at the Officers' Club. One of my best friends, a young first lieutenant and Air Force Academy graduate, finally wangled his way into the 497th from another squadron. He was lost over the Gulf of Tonkin a few months later—at night.

Night Owls
Tune: "Bye Bye Blackbird"

Here we stand down on the ground,
We won't take off till the sun comes down,
We fly Night Owls.
Go in low and come out fast,
Keep those fighters off our ass,
We fly Night Owls.

No one here can ever understand us,
You should hear the horseshit that they hand us;
Mix those drinks and mix them right,

Because we're standing down tonight,
Night Owls we fly.

Nimrod

Since night flying is inherently more dangerous than day flying, it is also even more rewarding when a night mission is just moderately successful. A "nimrod" is simply a hunter, but since Nimrod in the Bible is a mighty king, great-grandson of Noah, and also a great hunter, awarding his name to the truck killers in the next song raises the action to epic proportions, especially when the lyrics are well matched with the haunting melody of the 1949 Stan Jones American classic, "Riders in the Sky." Again, a song from 1968–69.

Nimrod
Tune: "Riders in the Sky"

An old VC truck driver went out
One dark and rainy night;
He went to drive that dark trail
Without a beam of light,
And knew that Uncle Ho Chi Minh
Would be so proud of him,
So he loaded up his POL
And he headed out for Vinh.
Nimrod, Nimrod, those truck killers of the night!

He ran on through Mu Gia Pass,
There was no turning back;
He had to reach a truck park soon
Or be spotted by a FAC;
When all at once a fire
Lit up the sky that day;
He felt a sudden chill of fear
As it drifted down his way.
Nimrod, Nimrod, those truck killers of the night!

The call came through the night:
"This is Covey 105;

We've got flares enough
If you've got that truck in sight."
They bombed and strafed and flared
And blew that bastard up,
Oh, Nimrod, Nimrod,
Truck killers of the night!
Nimrod, Nimrod, those truck killers of the night!

Normandy's Sand

Dick Jonas's "Normandy's Sand" reflects the attitude of a number of U.S. fighting men who viewed service in the Vietnam War as a patriotic duty in the best traditions of World War II and Korea. Despite the loss and suffering his family has already endured, the persona in the song chooses to serve in Vietnam as a duty he owes his country because of what it has given him. The simple and moving patriotism expressed here is rare in Air Force songs of the Vietnam era.

Normandy's Sand

CHORUS *(repeat after each verse):*
    My daddy died on Normandy's sand,
    Trying to give the Frenchmen back their land;
    My brother died in Korea's deep and drifting snow,
    And if my country needs me, I'll go.

My daddy was a brave man, I heard my mama say,
He left home when I was only two;
— *I still remember tears of pain and pride mom shed that day,*
But daddy said, "It's what I have to do."

My brother looked a lot like my daddy, mama said,
On the day he kissed us both goodbye;
Mom cried again with the girl that he had wed,
My brother said that for the flag he'd die.

Again my country said to mom, "I need your son, M'am";
She gave so much and how it hurts, I know,

But this country gave me what I have and who I am,
And for my God and country I'll go.

Words and music by Dick Jonas, from *FSH Volume II, YGBSM.* © 1971 by Enchantment Music Co. Used with permission.

Northward Ho

"Northward Ho" parodies a 1927 Harry Woods melody that was popularly revived in 1948 and has been another piano bar favorite. The flyer would rather not bomb in North Vietnam, though directed to do so by orders from Seventh Air Force Headquarters in Saigon, which scheduled all combat sorties in Southeast Asia. In stanza 2 he urges his number-two man to stay with him during the attack and use ABs (afterburners) to enable them to perform the prodigious feat described in the last line—a metaphor often used elsewhere to describe the skillful capability of the truly superior pilot. Not a song for the refined audience, but it makes its point.

Northward Ho
Tune: "I'm Looking Over a Four-Leaf Clover"

I'm looking northward to Haiphong Harbor,
While SAMs on the ground look at me;
Seventh says, "Go−go,"
But I'd rather not;
It's right in the asshole
That I'll sure get shot.

I'm not complaining, I'm explaining,
So, Two, stay with me through the pass;
Jink through the jungle,
Make the ABs rumble,
And we'll fly right up our own ass!

Number One Clismas Song

"Number One Clismas Song" is also not for the refined audience, as it humorously contrasts a Christmas in Thailand in the first

three stanzas with the pilot's imagined combat mission in stanzas 4 and 5. Many combat flyers never got used to flying seven
days a week, even on "holidays." I know that I never did. I flew
26 days out of 31 in December, 1968, including Christmas Eve and
Christmas Day, and also New Year's Day, 1969. And though I have
very distinct memories of many things that occurred during my
year at war, I don't remember a single thing about Christmas Day,
1968, though my personal log tells me I flew a mission over Laos
that day in F-4D tail number -681 for an hour and fifty minutes
with my wing commander, Col. Buck Pattillo, in my front seat.
Christmas was, unfortunately, just another day in the air war for
us. Perhaps this irony is why most Christmas songs from Vietnam are grotesque.

This song parodies the supposed Thai pronunciation of
the consonant "r" as "l," as in "Clismas," "Melly," and "lice," although
I cannot remember a Thai ever talking that way. "Samlars" are Thai
pedicab drivers who provided a favorite form of transportation
for off-duty fighter pilots around the streets of Ubon. "Geckos"
are small lizards, and "Tee Lucks" are willing Thai women, or com-
bination girlfriends and mistresses. Stanzas 4 and 5 are graphic
and coarse, if quite well written, and stanza 6 tells us that this
particular Thai Christmas was probably in 1967, at Ubon, home
of the 8th Fighter Wing Wolf Pack, where Col. Daniel ("Chappie")
James has just arrived to assist the wing commander, the famed
Col. Robin Olds. "Chappie" later became one of the few black
Americans to become a general in the U.S. Air Force and was
a hero of the air war over Vietnam in his own right.

This Air Force version parodies a song written in 1946 by
Mel Torme and Robert Wells that has become a U.S. Christmas
season classic. Mel Torme would doubtless find this version interesting, but I suspect he wouldn't like it. To appreciate this
song fully, I guess you had to have been there.

Number One Clismas Song
Tune: "The Christmas Song"

Chestnuts roasting on a Thailand fire,
Bullfrogs singing in the choir,
Samlars singing "Ho, Ho, Ho,"
It's Melly Clismas, you know.

Geckos clawling closs the cold bare floor,
Flied lice cooking on the stove,
Tee Lucks kissing neath the mistletoe,
It's Melly Clismas, you know.

Sweet lips waiting for my tender kiss,
Garlic breath gets in my way,
VCs roasting in a napalm fire,
Melly Clismas, Uncle Ho.

Cripples limping down a small side street,
Napalm rising at their feet,
I dropped it low but they went too slow,
Melly Clismas, dear Ho.

VC making love near rice paddy,
Tee Luck's eyes are all aglow,
Twenty mike-mikes up his ass,
Tee Luck's screaming, "Go, go, go!"

Wolf Pack sends greetings from old Robin Olds,
Chappie joined him over there,
We'll carry on, the stars will be bright,
Over Ubon Ratchathani tonight.

Ode to a Great Fuckin' SAR Effort

The next song, though not about Christmas, employs the melody of a popular Christmas song. Unprepared air crews are hurriedly launched to support a SAR effort, a Search-and-Rescue mission to help a downed American flyer. The pilot's flight encounters heavy hostile fire and is finally separated, and the crippled leader and his backseater are forced to eject. The conversation between the two crew members reveals that the aircraft commander has been shot down on his first mission over North Vietnam (his first "counter"). Fighter pilots would especially enjoy stanzas 4 and 5. In this song a mission that begins as a SAR effort ends with some of the rescuers needing a SAR effort themselves, making the song's title ironic.

Ode to a Great Fuckin' SAR Effort

Tune: "The Night Before Christmas"

One fine day, just last summer ('twas prior to a raid),
The jocks were hung over from screwing the maid;
So with canopies open and heads hung in grief,
Their sorrows were many, their crew rest too brief.

The mission commander, by some marvelous feat,
Got them to the Anchor, cycled through, then did meet
With those beautiful Thuds spread in "pod"—quite a force!
The Phantoms moved in like the old Trojan horse.

The MiGs had been scrambled, were headed out east,
And the gunners were hosing eighty-fives at our beast!
"Why the hell should they hate me?" I cried in dismay,
"I'm egressing, you bastards, so play it my way!"

But my cry went unheeded as our bird took a hit,
And I knew there and then things had just turned to shit;
Though my chances were nil there was fuck else to do,
But head for the Black with our whole fuckin' crew!

So in anger, and pissed, did we drop the whole load
On that cock-suckin' gunner's kids, wife, and abode!
There was no goddamn grief as I cried out with glee,
"Eat your heart out, you bitch, for you'll never get me!"

So with eighty percent (that was all we could get)
We headed for North Point with hopes of a Tet,
But 'twas mostly in vain as we swung past the Red,
I knew that my ass was fuckin' near dead.

'Cause Yen Bai came alive like the Fourth of July!
The flak was so thick that I wanted to cry,
As my two, three, and four broke down, left, then right—
Leaving us solo in the dwindling light.

"Well, ol' buddy," my number one GIB says to me,
"It looks like there's just gonna be me and thee,
And with your goddamn luck we should punch out at 10—
So the rest of the fall we can take with a grin."

"For I just know goddamn well as I sit here in fright,
That both fuckin' chutes were packed wrong last night,

And I want you to know," he hastened to add,
"That in case we don't make it, please don't get mad!"

"It isn't my fault that the pod didn't work—
I told you that twice, you dumb fuckin' jerk!
A tank didn't feed, the doppler was short,
You said we'll get our counter—no matter what."

"Well, you've got your first counter, it may be your last,
Unless this old whore can take one more blast!"
Shut your trap and eject was the word of the day,
So we punched, not at 10, but at 2, so they say. . . .

Old 97, the O-1E

The title of "Old 97, the O-1E" links this song thematically to an earlier 1927 song with lyrics by H. S. Hansell, Jr. The melody was from an even earlier song written by Henry Whitter in the late 1800s, "The Wreck of the Southern 97," which imitates "Casey Jones." The melody was quite familiar to Vietnam flyers through the Kingston Trio's hit of the late fifties or early sixties, "The MTA," and is also used in Vietnam in "GIB Named Richard" and "The Phu Cat Alert Pad." There was a Korean version, as well, featuring the F-86 fighter.

Our Vietnam version is a serious, graphic narrative about a forward air controller flying an O-1E, a small Cessna single-engine spotter plane, which began being replaced in Vietnam service by the O-2 in 1966. The FAC is trying to help friendly troops surrounded by Viet Cong by directing a flight of F-100 fighters to hit the hostile positions. In essence, the FAC is a "bird-dog" who spots, calls out, or marks the target for the fighters to see. In this case the enemy fire is extremely heavy, and though the FAC bravely does his job, he is killed while the friendly troops are blessing the F-100 pilots for saving them. This serious narrative is one of the finest songs in this collection—here, one man is merely helping his fellows with no politics involved. The story is well told and suits its melody, while the muted yet moving chorus could well apply to all American servicemen missing in Vietnam.

Old 97, the O-1E

Tune: "The Man Who Never Returned"

There were ninety-seven planes lined up on the apron
As far as the eye could see,
Now the first ninety-six were of modern construction—
The last was an O-1E.

Well, a handsome young captain stepped up to Operations,
For FAC-ing was his line,
"Now if the first ninety-six belong to the majors,
Old 97 is mine."

So he climbed into his Cessna, his carbine beside him,
His rockets tucked snug beneath his wing,
When a cry came from the ground commander,
"Charlie's got us in his ring!"

CHORUS:

    Well, did he ever return?
    No, he never returned,
    And his fate is still unlearned;
    He may lie forever in that Vietnam jungle—
    He's the FAC who never returned.

The ceiling was low and the rain was a-fallin'
The birddog was pitchin' all about,
But he said to that soldier, "No sweat, brother—
TAC air will get you out."

Soon the fighters arrived, they were F-100s,
They called down to our FAC,
He told them it was rough but to follow his directions
And this one they could hack.

Now Charlie didn't like the sound of that birddog,
And the bullets began to fly,
He said "If that airman brings in those fighters
Then he is going to die!—

CHORUS

Now the leader rolled in and he asked for the target,
The FAC told him where to aim his guns,

With unerring eye he smoked out Old Charlie
Until he had 'em on the run.

Oh, the battle was hot and too much for Charlie,
And the soldiers began to shout,
"God bless you fighters for savin' our asses
And drivin' those VC out!"

But no one noticed the crippled Cessna
As he made his final bow,
But one of those bullets had found its target
And Charlie had kept his vow.

CHORUS

Old Smoky

A traditional American folk song, "Little Makee," dating from 1916, provides the melody for the 1951 arrangement of "On Top of Old Smoky" by Fred Barovick. The melody was almost immediately used in Korean War Air Force songs and remained highly popular through Vietnam in "Old Smoky," "On Top of Old Thud Ridge," and "On Top of the Pop Up."

"Old Smoky" of the next song refers to the aircraft, which isn't identified until the final stanza, for this is a shaggy-dog story with a surprise ending, probably written in the same spirit as "B-52 Takeoff" by a fighter pilot. Read the first eight stanzas straight, and then stanza 9 will take care of itself.

Old Smoky
Tune: "On Top of Old Smoky"

Flying over old Cam Ranh
En route to the North,
My hands got so shaky
From the thoughts that came forth.

The sun was bright shining,
The sky it was clear,
But my heart it did falter,
I was frozen with fear.

As we crossed the border
I thought I would die,
But my fearless commander,
Oh, how well he did fly.

With this inspiration
What more could I do?
I screwed up my courage
And pressed on anew.

We started our bomb run,
The sights I did set,
We rippled our bombs off,
Then wiped off the sweat.

We turned toward the Tonkin
With the engines full bore;
She really was smokin'
Like a two-dollar whore,

When once past the coastline,
With a sigh of relief,
We'd gotten the job done
Just as it had been briefed.

This mission accomplished,
So important to me,
They're sure to award us
Our first DFC.

I'm an outstanding airman,
This story is true,
For I'm a copilot
On a B-52!

Old Weird Harold

Of his original song "Old Weird Harold" Dick Jonas says,

> Obviously fictitious. The element of surprise in battle is some-
> times quite hard to come by. We surmised in jest that our ap-
> proach to the target was announced ahead of time by a dis-
> graced and dishonored MiG jock whom we dubbed "Old

Weird Harold." He doubtless had been banished to the provinces for landing sans gear or running out of gas or some other unprofessional caper. Perhaps he became chief of their counterpart to our now obsolete "Ground Observer Corps." Without doubt, someone told the people who manned the target defenses that we were on the way. It was too hot when we got there to have been otherwise. "Old Weird Harold" . . . or somebody.

The Wolf Pack's revenge on Weird Harold in the last few stanzas, involving Ho Chi Minh's outhouse, seems appropriate to Dick Jonas's country upbringing.

Old Weird Harold

I will sing you a song about Weird Harold,
I will tell you a tale fraught with fear,
How the Wolf Pack put the word on Weird Harold,
How we shoved it into Weird Harold's ear.

Now the Wolf Pack knew all about Weird Harold,
How he laid in the weeds on Thud Ridge,
How he talked on the phone line to Hanoi
Every time the 8th Wing tried to bomb the bridge.

So one day we all strapped on our Phantoms,
Lit the burners and leaped off the ground;
We had sent out a message to Harold,
Saying, "Harold, we're Hanoi bound."

Come fly with me down the Red River Valley,
Down Thud Ridge to the north side of town;
Pay no mind to the MiGs and the SAM sites,
Nor the AAA that's bursting all around.

Oh, we're gonna fix old Weird Harold's wagon,
Yes, today we are gonna cut him down;
Old Weird Harold, I know you are listening,
Tell old Uncle Ho the Wolf Pack's going to town.

Well, the Wolf Pack crossed over the valley,
Down the ridge to the north side of town;
Took it down once or twice for a SAM break,
Then we rolled into the slide and started down.

Now, it happened that behind Ho's cabin,
Stood a little house old Ho loved so well,
With a half-moon on the door, a real two-holer,
'Twas upon this little shack the bombs had fell.

Oh, that poor little house turned into sawdust,
All except that beloved two-hole seat,
And it sailed high and far into the distance,
And it landed smack at Weird Harold's feet.

Harold took this to mean he'd been rewarded,
So he painted that two-holed seat in red,
And just over each hole he wrote "Weird Harold,"
Now he wears Ho's toilet seat 'round his head.

That's my story of poor old Weird Harold,
How the Wolf Pack made Ho a nervous wreck,
How the Wolf Pack fixed up old Weird Harold,
When he hung that two-holed seat 'round his neck.

Words and music by Dick Jonas, from *FSH Volume II, YGBSM.* © 1971 by
Enchantment Music Co. Used with permission.

O Little Town of Ho Chi Minh

Although again not about Christmas, "O Little Town of Ho Chi
Minh" uses a Christmas melody written in 1868 by Lewis H. Red-
ner and first popularly published in 1920 with lyrics written in
1868 by Phillips Brooks. Though defended by rings of Soviet
SA-2s (surface-to-air missiles), Hanoi is not safe because the U.S.
F-105 pilots are too dogged, their toss-bomb computers too
deadly accurate. This Air Force version was composed prior to
February, 1968, when U.S. president Lyndon Johnson restricted
the bombing of North Vietnam to the area stretching 120 miles
north of the DMZ separating North from South Vietnam.

O Little Town of Ho Chi Minh
Tune: "O Little Town of Bethlehem"

O little town of Ho Chi Minh,
How safe you think you lie;

Beneath your ring of SA-2s
You think the Fives won't fly;
Yet through the cloud deck raineth
A deadly trail of bombs;
Too late for fear, the end is near.
How about that TBC?

One Hundred Missions

"One Hundred Missions," a Vietnam original, uses a melody from 1863 by Patrick S. Gilmore that was rearranged in 1945 for World War II use by Buddy Kaye. While the Civil War song joyfully describes the wonderful welcome to be given to returning war heroes, the Vietnam version verbalizes the feelings of flyers who can't return—yet. The singers are Iron Hands, or F-105 Wild Weasel pilots from Takhli Royal Thai Air Force Base.

U.S. combat flyers were supposed to return home after completing either 100 missions over North Vietnam or a calendar year of combat flying, whichever came first. Someone has changed those rules, but these flyers of especially dangerous missions are good soldiers who will do what they're ordered to —though they obviously don't like it.

One Hundred Missions
Tune: "When Johnny Comes Marching Home"

One hundred missions we have flown, aha, aha,
One hundred missions we have flown, aha, aha,
One hundred missions we have flown,
One hundred bridges we have blown,
But you can't return till Lyndon gives the word.

From one to one hundred we did count, aha, aha,
From one to one hundred we did count, aha, aha,
From one to one hundred we did count,
But now one half or more don't count,
And you can't return till Lyndon gives the word.

They said they'd give us combat pay, aha, aha,
They said they'd give us combat pay, aha, aha,

They said they'd give us combat pay,
And then the bastards took it away,
But you can't return till Lyndon gives the word.

We're Iron Hands from old Takhli, aha, aha,
We're Iron Hands from old Takhli, aha, aha
We're Iron hands from old Takhli,
Our hearts beat fast, we think we'll pee,
But you can't return till Lyndon gives the word.

The Weasels fly around alone, aha, aha,
The Weasels fly around alone, aha, aha,
The Weasels fly around alone,
With half a flight they head for home,
But you can't return till Lyndon gives the word.

The force rolls in amidst the flak, aha, aha,
The force rolls in amidst the flak, aha, aha,
The force rolls in amidst the flak,
One half or more won't make it back,
But you can't return till Lyndon gives the word.

Not many will return alive, aha, aha,
Not many will return alive, aha, aha,
Not many will return alive,
Who flew the bloody 105,
But you can't return till Lyndon gives the word!

One Hundred Sixty VC in the Open

The persona in the next song is a forward air controller who obviously likes his work. He catches a good-sized force of Viet Cong with their North Vietnamese advisers out in the open and calls the Direct Air Support Center for a fighter attack. These enemy troops are in big trouble once the FAC accurately marks their position with his white phosphorus rockets and the F-100s tear in on them with cannon, napalm, and cluster bomb units. This FAC is probably working an area of South Vietnam. Like "Armed Recce," this song is by W. F. ("Toby") Hughes, who also wrote the classic "Tchepone." Here Toby adapts the melody of Marty Robbins's "One Hundred Sixty Acres in the Valley."

One Hundred Sixty VC in the Open
Tune: "One Hundred Sixty Acres in the Valley"

I've got one hundred sixty VC in the open,
And ten or twenty North Vietnamese;
I've got to get some air, put a strike down there,
Before they can make it to the trees.

I've got one hundred sixty VC in the open,
It's a target that you don't get every day;
So I call the DASC and I quickly ask
To please get the fighters on their way.

Number One should have a gun,
And a load of what we call incendi-gel;
Send Number Two with CBU;
When they get here we can really give 'em hell!

I've got one hundred sixty VC in the open,
I've got a flight of F-100s up above,
I've got my Willy Pete smoking at their feet,
It's the kind of situation that I love.

Words by Toby Hughes, © 1968. Used with permission.

On Top of Old Thud Ridge

The first six stanzas of "On Top of Old Thud Ridge" appear elsewhere as a separate song titled "On Top of Old Hanoi." Unlike "Old Smoky" and "On Top of the Pop Up," this next song closely parallels the source song's original lyrics in stanzas 1–4. In this song the F-4 pilot experiences both the danger and the monotony (stanzas 6–8) of flying combat. This seems the least interesting of the three Vietnam songs that use the same 1916/1951 melody.

On Top of Old Thud Ridge
Tune: "On Top of Old Smoky"

On top of old Thud Ridge,
All covered with flak,

I lost my poor wingman,
He'll never get back.

For flying is a pleasure
And dying a grief,
And a quick-triggered Commie
Is worse than a thief.

For a thief will just rob you
And take all you save,
But a quick-triggered Commie
Will send you to the grave.

The grave will decay you
And turn you to dust;
Not a Commie in a thousand
Can an old F-4 trust.

Now when the bad weather
Keeps the ships down,
All day we can hear this
Horrible sound:

"Attention all pilots,
Now listen to this,
There'll be a short meeting
That you dare not miss."

They'll give us some lectures,
Then give us some more,
But we have all heard them
Twenty-five times or more.

Now listen you trainees,
You can't fight the group,
Whatever they tell you
Is superfluous poop.

Now the moral of this story
Is easy to see,
Don't go to Haiphong
Or old Quang Khe.

On Top of the Pop Up

"On Top of the Pop Up" reveals an F-105 pilot's distrust of information on target defenses supplied him by Electronic Intelligence (stanza 4). The first four stanzas describe the situation effectively, while stanzas 5 and 6 remind other pilots to keep moving their aircraft around ("jinking") over the target, or it'll be a long walk back to Takhli Royal Thai Air Force base if they have to bail out from a crippled ship.

On June 16, 1968, I flew an F-4 combat mission over North Vietnam with a lieutenant colonel in my front seat whom I'll call Colonel Crush, who scared me silly. Right after weapons release during a dive-bombing pass, instead of jinking the F-4 left, right, up, and down to deter enemy groundfire during an especially vulnerable part of our bombing pass, Crush leisurely leveled off at about 7,000 feet, slowed down, and turned right with his right wing down so he could see how well he had bombed. I couldn't believe it—he acted like he was working some peaceful desert bombing site in the United States. Flak started to burst around us as I yelled at him to quit acting like a tourist and get us out of there. As soon as I could after we got back to base, I told my scheduling officer not to put me on any more missions with Colonel Crush, and told him why. Less than a month later, on July 6, 1968, Colonel Crush was shot down, and he and his young lieutenant backseater were captured.

On January 28, 1969, I flew a mission over North Vietnam with a Lieutenant Colonel Moon, who did the same crazy thing that Crush had done after we released our bombs. Once again, I asked not to fly with Moon, and on March 10, 1969, less than two months later, he was shot down over Laos. His backseater was picked up, but Moon was captured and either died or is still missing. I flew with a total of 54 F-4 pilots during my year with the Wolf Pack, and Crush and Moon were the only two I wouldn't fly a second mission with. As I think of Crush, Moon, and these two incidents, even today, I feel a terrible sadness.

On Top of the Pop Up
Tune: "On Top of Old Smoky"

On top of the pop up
And flat on my back,

I lost my poor wingman
In a big hail of flak.

Guard channel was silent,
The sites were all dead,
Until we rolled in
And looked up ahead.

The sky filled with fireballs,
The missiles flashed by,
Sweet Mother of Jesus,
We're all going to die!

Number Two called out, "I'm hit,
I'm going to bust";
Not one goddamned ELINT
A poor jock can trust.

So come, you young pilots,
And listen to Dad,
Forget about jinking,
And your ass has been had.

They'll hit you and burn you,
Their flak reaches far;
It's a long walk to Takhli,
And a beer at the bar.

Our Leaders

The first stanza of "Our Leaders" describes a recurring problem in the lives of American fighter pilots—restraints upon their high spirits imposed by senior officers worried about their own promotion to star, or general officer, rank. Another conflict is often over tactics, as seen in stanza 3. In fact, stanzas 3, 4, and 5 shift to another, more serious problem that especially plagued combat flyers and commanders in the field during most of the Vietnam War—the running of an air war by authorities who were further and further removed from the action, from the Joint Chiefs of Staff (JCS) through the secretary of defense, Robert S. McNamara, up to the ultimate authority, the commander in chief,

Pres. Lyndon Baines Johnson. The pilots' reaction to the decisions of higher echelons are unmistakably stated in the chorus. The song, composed prior to McNamara's resignation on February 29, 1967, uses the melody from a 1948 hit by Peggy Lee and Dave Barbour.

Our Leaders

Tune: "Mañana"

At Phillips range in Kansas
The jocks all had the knack,
But now that we're in combat
We've got colonels on our back.
And every time we say, "Shit-hot!"
Or whistle in the bar,
We have to answer to somebody
Looking for a star!

CHORUS *(repeat after each verse):*
Our leaders, our leaders,
Our leaders, is what they always say,
But it's bullshit, it's bullshit,
It's bullshit they feed us every day!

Today we had a hot one
And the jocks were scared as hell;
They ran to meet us with a beer
And tell us we were swell,
But Recce took the BDA
And said we missed a hair;
Now we'll catch all kinds of hell
From the wheels at Seventh Air!

They send us out in bunches
To bomb a bridge and die,
These tactics are for bombers
That our leaders used to fly;
The bastards don't trust our colonel
Up in wing, and so I guess,
We'll have to leave the thinking to
The wheels in JCS!

The JCS are generals,
But they're not always right,
Sometimes they have to think it over
Well into the night;
When they have a question
Or something they can't hack,
They have to leave the judgment to
That money-saving Mac!

Now Mac's job is in danger
For he's on salary, too;
To have the final say-so
Is something he can't do;
Before we fly a mission
And everything's OK,
Mac has to get permission from
Flight leader LBJ!!

The Panther Pack Is Prowling

North and South Vietnamese women sometimes fought along-side their men during the Vietnam War. The next song tells of the truck driver Ling Po's woman, who wishes to masquerade as a man (stanza 3) so she can return with him on his route back north to Quang Khe, about 40 miles north of the DMZ. The Panther Pack (stanza 1), an American fighter unit, poses a serious threat to her beloved, but Ho Chi Minh allegorically grants her wish in stanza 4. Ling Po's woman represents all those like her whose love and courage Uncle Ho commends. Quite moving in its simplicity of language, this song is not only a sympathetic portrayal of the enemy, but of humankind at its very best.

The Panther Pack Is Prowling

The Panther Pack is prowling,
Ling Po has to drive,
And I'm afraid he won't make it
Back to Quang Khe alive.

I'm afraid he won't make it,
It grieves my heart so,
Won't you let me go with him,
Please, Uncle Ho?

I'll tie back my hair,
The People's uniform I'll put on,
And I'll pass as your gunner
As we drive along.

I'll pass as your gunner,
No one will ever know;
Won't you let me go with him?
"Yes," said Uncle Ho.

Parties, Banquets, and Balls

The next song exists in both World War II and Korean versions, as well as in Vietnam, with a simple name change of the president in line 3 from Truman in World War II to Johnson or Nixon in Vietnam. The song pokes fun at the notion that the social niceties of political protocol can avert war, with the final line both insinuating strong disagreement with the president's views of lines 3–5 and suggesting that when war does ensue, it will be the organs of manhood that will be needed to bring peace. A particularly courageous fighter pilot was said to have "balls of brass." The original melody was by Albert von Tilzer in 1708.

Parties, Banquets, and Balls
Tune: "Take Me Out to the Ballgame"

Parties, banquets, and balls, boys,
Parties, banquets, and balls,
As President Johnson [Nixon] has said before,
There's only one way to stay out of war;
That's with parties, banquets, and balls, boys,
Banquets and parties and balls;
We'll have parties and banquets,
Banquets and parties,
and balls, BALLS, BALLS!

The Phu Cat Alert Pad

"The Phu Cat Alert Pad" is another song from the F-100 pilots at Phu Cat Air Base, South Vietnam. In this narrative, the pilots are launched from standby, or alert status to help out friendly forces under attack. The Bats carry a "soft" load of rockets, cannon, and napalm rather than heavy bombs, the former ordnance especially useful for the precise work needed to hit the nearby hostiles without killing "friendlies" by mistake. The weather is extremely bad (the usual fighter pilot would call it "dog-shit"), yet the mission is highly effective, as stated in stanza 7. Referring to napalm victims as "crispy critters" is a bit grotesque, even if they were the enemy; I don't know if the popular American breakfast cereal of that name had yet been created when this song was written.

The story is based on an actual event of late August, 1968, when two Bat F-100 pilots, John McClelland and Jim Druhl, helped save a besieged U.S. Special Forces camp from a strong VC attack. For their efforts, both pilots were given the Silver Star, America's third-highest award for gallantry in action against enemy forces. For information on the rousing melody, see "Old 97, the O-1E."

The Phu Cat Alert Pad
Tune: "The Man Who Never Returned"

Well, the hail came down on the Phu Cat alert pad,
And the lightnin' rolled through the night,
And the jocks looked out at that hell-roarin' weather,
'Twas a piss-sorry night for a flight.

Well, the red phone jangled in the Phu Cat alert pad,
Sayin' "Scramble a soft load Bat,"
And the jocks all trembled as they zipped on their G-suits,
Said "I really ain't believin' that!"

Well, they went to the ground for the scramble information,
Found an outpost was under attack;
And they thought, "My God, what a fucked-up occupation;
In this weather I will never get back!"

But they smoked all the way with a vector from the radar
Till the flares came into view;

And the FAC said, "Bats, there's a fuckin' lot of groundfire,
But it's only .50 cal and ZPU."

And that old FAC rolled 'em in and he marked her with a rocket
As the tracers came sailing by,
And then Lead turned final and he said, "I've got it,"
Then he punched and let his napalm fly.

Number Two turned final mighty close to terra firma,
And he laid his napalm smoke;
He was pulling off the target just a strainin' at his hernia
When the forward air controller spoke:

"Take it high and give me cover while I figure out the damage,
Stand by for your BDA;
You got forty crispy critters, that's all I can manage,
Till I count 'em by the light of day."

Now listen, commanders, you must take warning
From this time on alert;
Never launch your fighter pilots in the night-time rainstorm,
They may leave you and never return.

The Phu Cat Star

The forward air controller in "Phu Cat Star" dislikes the orders
he has received from Gen. George S. Brown, Seventh Air Force
commander in 1969, reassigning him to work at Tan Son Nhut
Air Base, South Vietnam, in a nonflying job. The FAC, call sign
"Misty," would rather be a "star" at Phu Cat, the status of which
he defines humorously, than just another "ground pounder" at
headquarters. He realizes, however, as we do, that his new orders simply cannot be refused.

Phu Cat Star

Got a message just this morning,
Was signed by General Brown,
"Come work in my Command Post, boy,
Don't bring your guns to town";
I'm a Misty FAC at Phu Cat,

And I really would be missed;
I can tell that I've been screwed,
But I don't think I've been kissed.

CHORUS (repeat after the second verse):
    Phu Cat Star, that's what I are,
    Yodel-eedle-lay-hee,
    You oughta see my car,
    Got a big old Chevy six-pack
    With a broken right-hand door;
    Can't park it at the O-Club,
    I can't shoot my flares no more;
    Just back from old Sun Valley,
    That land I loved so well;
    Got lots of smoke and foliage;
    Them trees sure do catch hell!

I'm working up at Misty,
I can't fly that single-seat,
My friends all call me pushy,
But I sure think I'm neat;
My uniform's lopsided
From all the medals I got;
I'm a big star here at Phu Cat,
No thanks, Tan Son Nhut,
No thanks a lot!

Pop Goes the Weasel

"Pop Goes the Weasel" uses a traditional English dance melody from 1853. Here the Wild Weasels, or F-105s, roll in with high-explosive incendiary (HEI) bombs and 500-pounders ("Lady-fingers") to hit an enemy SAM site that has been clearly located and marked by a white phosphorus ("Willie Peter") rocket. As seen in stanza 3, the air war may be over Vietnam, but the enemy missiles are Soviet. The Weasels are obviously proud of their special mission of striking hostile SAM sites, and the circular melody with its short lines gives the destruction of SAM sites by Weasels a kind of curious inevitability and appropriateness.

Pop Goes the Weasel

Tune: "Pop Goes the Weasel"

Around and around the SAM site
The missile chased the Weasel,
The Weasel got pissed, the SAM got zapped,
Pop goes the Weasel!

Willie Peter showed us where
To roll in to displease 'em;
One more pass with HEI,
Pop goes the Weasel!

Ladyfingers did their job,
Did more than just tease 'em,
The Russian techs got all pissed off,
Pop goes the Weasel!

We look around for SAM sites,
We grab their balls and squeeze 'em,
They show their ass, we shoot it off,
Pop goes the Weasel!

Puff

As early as April, 1966, the U.S. Air Force modified for use in Vietnam the venerable C-47 cargo and troop transport with rapid-firing 7.62-mm cannon and other special equipment. This pre–World War II aircraft was redesignated the AC-47 (attack-cargo) and soon took on the nickname "Puff, the Magic Dragon," a name made popular in the 1963 movie song by Leonard Lipton and Peter Yarrow, which supplies the melody for the Vietnam song "Puff."

The C-47, the military version of the DC-3, had been dubbed "gooney bird" since World War II because of its clumsy appearance. The song, probably composed by a fighter pilot of a much faster, more modern jet aircraft, pokes fun at the AC-47, even calling it an FC-47 (fighter-cargo) in stanza 4. I myself flew more than 500 hours in C-47s out of Tucson's Davis-Monthan Air Force Base from 1962 through 1966 to keep up my flying proficiency while the Air Force sent me to the University of Arizona to complete my graduate work. I certainly did not consider "the goon" my favorite plane to go to war in. However, Puff, later called Spooky, proved to be a highly useful weapon against VC ground troops, even though its crews doubtless took a lot of ribbing from other pilots. The bloody toll that Puff could take against VC is graphically portrayed in the John Wayne movie *The Green Berets*. All U.S. Air Force AC-47 gunship units in South Vietnam were deactivated in fall, 1969, and the aircraft were turned over to the South Vietnamese Air Force for them to use.

Puff

Tune: "Puff, the Magic Dragon"

Puff the tragic wagon
Came across the sea;
Conceited turds in gooney birds,
They came to kill VC.

The VC shook in terror
Whene'r they appeared,
The mini-ones with mini-guns
A'sticking out their rear.

Puff the tragic wagon
At Da Nang by the sea,
Though Rinkelman, in Number One,
His waist is sixty-three.

The FC-47
Flies all afternoon,
Half a day of boredom in
A silly, fuckin' goon!

Puff, the Magic Dragon

This second, more serious work about the AC-47, which well-known singer of Air Force songs Oscar Brand honored in his own "The Winged Methuselah," is also a far better song than "Puff." Stanzas 2 and 4 mingle beauty and terror as powerfully yet simply as do any lyrics in this collection. The persona has served on the Dragonship, as we begin to learn in stanza 6, and has earned his way home, where the legend of the AC-47 Magic Dragon will live on even to the third generation (stanza 7), yet our singer has no regrets at walking away from this aircraft he loves. For every thing under the sun there is a season.

Puff, the Magic Dragon

Tune: "Puff, the Magic Dragon"

Well, Puff, the Magic Dragon,
A bird of Cam Ranh song,
Came to fly the evening sky
In a land called Vietnam.

Puff, the Magic Dragon,
Came across the sea,
To write his name in tongues of flame
In the hearts of all VC.

When the grunts are deep in trouble,
And Charlie's all around,
The flare smokes rise into the skies
And leave fires on the ground.

The VC's mortal terror
Starts when the minis cry,
And the Dragon's breath of sudden death
Comes streaming from the sky.

Yes, Puff will still be flyin';
From One Corps down to Four,
Till Charlie's gone and the evening sun
Is like the year before.

But I'll remember always
The ground troops' grateful cry,
When fire streamed and Charlie screamed
At the Dragon in the sky!

Now dragons live forever,
And the Puff is just the same;
The Gooney Bird will still be heard
When "Grandpa" is my name!

It will have to roam the skies,
But friends, not with me;
I'm going home, no more to roam
In that land across the sea!

(Repeat verses 1 and 2)

Pull the Boom from the Gashole

Of his song "Pull the Boom from the Gashole," Dick Jonas says:

> Not a particular story, but similar instances happened again
> and again. An awful lot of jocks are still flying today because
> the Jolly Greens, the Sandys, and those big beautiful flying
> tankers hung it out far enough to snatch them to safety. The
> boom is the long rigid pipe extending from the tail of the
> KC-135, through which it transfers fuel from its own tanks to
> the in-flight refueling receptacle on the fighter. People who
> fly and fight love each other; it's comforting to know that when
> you get into trouble, the whole U.S. Air Force—and Navy and
> Marines, too, for that matter—are there to bail you out. This
> is a story with a lot of happy endings.

The song begins with its chorus, in which Wolf Pack Lead,
an F-4 Phantom from Ubon, Thailand, is taking on fuel to go
back to North Vietnam to aid in the rescue of Wolf Pack Two,
who was shot down by enemy automatic-weapons fire (ZPU). A
propeller-driven A1-E Sandy goes in with napalm and .50-caliber
machine-gun fire to clear the area of bad guys, and then Wolf
Pack Two is successfully picked up by an HH-3E helicopter, or
Jolly Green Giant, and taken to Nakhon Phanom (NKP), a U.S. air
base on the Mekong River near the Thai-Laotian border, where
he celebrates his rescue with a Thai beer (Singhi) in his hand and
a pretty young girl (poo-yeng) on his knee.

Pull the Boom from the Gashole

CHORUS *(repeat after each verse):*
Pull that boom from the gashole, tanker, let me go,
Clear me out of the anchor track before the sun sinks low.
I got a buddy on the ground up north in Route Pack Four,
Pull that pipe from the gashole, boomer, let me go.

We rolled in on a bridge up north about daylight,
And the guns on the ground were lookin' for a fight.
Pullin' out we got hosed pretty good with ZPU,
And they shot off the starboard wing of Wolf Pack Two.

Well, ol' Wolf Pack Two was on the beeper when he hit the ground,
I told him don't go nowhere, just hang around.
I got a Jolly Green coming in in a little while,
So hang loose, old buddy, we'll bring you home in style.

Well, ol' Sandy came in first with nape and fifty cal,
And that super Jolly Green looked good as a big-eyed gal.
Wolf Pack Two spent the night down south at NKP,
With a tall Singhi and a poo-yeng on his knee.

Words and music by Dick Jonas. © 1981 by Enchantment Music Co.
Used with permission.

Put Your Beeper on the Air

The next song has some similarities to "Hallelulah" I and II, with
which it shares its melody (for notes on the melody, see "Cruising over Hanoi"). "Put Your Beeper on the Air" was doubtless
composed by a flyer of the SAR (search and rescue) force, whose
duty was to attempt to rescue downed American flyers. In the
first stanza, sleeping fighter pilots reject in a dream Gen. William Westmoreland's praise of the rescue forces. This reference
dates the song between 1964 and 1968, when Westmoreland was
overall U.S. commander in Vietnam, while the reference to the
F-4 pilot with six MiGs on his tail in stanza 2 indicates that the
song was composed between April, 1965, when U.S. aircraft were
first engaged by MiGs, and February, 1968, when Pres. Lyndon
Johnson halted our missions over the Hanoi area.

   The next five stanzas each feature a pilot in trouble who
desperately calls on the rescue forces, call sign Crown, who are
circling in an area just away from but readily accessible to the
target areas. The Phantom pilot in stanza 2 is in serious trouble
through no fault of his own, as is the pilot in stanza 3, who seeks
help from a Pedro (small rescue helicopter) after crashing at his
home base, and the F-101 Voodoo pilot in stanza 5.

   However, the pilots in stanzas 4 and 6 have both "screwed

up" in various ways. The first has bombed too low and then stalled his aircraft by pulling up too sharply from his bombing pass, while the B-57 Canberra pilot failed to check his survival radio ("beeper") at the assigned time. But whether these pilots are in trouble because of their own fault or not, in the final stanza the rescue flyer affirms his dedication to picking them up. He can do that most safely if they ditch in the Gulf of Tonkin. For a rescue in the face of hostile fire, see "The Ballad of Jeb Stewart." All of the fighter pilots I knew had nothing but respect for SAR personnel—we knew we could count on them.

Put Your Beeper on the Air
Tune: "Throw a Nickel on the Drum"

It was midnight in Vietnam, all the pilots were in bed,
When up stepped Westmoreland, and this is what he said,
"Pilots, gentle pilots, how I love them one and all,
Rescue, gentle rescue," when a pilot shouted "Balls!"
Then up stepped a young pilot, and with a voice as bold as brass,
Said "You can take these rescue aircraft and shove them up your ass."

CHORUS (*repeat after each verse*):
    Oh, hallelujah, hallelujah, put your beeper on the air,
    There's a rescue aircraft there;
    Hallelujah, hallelujah, put your beeper on the air
    And you'll be saved!

Cruising round my orbit, doing one and thirty per,
When a call came from a Phantom, "Oh, won't you save me, sir?
I've got flak holes in my wingtips and my tanks ain't got no gas;
Mayday! Mayday! Mayday! I've got six MiGs on my ass!

"I shot my traffic pattern and to me it looked all right;
The airspeed read two-thirty, I really racked her tight,
When the airframe gave a shudder; the engines gave a wheeze,
Mayday! Mayday! Mayday! Some Pedros for me, please!

"It was split-S on my bomb run when I got too goddamn low,
But I punched that bloody button and I let those mothers go;
Put the stick back in my lap, when I hit a high-speed stall;
Come get me, Jolly Giant, I'm too young to die!

"They sent me up to Haiphong, the frag said no ack-ack,
But by the time I got there, my wings were mostly flak,

So I punched out of my Voodoo; it was too cut up to fly;
Come get me, Crown Alpha, I'm too young to die!

"I punched from my Canberra, and I landed all alone;
With my E and E equipment I made for a safe zone;
I tried to use my beeper, but the damn thing wouldn't go;
The squadron had 'em tested, but guess who didn't show?"

That wily fighter pilot, he's a skillful man, you know;
He can take those bombs and rockets and make that target blow,
But when he gets shot up and can make it to the sea,
I'll make a water landing and take him home with me.

The Red River Valley

Written in the late 1890s, "The Red River Valley" was popularized in the 1943 movie *King of the Cowboys*. A World War II song titled "The Po River Valley" used the melody, as does the Vietnam version following. In Vietnam the original title could again be used, not for the valley in Texas, but for the deadly one with the same name in North Vietnam. The fighter pilot laments the loss of his flight leader, Teak Lead, and in the final stanza says he will be praying at the briefing ("tickle the beads," or rosary), for today *he* will be using the jinxed call sign of Teak Lead. In fact, Teak flight lost its leader several times, and the call sign was finally retired, for fighter pilots have their superstitions too. At Ubon one of ours was that you shouldn't change anything in your life during your combat mission, or you might be shot down or killed. I knew flyers who wouldn't shave their mustaches—or grow one—for this reason. I myself grew and shaved two mustaches during my combat tour, for watching it grow helped make the time pass.

The Red River Valley
Tune: "The Red River Valley"

To the valley he said he was flying,
And he never saw the medal that he earned;
Many jocks have flown into the valley,
And a number have never returned.

So I listened as he briefed the mission,
"Tonight at the bar Teak Flight will sing,
But we're goin' to the Red River Valley,
And today you are flyin' my wing.

"Oh, the flak is so thick in the valley,
That the MiGs and the SAMs we don't need;
So fly high and down-sun in the valley,
And guard well the ass of Teak Lead.

"Now if things turn to shit in the valley,
And the briefing I gave, you don't heed,
They'll be waiting at the Hanoi Hilton,
And it's fish-heads and rice for Teak Lead!

We refueled on the way to the valley,
In the States it had always been fun,
But with thunder and lightnin' all 'round us,
'Twas the last AAR for Teak One.

When he came to a bridge in the valley,
He saw a duty that he couldn't shun,
For the first to roll in on the target,
Was my leader old Teak Number One.

Oh, he flew through the flak toward the target,
With his bombs and his rockets, drew a bead,
But he never pulled out of his bomb run,
'Twas fatal for another Teak Lead.

So come and sit by my side at the briefing,
We will sit there and tickle the beads,
For we're going to the Red River Valley,
And my call sign today is Teak Lead!

Republic's Ultra Hog

Still another song using the popular American folk melody "The Wabash Cannonball," "Republic's Ultra Hog" reflects neither patriotism nor the fighter pilot's usual love for his aircraft but rather the bitter cynicism of an F-105 Thunderchief pilot stationed at

Korat Royal Thai Air Base in northern Thailand. The opening two
lines of stanza 3, referring to Robert S. McNamara, secretary of
defense under Presidents Kennedy and Johnson, are especially
vitriolic. McNamara resigned in February, 1967, so the song was
composed prior to his departure at a time of heavy F-105 losses
over targets "fragged," or scheduled, in North Vietnam. On April
4, 1965, two F-105s from Thailand became the first U.S. aircraft
to be shot down by North Vietnamese MiGs during the air war.
For more on McNamara, see "Skoshi Tiger," stanza 6; for more
on an F-105 pilot's attitude toward his aircraft, see "Thud Pilot."

Republic's Ultra Hog

Tune: "The Wabash Cannonball"

Listen to the jingle, the gruntin' and the wheeze,
As she rolls along the runway by the BAK-9 and the trees;
Hear the mighty roarin' engine as you leap off in the fog,
You're flying through the jungle in Republic's Ultra Hog.

We came up from old Korat one steamy summer day,
As we pitched up on the target you could hear the gunners say,
"She's big and fat and ugly, she's really quite a dog,
She's known around the country as Republic's Ultra Hog."

Here's to McNamara, his name will always smell,
He'll always be remembered down in fighter pilot's hell,
He frags all the targets and sends us out to die,
He sends us into combat in Republic's 105.

Listen to the jingle, the gruntin' and the wheeze,
As she rolls along the runway by the BAK-9 and the trees;
Hear the mighty roarin' engine as you leap off in the fog,
You're flying through the jungle in Republic's Ultra Hog.

Saigon City

Using the same melody as "Here's to Old Bien Hoa," "Saigon
City" is similar in other ways as well. One major difference in
"Saigon City," however, is the persona's case of venereal disease
in stanza 3; another is the overall lack of irony.

Saigon City

Tune: "Sweet Betsy from Pike"

Here's to old Saigon, it's a hell of a place;
The way things are run is a frigging disgrace;
There's captains, and majors, and light colonels, too,
With their thumbs up their asses and nothing to do.

They stand on the flight line, they scream and they shout,
They scream about things they know nothing about;
For all the good they do, they might as well be
Shoveling shit on the Isle of Capri.

It's up in the morning and to the latrine;
It burns when I pee, 'cause I've been with a queen;
I've got it bad, and I'm telling you,
If you don't quit "short-timing," you'll have it, too.

When this year is over, we'll all go back home,
Back to our roundeyes and never more roam;
To hell with old Saigon and her misery,
To hell with old Saigon and all her VD.

Sammy Hall

The coarse, outspoken Sammy Hall has appeared as a character in Air Force songs since the Korean War. Just as his heroic alter egos in the daydreams of James Thurber's Walter Mitty enable him to vitalize his humdrum life, Sammy permits the U.S. fighter pilot to vent his anger, frustration, and obscenity in fictitious song in ways the professional military officer cannot—at least in public. The repeated final phrase of each stanza's first two and final lines alludes humorously to and contrasts with the refrain of a popular World War II song, "Bless Them All," which uses its phrase in a positive connotation. Sammy curses President Johnson in stanza 2 and the Joint Chiefs of Staff in stanza 4 and shocks us with his black humor in stanza 5. The absurdity of someone like Sammy getting a medal in stanza 7 is matched by the absurdity of where that medal is hung. This Vietnam version of "Sammy Hall" is highly original and probably the best I've seen from any war. The melody, from a traditional English ballad of the early 1700s published as "Wondrous Love" in 1835, may have become part of the U.S. Air Force song tradition because of its close social association with the Royal Air Force in World War II, when flyers from both the United States and England fought together, partied together, and sang together.

Sammy Hall
Tune: "Captain Kidd"

Oh, come 'round us fighter pilots, fuck 'em all,
Oh, come 'round us fighter pilots, fuck 'em all,
Oh, we fly the goddamn plane
Through the flak and through the rain,
And tomorrow we'll do it again
So fuck 'em all!

Oh, they tell us not to think, fuck 'em all,
Oh, they tell us not to think, fuck 'em all,
Oh, they tell us not to think,
Just to dive and just to jink,
LBJ's a goddamn fink,
So fuck 'em all!

Oh, we bombed Mu Gia Pass, fuck 'em all,
Oh, we bombed Mu Gia Pass, fuck 'em all,
Oh, we bombed Mu Gia Pass,
Though we only made one pass,
They really stuck it up our ass,
So fuck 'em all!

Oh, we're on a JCS, fuck 'em all,
Oh, we're on a JCS, fuck 'em all,
Oh, they sent the whole damn wing,
Probably half of us will ding,
What silly fucking thing,
So fuck 'em all!

Oh, we lost our fucking way, fuck 'em all,
Oh, we lost our fucking way, fuck 'em all,
Oh, we strafed goddamn Hanoi,
Killed every fucking girl and boy,

What a goddamn fucking joy,
So fuck 'em all!

Oh, my bird got all shot up, fuck 'em all,
Oh, my bird got all shot up, fuck 'em all,
Oh, my bird it did get shot,
And I'll probably cry a lot,
But I think that it's shit hot
So fuck 'em all!

While I'm swinging in my chute, fuck 'em all,
While I'm swinging in my chute, fuck 'em all,
While I'm swinging in my chute,
Comes this silly fucking toot
And hangs a medal on my root,
So fuck 'em all!

Shootin' Guns and Droppin' Bombs

The following is another song from the Bats at Phu Cat Air Base in South Vietnam. The Antonín Dvořák melody of 1896, rarely used in Air Force songs, provides a simple, lilting tune for a simple, clear set of lyrics. The composer was doubtless an F-100 pilot who was unashamed of his knowledge of classical music. The understatement of the first stanza works exceptionally well.

Shootin' Guns and Droppin' Bombs
Tune: "Humoresque"

Ever since I've started flying,
I had to work to keep from dying,
Specially since I came to Vietnam.

Seems on every combat sortie
That's when Charlie tries to zort me,
When I'm shootin' guns and droppin' bombs.

Someday when my tour is over,
I'll lay dreaming deep in clover,
'Bout you silly bastards droppin' bombs!

Sittin' in the Cab of My Truck

The Otis Redding hit of 1968, released shortly after his death in a plane crash in 1967, provides the smooth melody for another song about an enemy. It is comparable to "The VC Truck Driver's Blues." Hiding by day and driving by night, this North Vietnamese feels like a prisoner who wishes to escape (stanza 1, "filing my chains"). The driver left his home on the peaceful coast 30 miles north of the DMZ and came to the violent south to become a hero, just like so many other men who have gone off to war. However, the sights and sounds of combat quickly turn his hope to fear as he realizes the probable arrival of a hostile C-130 Spectre gunship ironically drawn to his area by the "red lead" gunfire of his own fellow soldiers. The concussions from exploding enemy bombs dropped nearby by radar from high altitude, or Sky Spot (see "GIB Named Richard"), have caused his ears and nose to bleed. Whether by design (the Spectre) or by chance (a Sky Spot), death is very close. Although an enemy, this man gains our sympathy while yet we cannot forget that he himself has been a purveyor of deadly arms and ammunition. The lyrics from the original Otis Redding song paint a relaxed, languorous scene which contrasts sharply with the plight of this all but doomed North Vietnamese.

Sittin' in the Cab of My Truck
Tune: "Sittin' on the Dock of the Bay"

Hidin' in the morning sun,
I'll be drivin' when the evening comes;
Watchin' the Phantoms pull in,
And I watch 'em pull back off again;
Well, I'm just a'sittin' in the cab of my truck,
Thinking this life ain't such a game,
Sittin' in the cab of my truck,
Filing my chains.

I left my home in Dong Hoi,
Headed for the DMZ,
I had somethin' to live for,
A people's hero I was going to be;

Well, I'm just a'sittin' in the cab of my truck,
Lookin' through the windshield at daylight rain;
Sittin' in the cab of my truck,
Filing my chains.

Here I sit havin' a king fit,
But God, I'm too scared to see the red lead,
'Cause it might just blow my only hope
Of not showing up on a starlight scope;
Well, sittin' here with britches so tight,
'Cause I think that Spectre's due back tonight,
Bleedin' from my ears and my nose,
From a Sky Spot that finally came close.

Well, I'm just a'sittin' in the cab of my truck
Watching the bombs fall through the rain,
Sittin' in the cab of my truck,
Yankin' my chain!

[Whistling; sounds of falling bombs directly overhead.]

Sixteen Tons

Merle Travis's 1947 song, popularized by Tennessee Ernie Ford in 1955, provides both title and melody for its Vietnam war parody, "Sixteen Tons." The pilot flies a DeHavilland C-7A, or Caribou, a small, reciprocating-engine troop and cargo transport. In stanza 1 he is scheduled for a flight to "Bung Bung," perhaps Ban Ban in Laos, but most probably somewhere in South Vietnam, as is Ca Mau, since his adversaries are Viet Cong rather than Laotians or North Vietnamese. The pilot has little chance at the Air Force Crosses, Distinguished Flying Crosses, or Bronze Stars won by many flyers over North Vietnam, since he merely gets an Air Medal for every specified number of Charlie Bravo flights he makes over South Vietnam or Laos, rather than Alpha flights over North Vietnam. His is not the most glamorous kind of flying, yet it can be quite dangerous. The pilot's own plane can "get him," or he may collide with a Huey, or small Bell UH-1 helicopter, as he drops supplies or even as he tries to land back at his own base. The ambiguous final line may also mean that his Caribou

will have doomed him with one engine knocked out unless a
Huey can pick him up after he crashes.

Sixteen Tons

Tune: "Sixteen Tons"

I woke up one morning when the sun didn't shine,
Got on my Honda and rode to the line,
I loaded sixteen tons of POL,
Fragged for Bung Bung, sure as hell.

CHORUS (*repeat after each verse*):
> *You carry sixteen tons and what do you get?*
> *Another Air Medal and a little more sweat;*
> *VC don't you get me, 'cause I can't go,*
> *I owe my ass to Charlie Bravo!*

I woke up one morning, it was drizzling rain,
Flying and bitching are my middle names,
An aerial drop south of old Ca Mau,
And the VC rifles went POW, POW, POW!

If you see me coming, better turn aside;
A lot of planes did and a lot of planes tried;
One engine turning, the other one still,
If a Huey can't get me, the Caribou will!

Skoshi Tiger

Although fighter pilots usually have great love for their aircraft,
they are often eager to move into a faster, more modern plane
such as the F-15 or F-16, when one becomes operational. However, the narrator in "Skoshi Tiger," probably an F-4 Phantom pilot with the 366th Tactical Fighter Wing at Da Nang, has little
respect for the newer Northrop F-5 Tiger. He's probably made
fun of the F-5 at the Officers' Club bar, only to have his own beloved F-4 belittled by the F-5 jockeys, so he retaliates in song.
The F-5's prototype first flew on July 30, 1959, and by 1962 the U.S.
government decided to produce the aircraft for its own use and
for sale to its MAP (Military Assistance Program) countries. What

better way to test the aircraft than in combat? So the U.S. Air Force sent a squadron of F-5s to Vietnam in 1965.

The F-5 was smaller and less powerful than the F-4 in almost every way. It had a length of 47 feet compared with the F-4's 63, a wingspan of only 29 feet compared with the F-4's 39, a gross weight of only 25,000 pounds compared with the F-4's 62,000, and could carry only 7,000 pounds of external payload compared with the F-4's capacity of 16,000 pounds. And while the F-5 had a top speed of Mach 1.64, the F-4 could hit Mach 2.0. Both aircraft had GE jet engines, but the F-5's two J85s produced only 10,000 pounds of total thrust, while the F-4's two J79s produced more than 35,000 pounds. To an F-4 pilot the F-5 looked like a toy, hence the song's title ("Skoshi" means "little" in Japanese) and the reference to "Skoshi Pussy" in stanza 8.

The first stanza criticizes the F-5's engine reliability, while stanzas 2 and 3 poke fun at its faddish newness and photographic overkill. Stanza 5 belittles the F-5's small wingspan, and stanza 4 derides the F-5's inability to start its engine with internally stored explosive charges, as the F-4 can. This last contrast is questionable, for most people I knew dreaded the few times we had to make cartridge starts in the F-4 because of the very real danger of a fire starting when the cartridges fired. More than once my frontseater and I hurriedly unstrapped and got out of an F-4 during a cartridge start because of fiery, smoking cartridges. Stanza 6 knocks both Secretary of Defense McNamara, who authorized the F-5, and the aircraft itself, with the pun "paper tiger." Stanza 7 extends an ironic welcome to the F-5 pilots, who are "rotten to the core," while stanza 9 declares that the F-5 would far better serve as a training plane for the Air Training Command (ATC) than as a combat fighter. The final stanza says that the Tigers, who may have been only on temporary duty (TDY) at Da Nang, will soon be returning to Bien Hoa Air Base in South Vietnam, where they were probably permanently stationed.

In fairness to the F-5 Tiger, it did indeed prove a reliable, easily maintainable, low-cost fighter. More than 2,500 were built for the United States and 30 other countries, and 2,000 were still flying as of April, 1987. Because of the Tiger's maneuverability, the U.S. Air Force and Navy use it to simulate an aggressor aircraft in training our pilots for air-to-air combat. As for the F-4 Phantom, the U.S. Air Force still uses more than 900 of them, compared with 50 F-5s, and is currently planning on modifying their power plants and electronic gear to enable them to serve well through the year 2000. Both the F-5 Tiger and the F-4 Phantom were excellent aircraft for the purposes for which they were designed.

"Skoshi Tiger" was composed between 1965 and 1967 and uses a popular melody of 1899 that was based on a traditional black American song of the 1850s, "When the Chariot Comes."

Skoshi Tiger

Tune: "She'll Be Coming 'round the Mountain"

Oh, they call them Skoshi Tiger when they come,
And they come in Freedom Fighters when they come;
If an F-5 flies on Sunday they must change the engines Monday,
But they'll all get airborne someday when they come!

Oh, they all will bring a camera if they come,
And they'll be on cinerama if they come,
And we all have a suspicion they may use real ammunition
Making color, wartime movies with their gun!

Oh, their planes go supersonic when they go;
They're transistor-electronic if they go;
The F-5's sophisticated and it's also overrated
For it will not fly in slush or sleet or snow!

By themselves the GE engines will not start;
The F-5 can't go without a power cart;
When it goes, it goes, I think, far as any kitchen sink,
Though it may go farther if the crews will fart!

Oh, their bomb load may consist of only four,
But their teeny weeny wing will hold no more;
If they had a bigger wing on that silly, fucking thing,
They would find a better use for that old whore!

Oh, they lumber down the runway when they roll,
And the pilot feeds it just a little coal;
If they took off from the grass they would surely bust their ass,
McNamara's paper tiger's in a hole!

But we're glad to have the F-5 here at war,
Though the pilots may be rotten to the core;

They may drink and they may swear [half-line is missing],
They'll be here aborting aircraft by the score!

Now we call them Skoshi Pussy when they fly,
For they can't quite get their ass up in the sky;
They may huff and puff their back up, if they ever have a crackup
There'll be bloody Skoshi Pussy where they lie!

They don't like the life at Da Nang by the sea,
They don't like to fly alone against VC,
So we'll give them all a treat, we will add another seat,
And will send the airplanes back to ATC—

But ole ATC will have to wait awhile,
For Headquarters cut new orders with a smile;
Now they'll not be going home, back to Bien Hoa they will roam,
For their TDY is going out of style!

So Long, John

"So Long, John" is the Vietnam version of a Korean War song,
"So Long, Mom." The Korean version, a better song, implies that
the war will lead to World War III and a nuclear holocaust that
will end the war "an hour and a half from now." Although removing the nuclear holocaust theme, the Vietnam version keeps the
references to dropping "the [nuclear] bomb" in stanza 1, and to
the length of the war in stanza 3. The pilot here is escorting a
Spectre, or AC-130 gunship, but his Spectre is forced to abort,
or cancel the mission, and the pilot escort is ordered to refuel
and escort still another Spectre, which will prolong his mission.
John is probably the escort pilot's roommate. The two lines of
stanza 1 referring to the Spectre's television capability echo an
interesting part of the Korean War version's first stanza:

So long, Mom, I'm off to drop the bomb,
So don't wait up for me.
And while you swelter down there in your shelter
You can see me on your TV.
While we're attacking frontally
Watch Brinkley and Huntley
Describing contrapuntally the cities
We have lost.

No use for you to miss a minute of
The agonizing holocaust.

During the 1950s, Chet Huntley and David Brinkley were probably America's favorite evening news team on television.

So Long, John
Tune: "So Long, Mom"

So long, John, I'm off to drop the bomb,
So don't wait up for me;
Escorting a Spectre in any old sector,
He can see me on his TV.

While we're on a bombing pass,
The Spectre's sparkling at the grass,
And gomers hose my little ass,
I'll try to smile somehow.

I'll be back to you when the war is over,
Two hours and a half from now—
"Your Spectre aborted—another tanker—"
Four hours and a half from now.

Song of the Wolf Pack

"Song of the Wolf Pack" pays tribute to the men of the 8th Tactical Fighter Wing, or Wolf Pack, stationed at Ubon, Thailand. The haunting melody is taken from the Stan Jones hit of 1949 sung by Vaughn Monroe. In 1967 Col. Robin Olds, the Wolf Pack's wing commander, led his men on a series of missions, sweeps specifically planned to destroy MiGs flying out of enemy air bases such as Kep and Phuc Yen, near Hanoi itself. This song probably commemorates that series of missions, one in which the Wolf Pack could take justifiable pride.

The song is quite "macho," especially stanza 4, though in 1967–68 we didn't use that word. In stanza 5 Wolf Pack Lead is too close to use a radar-guided Sparrow to shoot down his MiG, so he selects a heat-seeking Sidewinder. Robin Olds was a double ace in World War II, for he had shot down 12 enemy aircraft. He shot down 4 more in Vietnam and probably would have bagged the fifth he needed to become an ace in Vietnam as well had he not tried to use a Sparrow against a MiG once when he was too close in (or so I was told by an instructor of mine at Fighter Weapons School at Nellis Air Force Base, Nevada, who had flown with the Wolf Pack as a backseater on some of Olds's missions). Olds's charisma as an air combat leader is well portrayed in this song.

Song of the Wolf Pack

Tune: "Riders in the Sky"

Oh, pilots of the Wolf Pack, go to the briefing room;
The mission is a good one, to the MiGs it will mean doom;
We're going up to Hanoi, to Kep and Phuc Yen, too,
To write our bloody record in the annals of the blue.

We take off in our Phantoms to play our deadly cards;
The engines make our thunder and our eyes are steely hard;
We're on the way to battle the forces of the foe;
We're certain to destroy them, we'll seek them high and low.

CHORUS:

We battle today, and make our kills,
The Wolf Pack in the sky.

We cycle through the tanker, the tension starts to rise;
We go to meet our destiny awaiting in the skies;
We tune and arm our missiles as we streak across the black;
Our boss is in the forefront, leading the Wolf Pack.

We're showing on their radar, their hearts are full of hate;
They rise to meet the challenge, to meet their bloody fate;
They're headed for disaster, as any fool can tell;
If they dare to face the Wolf Pack, we'll shoot them clear to hell!

CHORUS

Wolf Pack Lead says, "Contact," they're MiGs, a flight of two;
I'm too close for the Sparrow, the Sidewinder will do;
I'll roll into the six o'clock behind the trailing MiG,
And let him have a missile, just like a fiery gig.

Oh, other flights engaged more MiGs, hot action filled the air;
The Wolf Pack's lust was sated before heading for their lair;

The enemy won't soon forget the awesome deadly toll,
As the 8th Wing troops return to base and make their victory rolls.

<small>CHORUS</small>

Son of Satan's Angels

A combat flyer has a very special relationship with the other members of his squadron, especially in wartime. Dick Jonas flew with the 433rd Tactical Fighter Squadron, or "Satan's Angels," of the 8th Tactical Fighter Wing. In a toast to his squadron, Dick once said, with unabashed patriotism and love:

> How shall I pay tribute to you? It is not possible to form the expressions to adequately represent what my heart feels for you. For the time it takes to fly your beautiful airplane 100 times into the enemy's homeland, you have been to me house and home, family and friend, comrade and brother. You have taught me the true meaning of courage, valor, prudence, discretion. With you I learned to dare, to stake my life against formidable odds, and you taught me to savor the intoxicating wine of victory. That I was one of Satan's Angels means to me that I have invaded the portals of hell with you, and there severely chastised the evil of tyranny in its abominable womb. That I was one of the Wolf Pack means that I have learned of you to be vicious and merciless in the defense of holy Freedom. You have made me one of the elite of the honored profession of military flying officers—a combat fighter pilot. While I was one of you I became acquainted with my God as never before. You helped me to know Him as an intimate friend, confidant, and counselor. I will not demean you by saying paltry words of gratitude, only that I salute you, brave comrades, and I bid you Godspeed.

In this lyrical salute to his squadron, Dick Jonas's chorus highlights his pride of membership as well as his loyalty to his squadron commander, Lt. Col. "Hoot" Gibson, an air-war ace in Korea and later leader of the U.S. Air Force aerial demonstration team, the Thunderbirds. The two stanzas show the pilot's personal courage in the face of enemy flak and MiG fighters, while the repetition of the chorus makes clear that the pilot's heroism is largely the result of his pride in the squadron in which he serves.

During World War II, Radio Berlin used Lord Haw-Haw and Axis Sally, and Tokyo used Tokyo Rose to try to demoralize listening American troops; the North Vietnamese used Hanoi Hanna over Radio Hanoi to try to do the same thing to us during the air war over Vietnam. While I was in Thailand from May, 1968, through May, 1969, I remember having heard Hanoi Hanna only once or twice early in my combat tour, but she must have been on the air quite a bit in 1966 and early in 1967 while Robin Olds, the Satan's Angels, and Dick Jonas were tearing up MiGs and targets near Hanoi.

Son of Satan's Angels

CHORUS (*repeat after each verse*):
> *I'm a son of Satan's Angels,*
> *And I fly the F-4D,*
> *All the way from the Hanoi Railroad Bridge*
> *To the DMZ;*
> *I'm one of old Hoot Gibson's boys,*
> *And mean as I can be,*
> *I'm a son of Satan's Angels*
> *And I fly the F-4D.*

> *There ain't a triple-A gunner up there*
> *That's anywhere near my class,*
> *'Cause I'm as mad as I can be*
> *And I'm in for one more pass;*
> *He hosed me down one time too much,*
> *And that one is his last;*
> *I look back at where he was,*
> *Hey, man, ain't that a gas!*

> *Hello, Hanoi Hanna, send your MiGs*
> *To meet their doom;*
> *Light 'em up and blast 'em off,*
> *Hoot's boys'll be there soon;*
> *I don't care if you are the gal with*
> *A mouth full of silver spoon,*

'Cause I got Sidewinders on board
That'll home on an AB plume.

Words and music by Dick Jonas, from *FSH Volume I*. © 1969 by Enchantment Music Co. Used with permission.

Spray On, Spray on Harvest Rice *and* Spray the Town

The next two are more Ranch Hand songs by flyers who dropped chemical defoliants. (See also "Battle Hymn of the Ranch Hands" and "I'm a Young Ranch Hand.") "Spray On, Spray on Harvest Rice," using a melody of 1908 by Norman Bales that was popularly revived in 1956, simply affirms that the sprayings will continue, despite the protests in the world forum of either British philosophers (Bertrand Russell) or French statesmen (Parole?). The harvests depended on by the Viet Cong will be destroyed to aid South Vietnamese president Nguyen Van Thieu and to antagonize U.S. antiwar activist Abie (usually "Abbie") Hoffman.

"Spray the Town," using a 1955 melody by Jerry Livingston, reveals the darker side of the same issue in horrible terms. The black humor and irony of the first two stanzas well set up the question in the song's final line, and the answer must be an emphatic "no!" Though defoliation missions were not to be flown over inhabited areas, the Ranch Hand here sets up a worst-case scenario that he obviously detests. War *is* hell.

Spray On, Spray on Harvest Rice
Tune: "Shine On, Harvest Moon"

Spray on, spray on harvest rice,
To get that crop;
Parole says that this is escalation,
And it's really got to stop.

Bertrand Russell says that this is not for you,
So spray on, spray on harvest rice, for Abie and Thieu.

Spray the Town
Tune: "Wake the Town and Tell the People"

Spray the town and kill the people,
Spray them with your poison gas;
Watch them throwing up their breakfast
As you make your second pass.

Get the spray pumps working double,
Slightly offset for the breeze;
See the children in convulsions—
And besides it kills the trees.

See them queue up in the market,
Waiting for a pound of rice,
Hungry, skinny, starving people—
Isn't killing harvests nice?

Springtime on the Red River

The next song is identical to the Korean War song from which it derives, except for the substitution of North Vietnam's Red River for Korea's Yalu River. The Robert Sauer 1929 melody was popularly revived in an American motion picture in 1945. Regarding stanza 3, airborne .50-caliber machine guns were extremely rare during the Vietnam War, if they were used at all. The Vietnam War adapter copied the Korean War song slavishly, but again, it's a pretty good song as is.

Springtime on the Red River
Tune: "When It's Springtime in the Rockies"

When it's springtime on the Red River,
And the MiGs come out to play,
And the contrails run in circles,
Fighter pilots earn their pay.

We'll hold our triggers steady,
When our sights are zeroed in;
We'll hold our glasses ready,
When they pass out rum and gin.

When it's springtime on the Red River,
And the napalm is in bloom,
And your .50s do the talking,
And it's just a MiG and you.

Once again you'll hear me whisper
That my fuel is running low,
When it's springtime on the Red River,
Then it's time for us to go.

Strafe the Town

Like "Spray the Town," the song "Strafe the Town" uses Jerry Livingston's popular 1955 melody, as well as horrible, more graphic
scenes of black humor. Here again a village is attacked, but by
fighter planes rather than Ranch Hands spraying defoliants. Just
as U.S. ground forces were not supposed to attack villages in-
discriminately and Ranch Hands were not supposed to spray
them, fighter planes were not usually supposed to attack them.
I knew one F-4 pilot, however, who lobbed a few leftover rockets into one every chance he got on the way back from a night
mission over Route Pack One, the area within 60 miles north
of the DMZ, because, as he said, "Those bastards down there
killed my best buddy." As far as I could tell, that village had been
abandoned for more than six months, so his gesture was symbolic rather than inhumane. And while North Vietnamese villagers—men, women, and children—could load munitions and
repair weapons in their churches and do other things to support North Vietnam's war effort, that fact doesn't justify the actions portrayed in this song in such bloody detail. Killing praying villagers as in stanza 1 is, of course, obscene, as is luring
orphans to their deaths in stanza 2. This song must be taken
ironically and is antiwar in the same vein as "Chocolate-covered
Napalm" and "Spray the Town." Such songs, though, embarrass
the U.S. government, since someone might miss the satire and
take the songs straight.

Only once during my year's combat tour was I ordered to
bomb a village. I was in the backseat of the lead aircraft of a
flight of four F4-D Phantoms scheduled for a bombing mission
over the Ho Chi Minh Trail in Laos. After air refueling we were

diverted to Route Pack One in North Vietnam to assist in a SAR (search and rescue) effort. An American pilot had tried to make the gulf in his crippled aircraft but had to eject and landed in a small lake just near the coast and was floating in the water waiting to be picked up. A village was about three miles away, and hostile forces from the village had apparently been moving around the lake to capture our guy.

Two other flights of fighters had been working with the rescue forces before we got there but had to leave, because their fuel was low. Each time a helicopter moved in to try to pick our flyer up, it was driven off by heavy ground fire, including automatic weapons. En route to the area my intercom had fouled up—I could hear my AC (aircraft commander) in my front seat, but I couldn't talk to him. I could also hear all the transmissions from outside the aircraft. The on-site airborne rescue commander first told us to lay some 500-pound bombs next to the road stretching about two miles from the village and running parallel to the east side of the lake. We put them in there, and the helicopter moved in but was once more driven back by withering fire. Apparently they had been trying to get this man out for a couple of hours, and finally, in desperation, I think, the rescue commander told us to put all the rest of our bombs into the village itself. I supposed he had tried everything else by now and was hoping the hostile forces near our man might run back to the village to help out after we bombed it.

I didn't like this order. First, if there were civilians in the village, even North Vietnamese, it seemed immoral to hit them, especially when anyone left in the village was not threatening our buddy on the ground. Second, on the practical side, if we did bomb the village and didn't succeed in getting our man out, we'd be increasing the likelihood that the enemy would kill rather than capture him. I'd heard tales of American flyers being beheaded on the spot by irate villagers in Laos. My intercom was still out, but my AC's hands were still full of airplane and he didn't have as much time to think as I did. I could hear my commander setting up aircraft two, three, and four to follow us in to bomb the village. Since I couldn't verbally discuss the authority, morality, or practicality of the order with my AC, all I could think of to do was to exert strong backward pressure on the stick as he dove into his bombing pass to show my objection. I'm sure he felt my pressure, but I'm not sure whether he got my message, for it was ambiguous. He might have thought I was merely warning him not to go in too low because of the heavy ground fire. We dropped the rest of our 500-pound bombs, perhaps 30 or so, right on the village, and then headed back home.

We were strangely silent as we rode in on the truck to debrief the mission. We were also strangely silent as we picked up coffee in our lounge and went into the debriefing room. Although we were saying nothing, I know that all eight flyers didn't like the order we had obeyed that day. As the flight leader, my AC talked about details of the mission from beginning to end, pointing out things we could have done better, but said nothing about the orders we had received or where we had dropped our bombs. It was as if those things had never happened. Later we learned that the downed pilot had not been picked up, and his fate was unknown.

Strafe the Town
Tune: "Wake the Town and Tell the People"

Strafe the town and kill the people,
Drop your napalm in the square;
Do it early Sunday morning,
Catch them while they're still at prayer.

Drop some candy to the orphans,
Watch them as they gather 'round;
Use your twenty millimeter,
Mow those little bastards down.

Strafe the town and kill the people,
Drop your high-drag on the school;
If you happen to see ground fire,
Don't forget the Golden Rule.

Run your CBU down main street,
Watch it rip off arms and hair;
See them scurry for the clinic,
Put a pod of rockets there.

Find a field of running Charlies,
Drop a daisy-cutter there;

Watch the chunks of bodies flying,
Arms and legs and blood and hair.

See the sweet old pregnant lady
Running 'cross the field in fear;
Run your twenty mike-mike through her,
Hope the film comes out real clear.

Super Constellation

Just as the aging C-47, B-26, and A-1E were pressed into Vietnam duty, so was the Air Force's version of the Lockheed Constellation, a pre–World War II commercial airliner used extensively by TWA (Trans World Airlines) for international flights. The Constellation was the last plane Orville Wright flew, and its Air Force version, the C-69, later the C-121, was used mainly for executive transport, including Pres. Dwight Eisenhower. With its 4,000 mile range, the C-121 was a natural for modification for electronic surveillance and airborne early warning as part of our nation's AWACS (Aircraft Warning and Control System), so the EC-121R saw considerable service in Vietnam and was especially valuable in warning U.S. aircraft of enemy attack.

The Super Constellation, however, was a strange sight, with its large, pancake-shaped radar dome mounted on the top center of its fuselage. These domes, perhaps 40 feet in diameter, plus a speckled camouflage paint job, made the EC-121R like its larger brother, the B-52, indeed appear a BUF, or "Big Ugly Fellow," even to pilots of the F-105, which though America's heaviest ever fighter aircraft, had only about one-third of the Constellation's weight to get airborne.

The song, with melody by Richard M. and Robert B. Sherman from the 1964 hit movie *Mary Poppins*, was written at Korat Air Base probably by a member of the 553rd Reconnaissance Wing, who most likely flew the "Super Connie" to war. The persona, J.J., is flying C-130s in Texas when he is suddenly transferred to the EC-121R program for training, probably at Otis Air Force Base in Massachusetts, the "northland" of stanza 2. The Connie was such a slow aircraft (stanza 3) that I heard one of its pilots once say that it took off at 120 knots, climbed at 120, cruised at 120, descended at 120, landed at 120, and taxied at 120. The aircraft was thus nicknamed "The Speed Brake," a retractable part on the trailing end of an aircraft's wings that can be lowered for quick deceleration. And even though the copilot had graduated from pilot training with a class ranking high enough for him to choose a far faster Phantom F-4C, the well-known "needs of the Air Force" had conspired with fate to land him in the Connie's right seat instead (stanza 4). I'm not sure what the BRT of stanza 4 was, but it was an important enough part of the plane's number 3 turbo-compound radial engine to cause the pilot to "feather" or turn off that engine when the part blows. Engine fires are another problem with a four-engined, propeller-driven aircraft like the EC-121R that critical Thud pilots would pounce on, but at least the Connie crew has warning buzzers and lights to alert them to those hazards (stanza 5).

Our songster is in obvious awe at the F-105 flyers cavorting around the Korat Officers' Club bar in their colorful, fancily adorned party flying suits (stanza 6) but doggedly defends his own aircraft, with its triple 48-feet high vertical stabilizers and 40-foot wide horizontal tail surfaces, which would dwarf the F-105's puny 20-foot high tail.

Stanzas 9 through 11 describe the EC-121R in combat, where it plays a vital if far less glorious role than did the F-105, which was credited with a total of 25 MiG kills during the war. Our pilot longs to return to the United States, often called "the Big BX," or Base Exchange, the store where you can buy almost anything. (Heaven was sometimes called "that big BX in the sky.") Perhaps only men and women who have been in a war and seen their small BX run out of soap, or not even carry it, can fully appreciate the "big BX" analogy. I certainly remember my own bug-eyed amazement on my first shopping trip to a U.S. supermarket after my year in Thailand, and many other Vietnam veterans have told me they had exactly the same experience. Whether we win the war or not, our flyer will return, but he will not miss the Constellation, a sentiment matching that of Dick Jonas's flyer, who in the ending of "Thud Pilot" says, "If I get my hundred and I'm still alive, / I'll have no grief, / Goodbye, Thunderchief, / My F-105." The song dates from 1967–68. The last EC-121R was retired in the mid-1970s, the last F-105 in the early 1980s.

Super Constellation

Tune: "Supercalifragilisticexpialidocious"

It's the extracamouflagilistic Super Constellation,
Even though the sound of it will cause you consternation,
If you fly it long enough it'll give you constipation,
Extracamouflagilistic Super Constellation!

When I was in Texas a'flyin' One-Three-Os,
My Wing Commander told me, "O J.J., you must go
Up to the far off northland, the land of ice and snow,
You'll fly the Lockheed Speed Brake, it's very, very slow!"

We fly and fly and fly and fly, and fly and fly and fly,
Because it takes so long for us to climb up in the sky,
But even after all of this we still aren't too high,
That's why the pilots sit around and all they do is cry!

One day the engineer yelled out, "We blew a BRT!"
The AC calmly turned around, said "Feather number 3,"
The young stud in the right seat screamed, "O dear Lord, why me?"
To think I finished high enough to get an F-4C!"

The Buf it doesn't have much speed, it really is quite slow,
It won't go anywhere if on its nose the wind does blow,
We fly around in circles, we go and go and go,
That is until the firelights begin to buzz and glow!

Now that we're in Thailand we share the base with Thuds,
O see them gaily walk around in all their fancy duds,
They sit upon the bar stools just sipping up the suds,
O gee! I wish that I could fly that great big ugly Thud!

Here's the story of speckled Buf, Lockheed's Super R,
It's gained less fame in the air than it has in all the bars,
But if you jeer a Connie man he'll answer without fail,
"I bet you mothers standing round can't handle that much tail!"

We spend our monthly earnings out chasing Thai poo-yings,
And nightly lifting mugs of cheer while dirty songs we sing,
We've learned our lesson very well on how to be a stud,
By watching all the throttle jocks who fly the Super Thud!

We have our own great hee-roes, each a wondrous guy,
And if you'll hear their hairy tales the drinks they'll gladly buy,

Once a mighty major brave was up where the VC roam,
He saw two shots of triple-A and brought the mother home!

We fly our speckled Bufs away up in the sky,
That's how we spend the whole damn week, just fly and fly and fly,
We fly in tiny circles round over near the fray,
But will we ever join the fight? You'll never see the day!

The flak that Charlie throws at us while in the dark 10 hours,
It's really such a pretty sight with all its sparkling showers,
It doesn't really scare us, or chill us to our bones,
Hell, half the crew is sound asleep while the rest eat ice cream cones!

I long for the time to come when I can get some rest,
And go back home to the big BX where the loving is the best,
Till the job be done, our tour complete, should either be the same,
And these damn Bufs go to TWA, the place from whence they came!

It's the extracamouflagilistic Super Constellation,
Number one priority in all of the nation,
McNamara chose it in a fit of desperation,
Extracamouflagilistic Super Constellation!

Tales That I Can Tell

"Tales That I Can Tell," another Dick Jonas song, is indirect and yet quite poignant. The first three stanzas build to the stark strength of stanza 4, and the final stanza closes the song with a sense of wonder and awe. A fighter pilot, at times, is capable of intense inner feelings and sensitivity. The tales that Dick Jonas tells more specifically in his other fine songs are hinted at here, and the singer must endure both pleasure and pain in telling them—yet they must be told.

Tales That I Can Tell

Oh, Lord, I got tales that I can tell,
Oh, Lord, what it's like down in hell;
Oh, Lord, I got tales that I can tell,
I got tales that I can tell, oh, Lord.

I know what it's like to sit and wait,
I know the misery of unknown fate;
Don't know whether I'll come back today,
I got tales that I can tell, oh, Lord.

I feel loneliness and fear and pain,
I've seen brave and daring deeds insane,
I've seen blood flow, but not in vain,
I got tales that I can tell, oh, Lord.

I've felt pity deep within my heart,
I've seen mothers' sons blown apart,
I've seen Satan's wicked fiery darts,
I got tales that I can tell, oh, Lord.

I've seen fire and thunder in the sky,
I've known men who weren't afraid to die,
I've seen men take eagle's wings and fly,
I got tales that I can tell, oh, Lord.

Words and music by Dick Jonas, from *FHS Volume I.* © 1969 by Enchantment Music Co. Used with permission.

Tay Ninh Mountain

The Tay Ninh Mountain of the next song is just over 3,000 feet high and is located in an area on the Laotian border just 70 miles north of Saigon. From Tay Ninh the Viet Cong could infiltrate into Saigon or nearby villages and military installations, strike, and then flee safely back to their jungle hideouts. Stanzas 1 and 2, mixing death and sensuality, beautifully sketch in the lonely susceptibility of men in war. And in Tay Ninh even the mountain tribesmen, the Montagnards, usually friendly to Americans, will betray one to the enemy. The danger here is intensely personal, both from treacherous human beings and hidden explosives, yet Viet Cong strongholds like Tay Ninh had to be challenged militarily.

Tay Ninh Mountain

They say don't go to Tay Ninh Mountain,
If you're fearin' for your life;

Old Victor Charlie's got a pretty young daughter,
She's out a'roamin' every night.

She'll ambush you and take your money
And Tay Ninh Mountain protects her there;
The Montagnards tell Victor Charlie
If a GI should enter there.

The roads are mined up Tay Ninh Mountain,
And you'll get stopped right in your tracks;
So if you go to Tay Ninh Mountain,
The chances are you won't come back.

Tchepone

Like "Thanh Hoa Bridge" I, "Tchepone" uses a popular American melody of 1870–90 which was revived in 1935–40; the openings of both songs are also similar. Located but 30 miles west of Khe Sanh, or 90 miles northwest of Hue, the heavily fortified Laotian town of Tchepone on the Ho Chi Minh Trail was a frequent target for U.S. air strikes. Hundreds of U.S. aircraft of all kinds were shot down over the Tchepone area by automatic weapons and 37- and 57-mm antiaircraft artillery fire.

About 600 feet above sea level, Tchepone had hills up to 1,200 feet high surrounding it on all sides. Twenty miles to the northwest was a peak 2,400 feet high; twenty miles to the northeast were jagged limestone ridges. Low-level attacks had to be very carefully planned and executed, for everything from pistols to 85-mm guns and SAMs could catch unwary U.S. flyers in a crossfire from the nearby hills. Most of us who flew in the Vietnam air war lost friends over Tchepone.

At Ubon, Thailand, we in the 8th Tactical Fighter Wing were only about 120 air miles from Tchepone and we could get there in 15 or 20 minutes, so we went there often. I especially dreaded missions over Tchepone, and my buddies and I couldn't understand why our leaders didn't use some imagination and drop in some U.S. troops once in a while to knock out the guns, even if they were in supposedly neutral Laos. But we launched no commando-like raids, and the guns near Tchepone just kept knocking us down, one after another, all through the war. Except for Thud Ridge near Hanoi, Tchepone today must be the largest junkyard of U.S. aircraft spare parts in the world.

In stanza 1, our hero, an F-4 pilot off duty, is conned into a mission over Tchepone by a sly colonel. Our F-4 pilot naïvely accepts the colonel's assignment and seems never to have heard of Tchepone before, which is unlikely, but the song wouldn't work as well without this premise. In stanza 4, as the Phantom Lead and his wingman are about to hit the town, the pilot feels sorry for his unsuspecting enemy, not knowing, as we do, that it's really he who is about to get the surprise as he flies into a hell of flak and tracers in stanza 6. By song's end our innocent F-4 flyer has learned a valuable lesson: stay away from Tchepone. But often we really didn't have that choice.

"Tchepone" was one of the most popular songs ever to emerge from the Vietnam air war. There were about a dozen versions of the song, but the original was by Toby Hughes, who flew F-4s out of Cam Ranh Bay in 1967–68 and also authored "Armed Recce" and "One Hundred Sixty VC in the Open." Toby told me that people were already singing "Tchepone" back in the States when he returned from his combat tour in 1968.

Tchepone

Tune: "The Strawberry Roan"

I was hangin' 'round Ops, just spendin' my time,
Off of the schedule, not earning a dime;
A colonel comes up and says, "I suppose,
You fly a fighter, from the cut of your clothes."
He figgers me right, "I'm a good one," I say;
"Do you happen to have me a target today?"
Says "yes," he does, a real easy one.
"No sweat, my boy, it's an old time milk run."

I gits all excited and asks where it's at;
He gives me a wink and a tip of his hat;
"It's three-fifty miles to the northwest of home,
A small, peaceful hamlet that's known as Tchepone."
(Ah, you'll sure love Tchepone!)

I go get my G-suit and strap on my gun,
Helmet, and gloves, out the door on the run;

Fire up my Phantom and take to the air;
Two's tucked in tight and we haven't a care.

In forty-five minutes we're over the town;
From twenty-eight thousand we're screamin' on down;
Arm up the switches and dial in the mills,
Rack up the wings, and roll in for the kill.

We feel a bit sorry for folks down below;
Of destruction that's comin' they surely don't know;
But the thought passes quickly, we know a war's on,
And on down we scream toward peaceful Tchepone.
(Unsuspecting, peaceful Tchepone.)

Release altitude, and the pipper's not right;
I'll press just a little and lay 'em in tight;
I pickle those beauties at two-point five grand,
Startin' my pull when it all hits the fan.

A black puff in front, and then two off the right,
Then six or eight more and I suck it up tight;
There're small arms and tracers and heavy ack-ack,
It's scattered to broken with all kinds of flak.

I jink hard to left and head out for the blue;
My wingman says, "Lead! They're shooting at you!"
"No bull!" I cry, as I point it toward home,
And still comes the fire from the town of Tchepone.
(Dirty, deadly Tchepone!)

I make it back home with six holes in my bird;
With the colonel who sent me I'd sure like a word,
But he's nowhere around, though I look near and far;
He's gone back to Seventh to help run the war.

I've been 'round this country for many a day,
I've seen the things that they're throwing my way,
I know that there're places I don't like to go,
Up in Mu Gia and in Ban Karai;
But I'll bet all my flight pay the jock ain't been born,
Who can keep all his cool when he's over Tchepone!

Words by Toby Hughes, © 1968. Used with permission.

The Thanh Hoa Bridge I

From March, 1965, until May, 1972, repeated U.S. air strikes were launched against the Thanh Hoa Bridge, called by the Vietnamese "The Dragon's Jaw." Spanning the Song Ma River just north of the town of Thanh Hoa, the Dragon's Jaw was built during seven years of heavy labor by the North Vietnamese to replace the one they themselves had destroyed in 1945 during their war with the French. Completed in 1964 and built to last, the new bridge was 540 feet long, more than 50 feet wide, and stood 50 feet above the river. A single railroad track ran down its center, with highways running on each side. Because of its importance in the flow of war supplies to the south, the Thanh Hoa Bridge was a vital, if formidable, target for U.S. pilots, and the difficulty we had in knocking it down, which thus gave it a strong symbolic value to our enemy, is well chronicled in John Clark Pratt's *Vietnam Voices*.

The first important American air strike against the bridge took place on April 3, 1965, involving 79 aircraft from Korat and Takhli in Thailand and from other bases in South Vietnam. Forty-six F-105 Thunderchiefs were armed with 250-pound Bullpup missiles and 750-pound bombs. Most were to attack the bridge, while some, together with F-100 Super Sabres, would try to suppress the enemy ground fire in the target area. The overall mission coordinator was Lt. Col. Robinson Risner, who later in the war became a famous American POW.

During the mission an F-100 and an RF-101 were lost, and although ten dozen 750-pound bombs and 32 Bullpup missiles had been launched at the Dragon's Jaw, it remained structurally sound after the attack. A similar raid the next day also met with little success, though more than 300 bombs scored hits on the bridge, and this time, on April 4, 1965, U.S. aircraft in Vietnam for the first time were engaged by enemy MiGs, in this case MiG-17s, and two F-105s and their pilots were lost. Both attacks damaged the rails and highways on the bridge, but these were repaired almost overnight. The Bullpups and 750-pound bombs were just not powerful enough to do the job.

In May, 1966, about a year later, U.S. military planners devised Project "Carolina Moon," a clever plan involving the dropping of a specially devised weapon, weighing two and a half tons and resembling a giant pancake eight feet in diameter and two and a half feet thick, into the Song Ma River near the bridge.

The devices would float down the Song Ma and detonate when their sensors detected the metal structure of the Dragon's Jaw—or so it was hoped. On the night of May 30 a C-130 dropped five of these special weapons into the Song Ma River near the bridge, but photo reconnaissance the next day showed no new damage to the bridge, nor were the weapons seen on the river banks or elsewhere. A second night mission took place on May 31, but this time the C-130 and its crew vanished en route, although an F-4 crew working the area reported seeing heavy enemy groundfire and a flash of light on the ground near the Thanh Hoa Bridge about two minutes before the C-130's scheduled drop time. Again, the Dragon's Jaw remained standing.

The attack in the next song probably takes place some time after "Carolina Moon," but yet early in the war, for the song appears in "Yankee Air Pirate," a songbook of the 355th Tactical Fighter Wing, an F-105 unit at Takhli in Thailand, dating probably from 1966–67. F-105s from Takhli took part in the first major attack on the Thanh Hoa Bridge on April 3–4, 1965, and no doubt made later strikes against it as well. Like "Tchepone," the song opens with a pilot scheduled by a colonel for a special mission, but here the similarity ends. The former pilot may be naive about Tchepone's dangers, but as seen in the chorus, this flyer knows full well how dangerous the Dragon's Jaw is. There is an especially powerful feeling of futility when you know that despite your best efforts and although you may die trying, you'll be aiming at a target that no one has yet succeeded in destroying.

At the end of stanza 3, our pilot's pride overcomes his fear, and he's humorously given a less-than-airworthy "Nickel," or F-105, to fly against the Dragon's Jaw. After finding the bridge on his own, our lone attacker drops his bombs and then almost has a midair collision with an enemy MiG as he pulls off the target. As he egresses the target area at low level, he's hit by a SAM and is forced to eject over the Gulf of Tonkin, from which, probably in his raft, he waxes philosophical. In combat, a sense of humor is essential for survival.

The Thanh Hoa Bridge I

Tune: "The Strawberry Roan"

I was hangin' 'round Ops in this sweaty clime,
Just cussin' the schedule and my lack of time,
When up walks this colonel and says, "I suppose

You're a trained killer by the looks of your clothes."
Well, I looked him up once and I looked him down twice.
I could tell by his sneer he weren't thinkin' nice.
So I said in a voice that was shakin' with fear,
"I am your man if you buy the beer."

CHORUS *(repeat after each verse):*
    Oh, that Thanh Hoa Bridge,
    Oh, that Thanh Hoa Bridge,
    They've flak and missiles,
    You're some sitting duck;
    At downing good pilots
    They've had lots of luck;
    Oh, that Thanh Hoa Bridge!

The colonel then said, "I've got a place in mind
Where you can go if you're not blind;
They've flak and MiGs and SAMs and such,
I need a man that's good in the clutch."
I got all het up and asked what I'd get,
'Twas a kick in the ass if I didn't hit;
I told him I'd go cause they haven't found
A target in hell that I couldn't pound.

We jump in his car and go to the line,
Then he stops by a Nickel that's tied up in twine.
"This is your bird, now get on your way."
I could tell at a glance I'd sure earn my pay.
I crank the beast up and I taxi on out,
As I leave the chocks I can hear the chief shout,
"The oil pressure's low, the water don't work,
And the stab aug's got one hell of a jerk!"

I give him a grin and waggle my thumb,
This one's a counter and I'm not so dumb.
Well, I take on off at two hundred per,
I got two on the wings and full-loaded MER.
I struggle on up to ten thousand feet,
"Send down the tanker or we'll never meet."
Well, I take on my gas and head out on course;
I call for a steer until I am hoarse.

But Lion is down and Invert won't say,
And Brigham says I'm not going his way.
Well, I'm off on my own and all for the best;
Those bastards don't know the East from the West.
Now I get over Thanh Hoa and I look for the bridge;
They said it was south but it's east of the ridge;
I roll in on my run; it looks easy as pie,
Till the flak starts burstin' and coverin' the sky.

I coolly compute all the mils I will need,
And calmly adjust both angle and speed.
I check my drift and with the bridge in my sight,
I mash on the button and pull off to the right.
Well, I check back at six and I see this big bird,
He's a-closin' in fast and he's sure ridin' herd.
As he flashes by there's a red star on each side,
It must be a MiG and there's no place to hide.

I head for the deck with all that she's got,
When along comes this SAM—my God, I've been shot!
While I'm driftin' down in my chute all alone
I'm finally convinced that I'm no smokin' stone.
I'm wishin' I was back in Kansas right now,
With a face full of horseshit, my hand on the plow,
But that ain't so and I'm down in the drink.
A day like today can sure make a man think!

The Thanh Hoa Bridge II

A third major mission directed against the Thanh Hoa Bridge took place on March 12, 1967, when three U.S. Navy A-4 Skyhawks, escorted by two F-8 Crusaders for protection from MiGs, hit the bridge with another new weapon, the Walleye Glide Bomb. The Walleye, a TV-guided bomb, had a 1,000-pound explosive warhead. Bombing in daylight to enhance their TV guidance capabilities, all three A-4s hit the specified aiming point on the Dragon's Jaw within a few feet of each other, but the results were much the same as on the earlier strikes. Even 1,000-pound bombs delivered with extreme accuracy were not enough to destroy or even seriously cripple the bridge. In February, 1968, U.S. president Lyndon Johnson ordered the bombing ceased above North Vietnam's 19th Parallel while peace negotiations continued. Thus the Dragon's Jaw, located some 50 miles north of the 19th Parallel, was spared further attack for over four years, during which time supplies continued to pour over the bridge to support the North Vietnamese and Viet Cong fighting in the South. Since peace negotiations came to an impasse, Pres. Richard Nixon ordered the resumption of the bombing of North Vietnam with Operation Rolling Thunder on April 6, 1972. The Dragon's Jaw again became fair game for U.S. air attacks as we sought to knock out what had become such a powerful symbol of North Vietnam's war-making capability. Both sides had lost a good deal already—we to destroy, they to defend and rebuild the Thanh Hoa Bridge.

Only a few weeks after Nixon's order, another major strike was planned against the bridge under Operation Freedom Dawn. On April 27, 1972, a force of 12 Wolf Pack F-4 Phantoms of the 8th Tactical Fighter Wing from Ubon, Thailand, set out to try to destroy the Dragon's Jaw. This strike force was armed with two more new weapons, Electro-Optical Guided Bombs of 2,000 pounds, and Laser-Guided Bombs in the 2,000- and 3,000-pound class. A special flying outfit had been experimenting with these new systems while I was at Ubon in 1968–69, and by 1972 these weapons were highly effective. The EOGB used a system similar to the Walleye's TV, which could be used in marginal weather, since the bombs would usually hit their targets if clouds did not obscure them when they were released. The LGBs, however, depended on clearer weather so they could follow their launching aircraft's laser beam down to the target. Since the weather was marginal that day, the F-4s carried both EOGBs and LGBs. The weather was bad enough that visibility was poor over the target area, and so five EOGBs were launched against it. The F-4s damaged the bridge enough this time that it was useless for vehicular traffic.

Although the Dragon's Jaw had been seriously weakened by this latest, most powerful attack, it took another mission, on May 13, 1972, to get the job done. This time 14 F-4s from the Wolf Pack were launched against the bridge in clear weather, armed with nine 3,000-pound and fifteen 2,000-pound laser-guided bombs plus forty-eight 500-pound conventional bombs. Despite heavy enemy ground fire, the mission was successful. No F-4s were lost or damaged, and the western span of the bridge was knocked completely off its 40-foot concrete support. The bridge itself was so twisted that it was useless for rail traffic for several months. Less than a year later, President Nixon ceased all hostile actions against North Vietnam, and the war was effectively over.

In "Thanh Hoa Bridge" II, Dick Jonas commemorates the successful final mission of his Wolf Pack comrades against the Dragon's Jaw. Dick says: "We tried a long time in the traditional way to destroy this bridge. A lot of us never came back because their gunners were so good. Then came the 'smart' bombs, and Thanh Hoa Bridge turned into a pussy cat—with its claws pulled and its fur blown away." And yet I suspect that today there may well be a bronze plaque on the Thanh Hoa Bridge saying in Vietnamese, "The Dragon's Jaw: The Bridge the U.S. War Dogs Could Never Destroy." In the second stanza, a tall Singhi is a popular brand of Thai beer.

Thanh Hoa Bridge II

CHORUS (repeat after each verse):
>   On the day Thanh Hoa Bridge saw the light,
>   The guys from the Wolf Pack went up north to fight.
>   We did our thing like we oughter;
>   We dropped that bridge in the water,
>   On the day Thanh Hoa Bridge saw the light.

>   There's a lot of good planes in the mud under Thanh Hoa Bridge,
>   And a lot of parachutes laying out on Thanh Hoa Ridge,
>   And the guys that took 'em north can't go nowhere,
>   All because of the guns on the ground around Thanh Hoa Bridge.

>   So we put our heads together one night around a tall Singhi,
>   Trying to figure out a way to kill a bridge
>   That didn't really wanna die.
>   We talked it up to the boys with bombs with the brains,
>   And they allowed to kill the Thanh Hoa Bridge wouldn't take no strain.

Words and music by Dick Jonas. © 1981 by Enchantment Music Co. Used with permission.

The 388th *and* The 390th TFW Song

Songs of individual flying units have been popular in the Air Force since World War II and earlier. Some of them are general enough to permit the substitution of the number of one squadron or wing for another. However, like Dick Jonas's "Son of Satan's Angels," the next two songs, "The 388th" and "The 390th TFW Song," are original with the Vietnam War and were both composed in 1967 or early 1968.

The 388th Tactical Fighter Wing, flying F-105 Thunderchiefs out of Korat Royal Thai Air Force Base, located about 100 miles northeast of Bangkok, took part in the early strike against the Thanh Hoa Bridge in March, 1965. They also flew many other dangerous missions over various targets in the Hanoi area. Their song is serious and straightforward, reflecting not only their unit pride and dedication but their pride in their aircraft in stanzas 5 and 6, as well. Like the F-4 Phantom, Thud pilots preferred to fight enemy MiGs at lower altitudes, where their maneuverability was more equal to that of their adversaries.

"The 390th TFW Song" comes from "A Fighter Pilot's Hymnal," the songbook of the 90th Tactical Fighter Squadron of the 3rd Tactical Fighter Wing stationed at Bien Hoa in South Vietnam. This songbook contains more than 300 songs derived from a variety of sources. Dick Jonas and I think the song is from an F-4 Phantom unit, probably a squadron rather than a wing, stationed at Cam Ranh Bay or Da Nang in South Vietnam. The sarcastic lyrics and colorful language of this song contrast well with the more noble sentiments of "The 388th," which precedes it.

The 388th

The 388th's going north today with bombs on every MER;
When we cross Red River, we'll do six hundred per;
The flak and SAMs will greet us from top, bottom, and the side,
And then the MiGs will tap us, to liven up our ride.

CHORUS *(repeat after each verse)*:
    Three Eighty-Eight, the best Air Force Wing,
    We're number one, so listen to us sing!

We're going to hit a target that we hit yesterday,
To sharpen up their gunners and earn our hazard pay;
We're going to use the same old route, which may to you seem strange,
But that will fool their planners, who think that we will change!

We're going to have to brave the SAMs and flak that we may face,
So that we can drop our bomb load on some defended place;
We may not like the place we go or the target we will hit,
But will do our very best, there is no doubt of it!

We're headed straight for old Hanoi, and when we get up there,
We'll drop our ordered payload just about anywhere,
On a bridge, a site, or railroad yard, or even right downtown,
To show that stupid Ho Chi Minh that he's a stubborn clown!

Maybe we don't turn so good when we are way up high,
But come on down into the weeds when you want to die;
We'll turn and fight and have your badge, if you want to play,
Down where we are better than MiGs in every way!

When you're flying way up north and want to stay alive,
There's just one Air Force airplane, the Thunder One-O-Five;
Now if you are a doubter of what we have to say,
You can take our glorious place, any glorious day!

The 390th TFW Song

Tune: "Hi, Ziggy, Ziggy"

Hi, ziggy, ziggy, fat little piggy, Blue Boar;
The F-4 is a fat whore without a bomb door;
Two engines to go, to see Uncle Ho,
And a tanker to feed her when dry, suck, suck, suck.

Hey MiGgy, MiGgy, I'm a little piggy, Blue Boar;
With our belly up, you're a sitting duck—oh shit, I missed!
It's back through the flak, with you on my back,
And a seat that is covered with crap, crap, crap, crap.

See the missiles come, you're a sitting duck, SAM site;
Hope the burners light, we don't want to fight, knock, knock, bat shit!
We'll drop all the bombs on North Vietnam;
We're going home empty tonight, dump, dump, dump.

Thud Drivers in the Sky

Like "Song of the Wolf Pack," the song "Thud Drivers in the Sky"
takes its stirring melody from the Stan Jones hit of 1949 made
popular by singer Vaughn Monroe. This song of bravado by pilots of the F-105 Thunderchief mixes humor and seriousness, fear
and courage. Stanza 3 is especially well done, revealing the pilot's very genuine respect for the crew chiefs who repair and
maintain his aircraft. We used to put the crew chief's name on
the aircraft he was responsible for and also tried to get him up
in the air in his own Phantom on a training mission or test flight.
He'd help strap us into our ejection seats before we took off and
helped us get out when we came back. When we returned after
a particularly dangerous mission, his smile seemed the most
beautiful sight in the world.

Thud Drivers in the Sky
Tune: "Riders in the Sky"

A 105 got airborne on a dark and windy day,
And as he raised his landing gear you could hear the pilot pray:
"Keep all those buckets in the wheel and I'll be safe and sound.
Don't let that fire go out, Dear Lord, till I am on the ground!"

CHORUS *(repeat after each verse):*
    Yippi-o, yippi-i-a-a-aye,
    Thud drivers in the sky.

Those flying fiends are here to stay, it's said they're very mean,
And all know we've been famous since 1917;
Though we may work on holidays, and weekends just the same,
Those pukin' pups make history, Oh, bless that famous name!

As our 105s take to the air, their tails are spouting flame,
The crews they all go through hell, but fly 'em just the same;
The crew chiefs work their asses off to keep 'em flyin' high,
And watch with satisfaction as their plane goes screaming by.

Day and night our pilots fight to live up to their name,
Other pilots come and go, but ours fly on to fame;
They're going to fly forever in that range so very high,
They cuss and cry, "LIVE OR DIE!" Thud drivers in the sky!

The Thud Driver's Theme

"The Thud Driver's Theme," probably from the 388th Tactical Fighter Wing at Korat, Thailand, uses a melody long popular with barbershop quartets, written by Tod B. Galloway in 1911 and revived by singer Rudy Vallee in 1936. This melody invites harmonizing and has been used for Air Force songs in World War II and Korea, as well as in Vietnam. Stanza 2 includes the usual amount of disrespect for those who run the war out of Seventh Air Force Headquarters in Saigon. Stanza 4 dramatizes a strike mission in which the lead F-105 gets hit by a surface-to-air missile, after which the other flyers must use afterburners (ABs) to increase their aircrafts' thrust to escape quickly. When sung in the Officers' Club, stanzas 1–3 might be rendered disharmoniously near the piano, while during stanza 4 the singers might act out the switching to afterburners by running around the room with arms outstretched.

The Vietnam War song "The Whiffenpoof Song," not reprinted here, is almost identical to "The Thud Driver's Theme." Line 7 in the former has "In a toast to a comrade who just fell," whereas the latter reads, "Sing they poorly, not too clearly, / Loud as well." Apparently the composers of the latter version were more self-conscious about their group's singing ability.

The Thud Driver's Theme
Tune: "The Whiffenpoof Song"

From a hootch in Southeast Asia
To the place where aces dwell,
To the bars in old Korat
We know so well,
Sing the fighter jocks assembled
With their glasses raised on high,
Sing they poorly, not too clearly,
Loud as well;

We will throw our glasses wildly
And throw our bombs as well,
Till the finks at Seventh Air Force go to hell!

We're poor fighter jocks who have lost our way,
Help—Help—Help—

We flew to the town of Hanoi today,
HELP—HELP—HELP—

Steely-eyed pilots up in the blue,
Lead got zapped by an SA-2,
Let's haul ass or they'll zap us too,
A _____ B_____ now!!

Thud Pilot

Dick Jonas says,

> The Phantom wasn't the only jet fighter with a piece of the action in that fracas [Vietnam], although you'd never know it by listening to a bunch of Phantom pilots. There was the F-105 Thunderchief, most of us called it a Thud, but never with an ounce of disrespect. There's enough pure, raw courage in one Thud pilot to make heroes out of an entire bomber squadron. I've watched those F-105 drivers baby that monstrous bucket of bolts into places the Devil himself wouldn't go. They'd come roaring in, peel off in a screaming dive, point that thing at the ground, and pray, I reckon. You see, the Thunderchief doesn't carry but one pilot, and I used to wonder just how lonesome it got for those guys, nobody to talk to like in the Phantom, except the Lord, maybe. One engine, one seat, one set of eyeballs, and one pilot. Yep, among fighter planes the Thud was sort of the last of the red hot mamas. Now it's true that to a Wolf Pack fighter pilot there isn't a plane anywhere that can hold a candle to a Phantom, but I'll give you a little tip. Don't ever bad-mouth a Thud or a Thud pilot where a Phantom driver can hear you. It might cost you a few teeth."

Stanza 1 of "Thud Pilot" clearly reveals the close communion between pilot and aircraft, but fear is part of that union as well. Stanza 2 pokes fun while praising the Thud, which takes more than 10,000 feet to get airborne. Fear is again evident, as it is in stanza 3, which also begins with the pilot's respect for his F-105. In stanza 4, however, the pilot tells us that, as much as he loves his plane and is grateful for the fear and danger she has brought him through, once he has finished his 100 required missions and can go home, he's willing to bid her farewell.

Thud Pilot

I'm a Thud pilot, I love my plane;
It is my body, I am its brain;
My Thunderchief loves me, and I love her, too,
But I get the creeps
With only one seat,
And one engine, too.

She's faster than lightnin', it says on her dials;
To get a Thud airborne, takes only two miles;
She's packed with transistors, black boxes, diodes,
But stay alert
'Cuz you might get hurt
When she EXPLODES.

She totes more bombs than a B-17;
My F-105 has a gun and she's mean;
But there is one thing that curdles my blood,
It's lonesome up there
Alone in the air
In my single-seat Thud.

I love my Thud and she loves me, too,
But she soaks up flak like a magnet can do;
If I get my hundred and I'm still alive,
I'll have no grief,
Good-bye, Thunderchief,
My F-105.

Words and music by Dick Jonas, from *FSH Volume I*. © 1969 by Enchantment Music Co. Used with permission.

Trees

"Trees" is another song from the F-100 pilots, or Bats, at Phu Cat Air Base, South Vietnam. In the Hollywood film versions of air attacks, every mission has a spectacular payoff in destroyed factories, bridges, or enemy airfields. For the fighter pilot, however, many missions over Southeast Asia were routine, and the results of his work, even in the face of extreme danger, as often as not were negligible. After two or three bombing or strafing runs he would often hear the forward air controller call, "No positive bomb damage assessment due to smoke and haze." The songwriter here does an excellent job in building up to his anticlimax in stanza 5. The U.S. naval ship *Pueblo* was captured by the North Koreans in January, 1968, and the song was composed shortly thereafter when the Bats arrived from Sioux City, Iowa, in February. Stanzas 1 and 2 humorously have the Air Guard coming to the rescue of the U.S. Air Force.

For operational purposes, South Vietnam was divided into four areas, I, II, III, and IV Corps, extending southward just below the DMZ in I Corps (pronounced "eye-core") down to the Mekong Delta and Ca Mau Peninsula in IV Corps. VC and North Vietnamese troops in I Corps, where the Bats are working in stanza 5, were especially skillful at camouflaging real targets and creating false ones. Without a doubt, many of our strikes were against suspected rather than verified targets.

Trees

> They called out the Air Guard to go fight the war,
> To help with the tactical air;
> To free the Pueblo would be better by far;
> We've got to be doing our share.
>
> We crossed the Pacific without any strain,
> The Air Force was sure in a jam;
> We landed at Phu Cat with twenty-two planes,
> Bad weather ahd hazards be damned.
>
> We started our checkouts with utmost dispatch
> To get all the aircrews all armed;
> And the pilots were qualified ten in a batch
> Just to get in the Vietnam War.
>
> The armorers all loaded us up to our max
> With napalm and high drags galore,
> And Uncle Sam bought them with an increase in tax
> Just to wrap up the Vietnam War.
>
> Now we're scrambled to targets all over I Corps
> In sorties of two planes or three;
> But what kind of targets was all of this for?
> My God, all we're bombing is trees!

Twelve Days in Ranch Hand, Twelve Days of Combat, *and* Twelve Days of Tet

The next three songs are all parodies of the same traditional English Christmas carol, which dates from about 1700 and has been popular in the United States since the 1950s. "Twelve Days in Ranch Hand" reflects the activities of our C-130 chemical defoliation crews, with "nozzles leaking" on the ninth day.

"Twelve Days of Combat" is from the fighter pilot's point of view, and since he has MiGs to chase on his fifth day, the song pre-dates February, 1968. The war is beginning to get serious, so there are "senators snooping" around on the ninth day, while on the twelfth, Thai poo-yings, or young maidens, are waiting for a downed U.S. flyer to be rescued by Sandys and choppers.

"Twelve Days of Tet" transfers the Christian Christmas to the Vietnamese holiday in late January, at which time there was a big enemy offensive in South Vietnam in 1968. Lacking the sardonic humor of "Number One Clismas Song," this third song straightforwardly lists the kinds of weapons carried by the F-4C, though there is some humor in the introduction. Santa Claus gives out presents at Christmas, but for Tet the weapons are gifts to our pilot from his deputy commander for operations (DO). The understated humor in these three songs effectively matches the light, lilting melody.

Twelve Days in Ranch Hand
Tune: "The Twelve Days of Christmas"

On my first day in Ranch Hand,
My foreman gave to me,
A province he said to plumb tree.

On the second day . . .	2 smoking engines. . . .
third day . . .	3 goddamn lifts. . . .
fourth day . . .	4 runs through A Shau. . . .
fifth day . . .	5 weeks at Da Nang. . . .
sixth day . . .	6 slopes a'sleeping. . . .
seventh day . . .	7 Purple Hearts. . . .
eighth day . . .	8 ship formation. . . .
ninth day . . .	9 nozzles leaking. . . .

tenth day . . .	10 clicks of rubber. . . .
eleventh day . . .	11 hits by .50s. . . .
twelfth day . . .	12 more days to go. . . .

Twelve Days of Combat
Tune: "The Twelve Days of Christmas"

On the first day of combat,
The Air Force gave to me,
A pilot in a teak tree.

On the second day . . .	2 rocket pods. . . .
third day . . .	3 fuel tanks. . . .
fourth day . . .	4 AIM-9s. . . .
fifth day . . .	5 MiGs to chase. . . .
sixth day . . .	6 750s. . . .
seventh day . . .	7 SAMs a-singing. . . .
eighth day . . .	8 flak sites firing. . . .
ninth day . . .	9 senators snooping. . . .
tenth day . . .	10 Sandys searching. . . .
eleventh day . . .	11 choppers whirling. . . .
twelfth day . . .	12 poo-yings waiting. . . .

Twelve Days of Tet
Tune: "The Twelve Days of Christmas"

On the first day of Tet,
My DO gave to me,
A gun on my Phantom F-4C.

On the second day . . .	2 CBUs. . . .
third day . . .	3 rocket launchers. . . .
fourth day . . .	4 high drags. . . .
fifth day . . .	5 hand grenades. . . .
sixth day . . .	6 Sidewinders. . . .
seventh day . . .	7 750s. . . .
eighth day . . .	8 charging Sparrows. . . .
ninth day . . .	9 nasty napes. . . .
tenth day . . .	10 tons of bombs. . . .
eleventh day . . .	11 Ladyfingers. . . .
twelfth day . . .	12 firecrackers. . . .

Uncle's Nephews

"Uncle's Nephews" is another Dick Jonas song reflecting his fine historical sense and love of country and freedom. Stanzas 1 through 5 ring out America's successful defense of its own freedom and that of its allies, but stanza 6 now seems powerfully ironic. The Republic of South Vietnam surrendered to the North Vietnamese on April 30, 1975, after America withdrew from the war, and Saigon is now Ho Chi Minh City. But for Dick Jonas and for many others of us who fought there, South Vietnam was not let down by Uncle's nephews—the American fighting men— but rather by political considerations over which we had no control.

Uncle's Nephews

In 1776 Great Britain said, "You'll buy my tea";
She didn't think my Uncle would deny that mad decree;
A few of Uncle's nephews went and dumped it in the sea,
And colored Boston's Harbor brown with old King George's tea.

Two hundred sixty men were killed the day we lost the Maine;
Uncle's nephews fought and won the war we had with Spain;
The charge that Teddy Roosevelt led up San Juan's terrain
Showed all the world that fighting Uncle's nephews was insane.

In 1917 ole Uncle said to Kaiser Bill,
"You've gone too far this time, and stop you now I think I will";
So Uncle's nephews once again took up their guns to kill,
And stopped the armies which were led this time by Kaiser Bill.

December 7, '41, the sky was clear and blue,
Pearl Harbor's blood told FDR exactly what to do;
Hitler, Tojo, Mussolini, met their Waterloo,
When Uncle's nephews went to war against that evil crew.

In 1950 North Korea tried us on for size;
There were so many Uncle's nephews, we shot them down like flies;
We fought them on the land and sea and fought them in the skies,
And proved to them no one believes their stupid Marxist lies.

The Communists in Southeast Asia know they're in a jam,
They won't defeat the brave nephews of my old Uncle Sam;

Ho Chi Minh and Mao Tse-tung won't take South Vietnam;
There are too many nephews there of my rich Uncle Sam.

Up in That Valley

"Up in That Valley" vividly portrays the highly dangerous combat missions flown over the Hanoi area of the Red River Valley
in North Vietnam by F-105 Thunderchief pilots from Takhli Royal
Thai Air Base, Thailand. The 1914 melody also appears as "Bir-
mingham Jail" and with other titles and was popularly revived
in 1944. The fast-paced lyrics of stanzas 3–8 contrast nicely with
the slower-moving melody—things happen fast in air combat, but
minutes over a heavily defended target seem an eternity. This
1967–68 song ends happily, however, as the pilot finishes his combat tour safely and heads home to the U.S., "mama," and the kids.

Up in That Valley
Tune: "Down in the Valley"

Up in that valley, that valley so low,
Where the SAM missiles flourish and the 85s glow.

The Thai Nguyen steel plant, the Hanoi railyard,
The bridges at Bac Giang, they've played their trump card.

The Iron Hands mill right, and the strike pilots flail;
The MiGs try to bounce us, but they always fail.

The MiG cap, he hollers, "There's bandits at twelve!"
"Launch!" screams the Weasel, "It's better in hell!"

The flak is a-burstin' right next to my hide;
All I can hear is, "You're lagging behind."

We're down on the bomb run, the target's in sight;
"Sweet Jesus," I'm thinking, "I'd better break right!"

We're breaking for Thud Ridge, what a beautiful sight;
Oh shit! I just noticed an overheat light!

My heart is a-pumping, I know I'm not dead;
Please, God, get this old Thud just out past the Red!

If I can get past that muddy old slough,
The Sandys and Jollys will pull me on through.

I'm past Ninety-seven, and now I can boast,
The rest I can finish out over the coast.

Where the tankers don't matter, although I must say
I often have seen it where they've saved the day.

Up in that valley, that valley of grief,
I hope all your flights there will always be brief.

Good-bye to that valley, so long to Takhli;
Don't bust your ass, buddy, I'm going home free!

The VC Truck Driver's Blues

"The VC Truck Driver's Blues" parodies a 1968 country music hit melody by singer Johnny Cash and pays tribute to the F-100 pilots of the Iowa Air National Guard as they complete their combat tour at Phu Cat Air Base, South Vietnam, in late 1968 or early 1969. The songwriter, a forward air controller, call sign Misty, has flown and worked with these Bats and is even part of their social life, for they have shared the same skies and the same dangers. In his song he creates a Viet Cong truck driver who hauls enemy supplies to the South. This VC in stanzas 1–3 tells how he always feels safer when his attackers are in F-100s with big HAs painted on their tails because he knows that these Air Guard Bats always let their bombs go all at once from too high an altitude to be effective. Here the Misty questions humorously the Bats' accuracy and courage. Stanza 4, however, reveals Misty's true feelings about his fellow flyers. Even today the Air Guard pilots from the 185th Tactical Fighter Group at Sioux City, Iowa, have big HAs painted boldly on their aircraft tails, but they no longer fly F-100s. Their new aircraft is the A-7D Corsair, a far more modern, faster, and more powerful attack and observation aircraft. If there's ever another Vietnam, the Bats will be there in style.

The VC Truck Driver's Blues

Tune: "Folsom Prison Blues"

"I hear that jet a'comin', on its tail a big HA;
No need to run for cover, 'cause they throw their bombs away;
Oh, I'm stuck here in Sun Valley, and they're bombing me;
Just keep sending those old Guard pukes; I know I'll get home free.

"I came in through Mu Gia, got hit near Ban Phanop;
It should've been all over, thank God for that Guard mob;
'Cause I'm stuck here in Sun Valley, and they're bombing me;
Just keep sending those old Guard pukes; I know I'll get home free.

"They release 'em from ten thousand, it's one pass and drop 'em all;
Never heard of old 'bombs-single,' all over the place bombs fall;
Oh, I'm stuck here in Sun Valley, and they're bombing me;
Just keep sending those old Guard pukes; I know I'll get home free."

(Now that's a song from Misty, and we've had a little fun;
They all know that we love 'em and admire the work they've done;
Oh, they came from old Sioux City, widely known as Bats;
And they're going home tomorrow; we gotta raise our hats!
Yes, they're going home tomorrow; we gotta raise our hats!)

Waltzing Matilda

Although many Americans are probably not aware of it, we had Australian soldiers and flyers fighting with us in Southeast Asia as members of the Southeast Asian Treaty Organization (SEATO). Australian sons died in the war just as ours did, and since the battle was raging closer to their part of the world than to ours, they were in some ways more dedicated to it than we were. Our failure in Vietnam thus became Australia's as well. We had a squadron of Aussie F-86 fighter pilots at Ubon, Thailand, when I got there in May, 1968, but they were pulled out in the next few months. Their parties were better than ours, their beef was better, their beer was better, and their air tactics were good. Several times after we returned from missions in our F-4 Phantoms, the Aussies would bounce us, and we'd go round and round in practice dogfights. "Waltzing Matilda" appears in this collection as a tribute to our Aussie fellow fighter pilots.

Composed in 1903 with words by A. B. ("Banjo") Paterson and music by Marie Cowan, the song was popularly revived in 1936 and 1941 and during World War II was sung with great gusto by servicemen of both countries. A "swagman" is a hobo, a "billabong" a water hole or stream, a "coolibah" tree a eucalyptus, and a "billy" is a stew. "Waltzing Matilda" means carrying a bundle on a stick. A "jumbuck" is a small lamb, a "tuckerbag" a small bag, and a "squatter" a landowner or cattleman. There may be differences in the vocabularies of American and Australian English, but in the war in Southeast Asia we both spoke the same language. Sydney, Australia, was a favorite place for R and R, and as did our predecessors in World War II, many of us were lucky enough to take respite from the war in that gracious and lovely city.

Waltzing Matilda

Once a jolly swagman camped by a billabong
Under the shade of a coolibah tree,
And he sang as he sat and waited till his billy boiled,
"Who'll come a-waltzing Matilda with me?"

CHORUS *(repeat after each verse):*
   "Waltzing Matilda, waltzing Matilda,
   Who'll come a-waltzing Matilda with me?"
   And he sang as he watched and waited till his billy boiled,
   "Who'll come a-waltzing Matilda with me?"

Along came a jumbuck to drink at the billabong,
Up jumped the swagman and grabbed him with glee;
And he sang as he stuffed that jumbuck in his tuckerbag,
"You'll come a-waltzing Matilda with me."

Up rode the squatter, mounted on his thoroughbred,
Up rode the troopers, one, two, three:
"Where's that jolly jumbuck you've got in your tuckerbag?
You'll come a-waltzing Matilda with me."

Up jumped the swagman, sprang into the billabong,
"You'll never take me alive," said he;
And his ghost may be heard as you pass by that billabong,
"Who'll come a-waltzing Matilda with me?"

Wand'rin' Man

I wrote this song myself one restless night about a month before I left for my flying combat tour in Southeast Asia in May, 1968. At that time I could only imagine and express in song the loneliness, doubts, and fear I was to feel during the coming year away from my wife, Jean, and our children. The loneliness, doubts, and fear I actually experienced during that year turned out to be even worse than I had imagined.

Wand'rin' Man

When I am weary and can't get no rest,
I long for my baby, the one I love best,
She knows what I'm missin', she knows what I lack,
She knows I'm a wand'rin' man, but I always come back.

It's been such a long time since I've seen her smile,
The sights are the same now, I hate every mile,
Will I ever find her? Will she wait for me?
Can she love a wand'rin' man that fights to be free?

The days are too long, that old sun doesn't shine,
How is my baby, is she doin' fine?
I'm so lost without her, I must find her soon,
These highways and byways will lead me to ruin.

There is no moon out, the stars are all dim,
Where is my baby, does she dream of him?
Does she think I'm lost now, does she think we're through?
Does she need somebody else so she won't feel blue?

It's been such a long time since I've seen her smile,
The sights are the same now, I hate every mile,
Will I ever find her? Will she wait for me?
Can she love a wand'rin' man that fights to be free?

© 1968 by Joseph F. Tuso

Way Down South in the Land of Rice

"Way Down South in the Land of Rice" refers to chemical defoliation missions probably flown over the Mekong Delta in southernmost South Vietnam. In stanza 1 the flyer describes the simple monotony of killing rice crops with deadly chemical sprays. In stanza 2 he says he is glad, however, to be flying defoliation missions rather than those protecting fighters over deadlier, heavily defended targets ("high suppression"), only to discover with terror that his own aircraft has just been hit on what he supposed a routine mission. The moral of this story is that whether a pilot flies high or low, fast or slow, he's playing a deadly game. For more on the Ranch Hands, see "Battle Hymn of the Ranch Hands," "Blowing in the Wind," "I'm a Young Ranch Hand," "Spray On, Spray on Harvest Rice," and "Spray the Town." The melody is taken from the Daniel Emmett song of the 1860s, which makes me suspect that the pilot who authored this was also from "way down south"—but in the United States.

Way Down South in the Land of Rice

Tune: "Dixie"

Way down south in the land of rice,
Where the Ranch Hands fly over once or twice,
It's dead,
It's dead,
It's dead, Ranch Hands.

I'm glad I'm not on a high suppression,
That's just not my type of mission,
I'm scared,
Oh, shit!
I'm hit, Ranch Hands.

The Weasel Song

One of the lengthier narratives in this collection, "The Weasel Song" features the Wild Weasels, or Iron Hands, pilots flying specially equipped F-105 Thunderchiefs used to protect strike forces from enemy surface-to-air missiles. Their most effective weapon was the Shrike, a ten-foot-long airborne air-to-ground missile. Escorting and working around the strike force, the Weasels would have to sidestep enemy missiles even as they attempted to hit the sites that launched them.

Hanoi, or "downtown," was heavily defended by a ring of Soviet-built missiles, and a common yet effective way to evade an enemy missile was to "take it down," or dive sharply. Four F-105s fly abreast preceding the strike force in stanza 2, launch a Shrike at a target missile site in stanza 3, and are in turn shot at by missiles in stanza 4. Their situation becomes even more dangerous when flak starts coming up at them from nearby Gia Lam Air Base, a MiG field just north of Hanoi.

Having used up their Shrikes, the Weasels drop cluster bomb units (CBUs) on the enemy missile sites in stanza 6. The Weasels are the last to leave the target area as the strike force leaves in stanza 7, and Bobbin Four has been hit. After in-flight refueling, they return to celebrate their mission—and life—at Korat, or Takhli Royal Thai Air Base. The bar talk turns to the many flying regulations they must observe, but despite these constraints, the Weasels, independent spirits, vow to "press on just the same." For more on the Weasels, see "Pop Goes the Weasel" and "Wild Weasel."

The Weasel Song

Oh, we joined the Weasel force,
When we finished the old course,
We thought we had a game
The missile for to tame;
After many trips downtown
No answer had we found,
Only "Take it down, Take it down!"

CHORUS *(repeat after each verse)*:
    Take it down, way down
    Take it down, way down,
    Down underneath that SA-2, to the bottom;
    After many trips downtown
    No answer had we found,
    Only "Take it down, take it down."

Off the tanker low,
Into fluid four we go,
Driving to the coast,

We run before the force,
We're about to face them all,
And are waiting for the call,
"Take it down, take it down."

In at ten thou' and point nine,
The signals painting fine,
We pull up to hose a Shrike,
Something they don't like;
Away the bastards roar,
And upward they do soar,
Time to take it down, take it down.

The sites that ring the town,
Our range have finally found;
Many missiles under way,
It's time for us to play;
Roll under to the right,
Red dots are now in sight,
Better take it down, take it down.

Back around again,
There's flak from Gia Lam,
Up for another Shrike,
Goes our weaving flight;
A missile bursts close by
And lower we do fly,
Down, take it down, take it down.

Hang on Bobbin Two,
We've got work to do,
Shrikes? We've shot the lot,
But a site's at ten o'clock;
So down the slide we go,
CBUs burst below,
Down, take it down, take it down.

Out behind the force,
Down the delta to the coast,
Tanks have long gone dry,
"Tanker" we do cry;
Holes in Number Four,

It's flying like a whore,
May have to take it down, take it down.

Back home on the ground,
All are safe and sound,
The Weasels rest once more,
Sites added to the score;
We gather around the bar,
No matter what the hour,
Time to drink it down, drink it down.
(Down to the bottom of the glass, to the bottom.)

The "Be No's" fence us in,
To fight is the greatest sin;
"Don't do this, and don't do that,"
Our leaders always blat;
Weasels press on just the same,
IRON HAND is a fighting game;
Down, take it down, take it down.

We've Been Working on the Railroad

A traditional American folk song from 1880 first published in 1894 provides the rollicking melody parodied in "We've Been Working on the Railroad." In this song, composed before President Johnson halted the bombing of the Hanoi area in February, 1968, the air crews have been bombing the Northeast Railroad, running from Hanoi to the Chinese border, but with no satisfying results. And as was often the case in Vietnam, though the target seems worthless, the work is highly dangerous. The missiles and 57- and 85-mm antiaircraft guns have knocked an American flyer out of the sky, and he sits in a tree near Hoa Lac, about 20 miles from downtown Hanoi, calling for a Jolly Green helicopter to come pick him up. Yet this downed American humorously consoles himself; since this is his first mission over North Vietnam, he has only 99 more to go to get his 100 and a ticket back to the States. Those of us who survived the war physically would perhaps not have survived it psychologically, except for our sense of humor.

We've Been Working on the Railroad

Tune: "I've Been Working on the Railroad"

We've been working on the railroad,
Every fucking day.
We've been working on the railroad,
Up Thai Nguyen way.

Uncle Ho ain't got no railroad,
No rolling stock or switches,
But Seventh frags us on the railroad,
Those dirty sons of bitches!

SAMs galore, 57s too,
85s will scragg your old yazoo!
Fuck, Shit, Hate, Shit Hot too,
So what the hell is new!

Someone's up a tree on Thud Ridge,
Someone's in the drink I know o-o-ow,
Someone's in the karst near Hoa Lac,
Shouting on the radio.

Shouting, Fee, Fi, Fiddly-i-oh,
Fee, Fi, Fiddly-i-oh, oh, oh, oh
Fee, Fi, Jolly Green, Oh,
Only ninety-nine more to go!

Where Have All the Flowers Gone? *and* Where Have All the Old Heads Gone?

The Pete Seeger hit "Where Have All the Flowers Gone?" (1961) provides the melody for the next two songs. The first describes the "food chain" of the horrors of war. Flowers are killed by U.S. Ranch Hands, or chemical defoliation crews, who are killed by enemy machine gunners, who are killed by U.S. fighter pilots. In the final stanza, the surviving Ranch Hands of stanza 1 and fighter pilots of stanza 3 console themselves with alcohol.

The second version, "Where Have All the Old Heads

Gone?" is even stronger and more bitter in its antiwar, protest tone. In stanza 2, all of the Vietnamese have become Communist Viet Cong, who go to repair a bridge bombed by U.S. flyers. In stanzas 4 and 5, our F-105 Wild Weasel pilots continue to fly missions against enemy missile sites (SAMs), even though the sites are inoperative. Meanwhile, our strike forces continue to bomb Hanoi, even though the Hanoi railroad is well defended. This song does an exceptionally fine job of portraying the monotonous and pointless repetition one experiences in war. In the final stanza, however, the veteran U.S. flyers, the "old heads," have at last learned what war is—they have all gone home. And yet, the war goes on.

Where Have All the Flowers Gone?
Tune: "Where Have All the Flowers Gone?"

Where have all the flowers gone, long time passing?
Where have all the flowers gone, long time ago?
Where have all the flowers gone?
Sprayed by Ranch Hands every one;
When will they ever learn? When will they ever learn?

Where have all the Ranch Hands gone, long time passing?
Where have all the Ranch Hands gone, long time ago?
Where have all the Ranch Hands gone?
Sprayed by .50s every one;
When will they ever learn? When will they ever learn?

Where have all the .50s gone, long time passing?
Where have all the .50s gone, long time ago?
Where have all the .50s gone?
Sprayed by [fighter call sign] every one.
When will they ever learn? When will they ever learn?

Where have all the [fighter call sign] gone, long time passing?
Where have all the [fighter call sign] gone, long time ago?
Where have all the [fighter call sign] gone?
Drunk with Ranch Hands every one.
When will they ever learn? When will they ever learn?

Where Have All the Old Heads Gone?

Tune: "Where Have All the Flowers Gone?"

Where have all the soldiers gone, long time passing?
Where have all the soldiers gone, long time ago?
Where have all the soldiers gone?
They've all gone to Vietnam;
When will they ever learn? When will they ever learn?

Where have all the Vietnamese gone, long time passing?
Where have all the Vietnamese gone, long time ago,
Where have all the Vietnamese gone?
They've all become Viet Cong;
When will we ever learn? When will we ever learn?

Where have all the VCs gone, long time passing,
Where have all the VCs gone, long time ago?
Where have all the VCs gone?
To fix the bridge that we bomb;
When will they ever learn? When will they ever learn?

Where do all the Weasels go, long time passing?
Where do all the Weasels go, long time ago?
Where do all the Weasels go?
O'er the ridge to meet the foe;
When will they ever learn? When will they ever learn?

Where have all the SAM sites gone, long time passing,
Where have all the SAM sites gone, long time ago,
Where have all the SAM sites gone?
They've been down, oh, so long;
When will they ever learn? When will they ever learn?

Where do all the strike flights go, long time passing,
Where do all the strike flights go, long time ago,
Where do all the strike flights go?
'Cross the fence again, I know;
When will they ever learn? When will they ever learn?

Where have all the flak sites gone, long time passing?
Where have all the flak sites gone, long time ago?
Where have all the flak sites gone?

Along the railroad, oh, so long;
When will they ever learn? When will they ever learn?

Where have all the old heads gone, long time passing?
Where have all the old heads gone, long time ago?
Where have all the old heads gone?
They've gone home; their tour is done;
You see, they've finally learned; oh yes, they've finally learned.

Whispering Death

Like "Hallelujah" IV, "Whispering Death" features the F-111A General Dynamics fighter known as the Aardvark (stanzas 4, 7). Test flown and delivered in the late 1960s, this aircraft first saw duty in Vietnam in the early 1970s, after the war had "trudged on for many years" (stanza 2). Stanza 1 gives us a new name for the F-111A, Whispering Death, for its terrain-following (TF) radar guides the deadly fighter toward its target on automatic pilot well below the effective range of hostile radar. The F-111A hits hard, silently, and without warning. Based in Thailand, the Aardvark was versatile enough to hit targets in North Vietnam and in both Southern (Saravane) and Northern Laos (PDJ, the Plaines des Jarres). In stanza 4 the songster is proud of the F-111A's ability to assist B-52s, or Bufs, but he is especially proud of her valiant crew members in stanza 5.

Stanza 6 highlights the Aardvark's involvement in air campaigns in 1972–73 over Cambodia and Laos, where the communist Khmer Rouge and Pathet Lao, respectively, held sway. The F-111A was a winner in Vietnam and stands ready to defend freedom as needed, a sentiment reminiscent of the once and future king concept of the Arthurian legend. As of January, 1990, there were still 330 F-111s on duty worldwide with the U.S. Air Force and they are expected to see use until the year 2000 and beyond. This simple, straightforward hymn of praise for one's aircraft can best be compared to "Puff, the Magic Dragon" and "Thud Pilot." Each song, although very different, is powerful in its own way.

Whispering Death

Tune: "Riders in the Sky"

To the frightful town of Hanoi
Came a stranger one dark night;
To Phuc Yen, Kep, and Haiphong
Came this stranger to the fight;
She flew low, she moved fast,
Two hundred feet TF;
To the Delta came this stranger
Known as Whispering Death,
Known as Whispering Death!

The war trudged on for many years,
Then one day she got her chance,
To fly and fight for freedom
And the cause to help enhance;
Colonel Nelson obliged,
He headed way out west;
He gathered up his fighters
And said "We'll do our best,"
He said, "We'll do our best."

She remained a stranger not for long,
Her victories were soon acclaimed,
She'd cut the Northeast railroad
And SAM sites she had maimed;
She hit hard, she hit true,
Her deeds you won't forget,
Nor the stress and strain of combat,
And of goin' out feet wet,
Goin' out feet wet.

Now, Aardvark's not a pretty name,
But here it earned respect,
And we're sure there are Buf drivers
Who'll swear she saved their necks;
We held our heads high knowin'
Of prestige she was to claim;
That sleek and silent fighter
With the strange and amusing name,
Strange and amusing name.

But the struggle wasn't easy
And the price we paid was high;
Many friends were lost for freedom,
But still our hopes were high,
That someday soon we'd see the end
And know the war would cease;
We'd be proud of Whisperin' Death
And how she helped to bring the peace,
Helped to bring the peace.

Her endeavors weren't confined
To the badlands way up north,
To the PDJ, Saravane, and Takeo
She burst forth,
The Khmer Rouge, the Pathet Lao
Were soon to meet their fate,
For the might of Whisperin' Death
They had realized too late,
Realized too late!

Now, my story has no moral,
For you see, it has no end;
What the 'Vark has done for liberty
She's prepared to do again;
We pray she'll not be needed,
But if conflicts do arise,
We'll be glad to fly her
Through dark and perilous skies,
Dark and perilous skies.

Whisperin' Death, Whisperin' Death,
To the Delta came this stranger
Known as Whisperin' Death,
Whisperin' Death!

Wild Weasel

"Wild Weasel" is a rollicking narrative about an F-105 pilot's adventures and final completion of 100 required combat missions over North Vietnam. The repeated last line of each stanza, or re-

frain, reflects the pilot's feeling of isolation during air combat,
yet pride in his excellent aircraft ("shit-hot fine bear") or his backseat crew member.

Despite the threats of enemy artillery, perhaps an 85-mm
gun in stanza 2 and an enemy missile in stanza 3, the pilot and
his comrades successfully destroy their target, an enemy surface-
to-air missile site in stanza 4. In stanza 5, the pilot tells us he's
won his own personal victory ("the big game") by crossing the
Mekong River ("the fence") 100 times, and he can now return,
alive, to the United States. For comments on the melody, see
"The Bat Song." In this song each stanza repeats the fourth and
last stanza line of the original tune to fit its five-line stanzas.

Wild Weasel
Tune: "Sweet Betsy from Pike"

Wild Weasel, Wild Weasel, they call me by name;
I fly up on Thud Ridge and play the big game;
I fly o'er the valleys and hide behind hills,
I dodge all the missiles then go in for the kills;
I'm a lonely Thud driver with a shit-hot fine bear!

Come weak guns, some weak guns, they're all off at once,
But don't worry fellows, for threats there are none;
There's a big one just looking at two o'clock now;
There's flak all around us, they're shooting, and how!
I'm a lonely Thud driver with a shit-hot fine bear!

Keep moving, they're shooting, the target's at eight;
Go burner, now roll in, don't pull it off straight;
A missile! a missile! Let's take it on down;
O God, where's that bastard? My flight suit's turned brown;
I'm a lonely Thud driver with a shit-hot fine bear!

Now pull it up, pull up, and head for the sky;
The missile's at two, boys, now watch it sail by;
There's smoke from the SAM site out there in the grass;
Set 'em up hot, boys, and we'll nail his ass;
I'm a lonely Thud driver with a shit-hot fine bear!

Wild Weasel, Wild Weasel, they call me by name;
I flew o'er the fence and I've won the big game;

One hundred, one hundred, I'm heading for home,
And o'er those damn hills I'll never more roam;
I'm a lonely Thud driver with a shit-hot fine bear!

Will the MiGs Come Out to Play?

"Will the MiGs Come Out to Play?" borrows its melody from a 1917 song by W. Ballard McDonald and James F. Hanley that was popularly revived in the late 1950s. Enemy MiGs did not always come up after our aircraft during raids over Hanoi in 1967–68, but the threat was always there. Some fighter pilots might display bravado and eagerness to engage the enemy when the MiGs did come up, but our hero here has no such feelings. His mission goes extremely well, but during each stage, in the refrain at the end of each of stanzas 1–4, he shows his concern for the MiGs and finally his desire that he not see any this day. But he does. Even though he completes his mission safely and is headed back to his base, Korat Royal Thai Air Base in Thailand, home of the 388th Tactical Fighter Wing, this F-105 pilot knows he's in for trouble when he sees that "glint of light, a speck up high." The song closes with our hero bobbing up and down in the Gulf of Tonkin after having been shot down by the MiG he feared might appear. Not an unhappy ending—he's been lucky.

Will the MiGs Come Out to Play?
Tune: "My Indiana Home"

When the SAMs start rising from old Haiphong harbor,
And the 85s start puffing round Kep Hay,
You will know your target's just beyond that mountain,
And you'll wonder if the MiGs will come to play.

Oh, you reach your pull-up point and start your pop up,
And the tracers seem to urge you on your way,
You see the bridge and as you start your roll-in,
And you'll wonder if the MiGs will come to play.

Oh, you've dropped your bombs and now you're off and running,
Jinking hard you're on your merry way,
And as you reach the jagged limestone ridges,
You'll wonder if the MiGs will come to play.

Oh, you've reached the coast and all the sea is friendly,
Your fuel is low, but "Not too low," you say,
I can make it back to Korat nice and easy,
If only the MiGs don't come out to play!

Oh, you're climbing now and starting to rest easy,
A drink of water helps you on your way,
But a glint of light, a speck up high, and you know
The MiGs have fi-nal-ly come out to play!

Oh, your burner's lit, you're diving down, you're running,
But his overtake is just too great today;
In your dinghy bobbing on the Gulf of Tonkin,
You wish the MiGs just hadn't come out to play!

Will There Be a Tomorrow?

Dick Jonas's beautiful ballad "Will There Be a Tomorrow?" is the most poignant personal meditation by a fighter pilot during the air war over Vietnam that I have come across. Of this song, Dick says: "A fighter pilot is certain sure of only a few things—himself and his airplane, the man flying his wing, and the present moment. The present moment—that's right now, today. He remembers names and faces and personalities for whom there is no now. And sometimes when he's alone with his heart of hearts, he'll shed a tear and say a prayer for his comrades of yesterday; and he knows that his own chances of becoming a member of yesterday are uncomfortably good. And so his philosophy becomes, 'Say it now, if it's worth saying; if it must be done, do it now; for there may be no tomorrow.'"

Will There Be a Tomorrow?

Can you say will the sun rise tomorrow?
Will there be any time left to borrow?
Will the poet make a rhyme, will there be any time?
Can you say will there be a tomorrow?

Seems to me I have been here forever;
Will this war ever end, maybe never;

Will the dawn still arrive, will I still be alive,
Or will I sleep alone here forever?

There's someone who I'm sure loves me only,
She's the one on my mind when I'm lonely;
Does she know, can she see, is she still true to me?
Does she know what it's like to be lonely?

From the sea comes the sun, dawn is breaking;
Soon the fight for my life I'll be making;
If I die over here, will they know, will they care?
Will there be joy, or hearts that are breaking?

Can you say will the sun rise tomorrow?
Will there be any time left to borrow?
Will the poet make a rhyme, will there be any time?
Can you say will there be a tomorrow?

Words and music by Dick Jonas, from *FSH Volume I*. © 1969 by Enchantment Music Co. Used with permission.

Wingman's Lament

The song "Wingman's Lament" uses the same melody as "Wild Weasel," and the fourth and final stanza line of the original tune is also repeated once here to give us the five-line stanzas. This song is much different in tone from "Wild Weasel." Our F-105 Thunderchief ("Thud") pilot is on a strike mission along with some F-4 Phantoms flying high cover to protect him from MiGs. He asks his lead 105 to slow up a bit in stanza 1 and shows how much disrespect he has for F-4s in stanza 2. After crossing over Cho Moi, about 50 air miles north of Hanoi, the strike force turns toward its target, suddenly encountering ground fire and bad weather.

The lead 105 goes past the target and dives for it too slowly, but rather than follow Lead, our pilot in F-105 Number Two attacks the target with better speed and a better angle. He nonchalantly lights a cigarette during his supposed "milk run" attack, only to be shocked back into the horrors of war when his plane is hit by a fated round ("golden BB"). Almost at once he loses engine pressure on his gauges ("P-1 and P-2") as well as much of his ability to climb or dive, since his control stick can no longer work his aircraft's horizontal tail surface ("slab").

Stanza 7 finds our laconic F-105 pilot as a POW in the infamous Hanoi Hilton, Hoa Lo Prison near Hanoi. Unlike "Wild Weasel," this song has an unhappy—if stoic—ending.

Wingman's Lament
Tune: "Sweet Betsy from Pike"

We turned the Red and Lead said, "Push it up,"
I used my burner and couldn't keep up;
I was dragging behind, it sure ain't no fun;
I said, "Leader, Leader, oh please, give me one."
I'm a lousy Thud wingman and a long way from home.

Flying above us were several F-4s;
They're 'bout as useful as tits on a boar;
They brief in the air and they pull other pranks,
Like bombarding Fives with their empty drop tanks.
I'm a lousy Thud wingman and long way from home.

We hit Cho Moi and then turned on our run,
The gunners below uncovered their guns,
I tell you the weather up there can change fast,
From clear and fifteen to a black overcast.
I'm a lousy Thud wingman and a long way from home.

Lead passed the target before he rolled in,
With three hundred knots, a capital sin;
And try though I did, and I tried as I pleased,
I had four hundred knots and twenty degrees.
I'm a lousy Thud wingman and a long way from home.

I rolled in and lit a fresh cigarette,
A few puffs of flak were nothing to sweat;
A damned golden BB met up with my plane,
Hey Coach, I think I will drop out of the game!
I'm a lousy Thud wingman and a long way from home.

P-1 and P-2 fall down through the red,
I begin to fear my Thunderchief's dead;
The slab and the stick, they soon separated;

By the finger of fate, I have been mated.
I'm a lousy Thud wingman and a long way from home.

The living at Hilton ain't very good,
I find the quarters as bad as the food;
The waiters, they give us a whole lot of lip,
But we don't have to pay, we don't have to tip.
I'm a lousy Thud wingman and a long way from home.

So listen, my friends, if you're flying today,
Keep it high, keep it fast, is what I say;
Keep up with your leader, but still, just the same,
You bet your own ass, is the name of the game.
I'm a lousy Thud wingman and a long way from home.

Wolf Pack's Houseboy

During the year I spent flying combat missions out of Ubon Royal Thai Air Base in 1968–69, my houseboy, Thon, was an important person in my life. He cleaned my room, made my bed, and shined my shoes, and for 100 baht ($5.00) a month, his wife did my laundry. We did have GI washing machines in a trailer on base that we could use, but after my whites turned out gray and my grays turned out whitish once or twice, I took up Thon's offer. After that, every few days my stuffed laundry bag would miraculously empty, and a few days later I'd find clean, neatly folded underwear, flying suits, and other clothes on my dresser ready to be put away. During that entire year I always had fresh laundry. Nor will I ever forget the many times I'd return to my room after an exhausting, frightening mission and see Thon shining my shoes on the stoop in front of my room. He'd look up, see me, flash me a big smile, and give me an enthusiastic "thumbs up" sign— everything is OK, I've returned safely.

If you were fair to your Thai houseboy (most of them were men, not boys), he would be fair to you. If you treated your houseboy poorly, then things just might disappear from your room—TEAC or Sony tape decks or amplifiers, Sansui speakers— our spoils of war via Japan, which even then was technologically astute. Or your bicycle might be stolen, if you had one. When I decided to buy a bike, Thon advised me to buy a "poo-ying" (girl's) bicycle because Thai girls didn't steal, he said, and Thai men wouldn't steal a poo-ying bike. He was right. I rode my Thai poo-ying bike around Ubon for about nine months and took it back to the States with me to give to my daughter Ann.

So the "ugly Americans" among us—and there were only a few—who treated their houseboys poorly might find objects missing. Not that their own houseboys necessarily stole them, although that was a possibility, but they would not report whoever did. Once things were stolen from a young lieutenant's room, and he told his houseboy about it. He and his houseboy had a relationship of mutual respect, and a few days later the missing objects mysteriously returned to the lieutenant's room, with no questions asked.

One day I was lying around getting some sun in the area near our hootches, or barracks, and saw some Thai workers changing the locks on some rooms under the supervision of a nonchalant U.S. airman who was leaning against a post reading a magazine. The replaced locks were supposed to improve security and cut down thefts. I chuckled, however, as I saw that after the locks were installed on certain rooms, one of the Thais would linger furtively behind the group long enough to cut a notch with a chisel next to the lock so it could easily be opened with a pocket knife or small screwdriver.

The Thais were polite, cheerful, and honest and loved their king and country, which was probably why there was as little thievery as there was at Ubon. But what a terrible temptation it must have been for a Thai houseboy to see casually lying about our rooms objects that to him, his wife, and children represented five or ten years of their total earnings. By and large, our houseboys were a wonderful group of people who helped make our wartime lives much more pleasant. And thus the ending to Dick Jonas's next song, "Wolf Pack's Houseboy," in some ways humorously treats the captured North Vietnamese MiG pilot with some respect. Our houseboys at Channel 51, or Ubon, probably would have treated him well, as would we, if he did his work. Dick Jonas says about "Wolf Pack's Houseboy": "Fantastic yarn, but not true. The acronyms are: TOC (Tactical Operations Center); AAA (Anti-Aircraft Artillery); SAM (Surface-to-Air Missiles); GIB (guy in the back seat)—rear cockpit crew member in the Air Force Phantom aircraft whose official name is WSO (Weapons Systems Officer)—they proudly call themselves 'Fightergators' for 'Fighter-Navigator.'

The Jolly Green was the rescue helicopter—more guts per capita than regulations would ever admit; 'Sandy' was the ancient but brave A-1, prop-driven rescue aircraft. Nope, it never happened, at least I don't think so; but just what if. . . ."

Wolf Pack's Houseboy

Seventh fragged us way up north
On a bridge that wasn't worth
Hanging out your ass to be shot at,
But they said, "You've gotta go,
Put the word on Uncle Ho,
You've no choice men, this is combat!"

So the boys in TOC pooped us up on what we'd see,
And Intelligence said, "Watch for SAMs;
MiGs are up, and triple-A
Will be thick as flies today,
Give 'em hell, the war is in your hands."

Well, we hit the tanker twice,
Then my blood ran cold as ice
When we dropped off and crossed the Red,
Barracuda understood,
He called out, "That launch is good,
Take it down right now or you'll be dead!"

Well, it almost makes me cry,
Down below I see bullseye,
Through the cloud of flak between the SAMs,
There's the bridge I came to bomb,
Lord, I'm scared, I want my mom!
Then my GIB said, "Pickle, pull, both hands!"

This is almost just like heaven,
Twenty miles from Ninety-seven,
We're home free, of that there is no doubt,
Then a MiG made one more pass,
Hosed a missile up my ass,
Then the bird pitched up and we punched out.

I can see the Phantoms go,
Round and round from here below,

They won't leave without my GIB and me,
And that MiG-21
Just got plastered with a gun,
And the pilot's frightened eyes I see.

Oh, he landed in a tree,
Only forty feet from me,
And I whipped out my .38,
I said, "Tell me how it feels,
When your MiG turns two cartwheels?
Come on down with us and here we'll wait."

"Hello, Chevy Lead up there,
This is Chevy Two down here,
With my GIB and the guy you just shot down,"
"Chevy Two, say what you mean,
I've called in the Jolly Green,
Just stay put and soon we'll have you found."

First I saw the Sandy come,
Making circles in the sun,
Then the Jolly Greens were overhead,
The MiG jock went up first,
I made him believe the worst,
"No tricks, boy, or I'll fill you with lead!"

Well, we brought that sonova gun,
All the way to Fifty-one,
Two took off, it's true, but three came back;
He won't fly the Phantom Two,
But here's what we're gonna do,
Make him HOUSEBOY for the WHOLE WOLF PACK!

Words and music by Dick Jonas, from *FSH Volume II, YGBSM,* © 1971 by Enchantment Music Co. Used with permission.

Yankee Air Pirate

During the air war over North Vietnam, Hanoi newspapers and government officials often referred to American flyers as Yankee Air Pirates who needlessly bombed civilian targets. Although they accepted the name with pride, American pilots would not accept charges of being inhumane. Dick Jonas says:

> A Phantom pilot's got a name for everything. His wife is affectionately called "mama." If he's not married, his sweetheart is a "dolly." He calls his airplane a "beast," a "bear," and a "hog," but nobody else can talk that way about the ship he flies, at least not in his presence. The folks up north have a name, too, for the guys who fly the Wolf Pack's Phantoms. They call us Yankee Air Pirates, and some of us ain't yankees atall, but I reckon that's OK. We've called them a few things, too. And well we might. The way they shoot at us with their SAMs and guns, it's a wonder we're not all nervous wrecks. And when you go rooting around at night up there and pull out of a dive and suddenly find yourself in the middle of the fireworks display of the biggest Fourth of July celebration you've ever seen in your life, well that's a good way to get old in a hurry, or a good way not to get old at all if you don't move it around and get out of there. Yankee Air Pirates, yep, that's what they call us, and probably a few other things too.

Yankee Air Pirate

I am a Yankee Air Pirate,
With D.T.'s and bloodshot eyeballs;
My nerves are all run down from bombing downtown,
From SAM breaks and bad bandit calls.

CHORUS *(repeat after each verse):*
   A Yankee Air Pirate, a Yankee Air Pirate,
   A Yankee Air Pirate am I;
   A Yankee Air Pirate, a Yankee Air Pirate,
   If I don't get my hundred I'll die.

I've carried iron bombs on the outboards,
Flown high cap for F-1-O Thuds;
I've sniveled a counter or two once or twice,
And sweated my own rich red blood.

I've been downtown to both bridges,
To Thai Nguyen, Kep, and Phuc Yen,
And if you ask me then I'm sure you can see
There's no place up there I ain't been.

The Yellow Rose of Hanoi

"The Yellow Rose of Texas," written in 1858 and popularly revived in 1955, was supposedly one of U.S. president Franklin D. Roosevelt's favorite songs. Its melody is used in "The Yellow Rose of Hanoi." Men at war think often of women – the good and the bad. This one thinks of one he'd rather not meet, Ho Chi Minh's daughter, whom he envisions as running the notorious POW camp, the Hanoi Hilton.

When I think of the women of the Vietnam War, I remember Tippy, our head bar girl at Ubon, who always had a cold towel handy to put over a weary fighter pilot's head after a mission – but you had to watch her, or she'd mischievously grab for your change off the bar. I remember Kathy, the young first lieutenant intelligence officer, who would brief us before our missions and call out as we were leaving the briefing room for our aircraft, "Be careful out there today, guys!" I remember a tall, blond, attractive Air Force nurse – and attractive women were exceedingly rare at Ubon – skillfully repelling the advances of a tipsy, lustful young fighter pilot without offending his ego; her fiancé was flying F-4s out of Udorn, and she understood fighter pilots.

I also remember the ecstatically happy face of a young, blue-jeaned, teenage bride I caught a glimpse of in a crowd after an on-base movie – somehow she had wangled her way over to Thailand to be with her man, a fuzzy-faced enlisted man. They were obviously much in love and could have been strolling down a lovely lane in a park back home. But especially I remember my wife, Jean, whom I saw only once in a year's time – Jean, who was taking care of our five kids, ages one to eight, while I was off to war. Those of us who flew in the air war over Vietnam and were able to come home to "mama and the kids" were lucky, yes, but I'll always believe it was Jean's love for me and my love for Jean that helped get me home safely. And for other American flyers, there were other Jeans. All of us remember them all.

The Yellow Rose of Hanoi
Tune: "The Yellow Rose of Texas"

There's a yellow rose in Hanoi
Who loves a fighter crew,
She runs the Hanoi Hilton

And she longs to welcome you!
Her father's name is Ho Chi Minh,
He has a long goatee,
And if you greet him nicely
He will let you stay for free.

CHORUS (*repeat after second verse*):
    Her eyes are shaped like almonds,
    And I'll give you a hunch,
    I don't want to meet her family,
    'Cause they're a nasty bunch;
    It's fish heads and rice for breakfast,
    And fish heads and rice for tea,
    But so long as they don't catch me,
    No fish heads and rice for me!

Oh, you may fly a Phantom,
Or you may fly a Thud,
But if you fly to Hanoi,
Better listen to me, bud;
You may talk of girls in Bangkok,
Or Los Angeles and such,
But the yellow rose of Hanoi
Is just a bit too much!

A ZPU Gunner

Just as "Old Weird Harold" gives us a snapshot of an enemy air-craft spotter and "Sittin' in the Cab of My Truck" introduces us to an enemy truck driver, "A ZPU Gunner" gives us an empathetic look at an active, aggressive enemy who turns out to be very much like an American flyer. This song flatters Dick Jonas's melody in his "Yankee Air Pirate." ZPU were lighter, more easily transported NVN (North Vietnamese) antiaircraft weapons. The smaller caliber ZPU were belt-fed, and the larger used clips, with projectile sizes ranging from 12.7, 14.5, to 23 mm, or in inches respectively, .50, .57, and .91. On missions over the remotest jungles we could still suddenly find yellow-orange streams of ZPU fire rising up toward us like the output of languid garden hoses, so easily could these weapons be moved around and so quickly set up. Their serpentine beauty could also be quite deadly, as over Tchepone.

Our ZPU gunner doesn't want to defend a dangerous SAM site. You'd think he would get a choice of assignment out of gunnery school, as our flyers usually do when they graduate with high standing from pilot training, but no. Instead of a safe stint in Northern Laos (Barrel Roll), he's put on a rock probably overlooking the much attacked Ho Chi Minh Trail. He next goes to the South Laotian panhandle (Steel Tiger) and turns in a respectable performance against enemy aircraft, probably using a larger, clip-fed 23-mm gun.

In stanza 5, like an American F-4 co-pilot or backseater, the gunner is promoted to Mu Gia Pass and a 37-mm gun, as the American would be "upgraded" to AC and the front seat. And just as the new AC's co-pilot carps at him from the backseat and is eager to take over the aircraft when the new AC goofs, so is our gunner plagued by his 37-mm backseat gunner (stanza 6). Stanzas 3 and 4 point out the gunner's endurance. His position can be bombed to bits one day, or so strike films will show, yet he will climb right back out of his hole the next day and shoot right back again. In stanza 7, NVN intelligence is so good that it enables the gunners to know their enemy well enough to spend their time appropriately, depending on who is scheduled to attack that day. Although humorous, this song expresses great respect for the enemy with almost World War II gallantry. We did all we could to kill him, and he did all he could to kill us, yet we were both more alike than different. Still, we didn't kill him in this song.

A ZPU Gunner
Tune: "Yankee Air Pirate"

CHORUS (*repeat after each verse*):
  A ZPU gunner, a ZPU gunner,
  A ZPU gunner am I;
  A ZPU gunner, a ZPU gunner,
  If they give me a SAM site I'll die.

I graduated at the top of my gunner's class,
I worked hard, you will agree,
But three classes behind, those guys that were blind
Got the same assignment as me.

So I asked for a Barrel Roll assignment,
I said "a shit hot young gunner I am,"
They gave me a block on top of the rock
Dodging CBU's and GAM's.

So I asked for Steel Tiger assignment,
I got there one bright sunny day;
That night by flare light they laid them in tight,
I wound up in O'Rourke's BDA.

Well, soon I crawled out of my spider hole,
I put a new clip on my gun;
The very next day, despite BDA,
I hosed down Falcon One-One.

Well, I went PCS to Mu Gia,
To a two-seater 37 upgrade,
But one thing I can't hack, it's that guy in the back
Telling me every mistake that I've made.

He reads me all of the checklist,
We prefire the gun in the pit,
But if I shoot a bit low or am just a tad slow
The first thing I hear is "I've got it!"

We read the Yankee frag daily,
We know who's flying, who's not;
We sit in the shade while the passes are made,
Reading sex magazines, smoking pot.

Final Movement

When we completed 100 combat missions over North Vietnam or a calendar year in the combat zone, whichever came first, we were finally free to go home. Just before we left, usually at a party honoring our departure, we were given a plaque signed by our fellow flyers as a memento of our friendship and shared experiences. Our farewell plaques at the 8th Tactical Fighter Wing had sentiments on them common to those used at other bases. My plaque reads:

THE FIGHTER PILOT

Say what you will about him—arrogant, cocky, boisterous, and a fun-loving fool to boot—he has earned his place in the sun. Across the span of fifty years he has given this country some of its proudest moments and most cherished military traditions. But fame is short lived and little the world remembers. Almost forgotten are the fourteen hundred fighter pilots who stood alone against the might of Hitler's Germany during the dark summer of 1940—and in the words of Sir Winston Churchill gave England "its finest hour." Gone from the hardstands of Duxford are the P-51s with their checkerboard noses that terrified the finest fighter squadrons the Luftwaffe had. Dimly remembered—the 4th Fighter Group that gave Americans some of their few proud moments in the skies over Korea. How fresh in recall the Air Commandos who valiantly struck the VC in their aging Skyraiders in the rain and blood-soaked valley called A Shau? And how long will be remembered the Wolf Pack F-4s over Route Pack Six and the flak filled skies above Hanoi? So here's a "nickel on the grass" to you, my friend, for your spirit, enthusiasm, sacrifice, and courage—but

An F-4 Phantom, heading home. *U.S. Air Force photograph*

most of all to your friendship. Yours is a dying breed and when you are gone—the world will be a lesser place. A MEMENTO TO OUR FELLOW FIGHTER PILOT Major Joe Tuso.

Below this message are 47 signatures of the kinds of men who fill the lyrics of the songs in this collection. I remember each of them in many ways, but I smile most when I remember them singing.

Glossary

Distances appear in nautical miles (NM). One NM equals approximately 1.15 statute miles.

AAA: Anti-aircraft artillery.

AAR: Air-to-air refueling, generally from a KC-135 jet tanker to an F-105, or other aircraft with an AAR capability.

Aardvark: Affectionate name for the General Dynamics F-111A.

AB: Afterburner, a device providing extra thrust to a jet engine; usually used sparingly because it consumes much fuel.

Abie: Abbie Hoffman, U.S. anti-war activist of the late sixties.

Abort: To cancel a flight mission, either before takeoff or in the air, because of aircraft or other problems.

AC: Aircraft commander, the pilot in charge of the aircraft.

Ace: A flyer credited with shooting down at least five enemy aircraft in air-to-air combat; also means "good."

Ack-ack: Antiaircraft artillery.

AD: An air division, usually consisting of several wings of aircraft operating out of different bases.

AFB: Air Force Base.

AIM-9, or Sidewinder: A close-range, heat-seeking, air-to-air missile especially favored against MiGs by such aces as Robin Olds and Steve Ritchie.

Airman-third: An extremely low-ranking Air Force enlisted person.

Air Medal: A U.S. decoration for valor or meritorious achievement during aerial flight.

Air patch: An air-to-ground radio relay system for voice communications.

Alpha Frag: *See* Frag.

Anchor: An air refueling area where tanker and receiver aircraft rendezvous.

Angels: Thousands of feet, e.g., six angels is 6,000 feet.

A-1E: A small, reciprocating-engine U.S. aircraft, a Sandy.

AR: Air refueling.

Arc Lights: Massive high altitude saturation bombing by B-52s.

Arnold, Hap: Henry H. Arnold (1886–1950), military aviation pioneer, commander of the U.S. Army Air Forces in World War II, and the U.S. Air Force's first five-star general.

A Shau Valley: About 20 NM (nautical miles) southwest of Hue in South Vietnam.

ATC: Air Training Command, which trains all U.S. Air Force flying and support personnel.

Auger in: To crash an aircraft.

Baby Huey: *See* Huey.

Bac Can: Enemy airfield 65 NM north of Hanoi.

Bac Giang: A city 25 NM north of Hanoi on the Northeast Railroad to China.

Bac Mai: An enemy airfield about 5 NM southwest of Hanoi.

Bac Ninh: A city 15 NM northeast of Hanoi on the Northeast Railroad to China.

BAK-9: An arresting cable system for stopping aircraft on a runway in emergencies or bad weather.

Banana Valley: Pilot-coined name for a geographical location.

Ban Ban: A city and airfield in Laos, 115 NM northeast of Vientiane near the eastern end of the Plain of Jarres noted for its heavy defensive flak.

Bandit: Any enemy aircraft.

Bandit call: A radio warning of the proximity or approach of hostile aircraft (*bandit*); a "bad bandit call" is a false alarm.

Ban Karai: A village in North Vietnam 20 NM west of Dong Hoi on the Laotian border.

Ban Laboy: A small town in Laos on the Ho Chi Minh Trail.

Ban Phanop: A village in southeastern Laos near the Ho Chi Minh Trail, about 50 NM east of Dong Hoi.

Barracuda: An aircraft, equipped with sophisticated electronic devices, that warns other U.S. aircraft of hostile missile threats or launches.

Barrios: An 8th Tactical Fighter Wing MiG fighter in 1967.

Bat: An aircraft identifier and radio call sign of F-100s stationed at Phu Cat Air Base in South Vietnam in 1967–68.

Bat Lake: Descriptive name for a North Vietnamese lake 12 NM north of the DMZ and 8 NM from the coast of the Gulf of Tonkin.

BDA: Bomb damage assessment, the results of a bombing mission ascertained from photos or other evidence.

Bear: An affectionate name for an aircraft; also, a backseat pilot or navigator in a two-seat, tandem aircraft.

Beast: An affectionate term for an aircraft.

Beep: The sound made by a downed flyer's emergency radio or "beeper" by which rescue aircraft fix his position.

Be-No's: Air Force regulations, which often begin, "There will be no . . ."

B-52: The Boeing Stratofortress, an eight-engine, heavy jet bomber; also called a *Buff*.

Bien Hoa: U.S. air base in South Vietnam just north of Saigon.

Bingo: Having minimum fuel on board an aircraft.

Bird: A more neutral term for an aircraft than *bear* or *beast*.

Birddog: A small, airborne compass.

Black boxes: Radar equipment, computers, or other electronic gear.

Black River: A strategically important river running parallel to and south of the Red River from the northwest to the southeast across North Vietnam.

Black Route: An aircraft reconnaissance route between the 17th and 18th parallels in North Vietnam.

BLC: Boundary layer control; air from the engine compressor of a jet aircraft directed over its wings to increase lift at slow speeds; the BLC light indicates when the air is becoming too hot for continued safe flight.

Blue Boar: An affectionate name for an F-4D Phantom.

Blue Four: An aircraft identifier and radio call sign; Blue Four is the number four aircraft in Blue Flight. *See* Flight.

Blue Route: Similar to *Black Route*.

Bobbin: An aircraft identifier and radio call sign.

Boeing Fortress: *See* B-17.

Boeing Stratofortress: *See* B-52.

Bogolofski: An 8th Tactical Fighter Wing MiG fighter in 1967.

Boom: An air refueling receptacle trailing from a tanker aircraft;

also the blast of noise on the ground when an overhead aircraft exceeds the speed of sound ("sonic boom").

Bounce: For one aircraft to be unexpectedly attacked by another.

Bravo, Bravo Frag: A mission flown over Southeast Asia, but not over North Vietnam. *See* Counter; Freebie.

Bridges, both bridges: Two large bridges near Hanoi.

Brief, briefing: To plan and discuss the tactics of a combat mission prior to takeoff.

Brigham: A ground-based, aircraft radar monitoring agency.

Bronco: A small U.S. aircraft, the Rockwell OV-10A, used for forward air control and quick-response ground support pending the arrival of jet fighters; the Bronco has two turboprop engines.

Brown, or Brown Anchor: An air refueling area in the Gulf of Tonkin.

Brown, General: George S. Brown, commander of the Seventh Air Force in Saigon and later Air Force Chief of Staff (1973–74).

B-17: The Boeing Flying Fortress, a WW II heavy bomber with four reciprocating engines.

Buf or Buff: "Big Ugly Fucker" or "Big Ugly Fat Fellow"; any large aircraft such as the B-52 or EC-121.

Bullpup: A 250-pound U.S. air-to-ground missile.

Bullseye: Nickname for Hanoi, the target of targets.

Bung Bung: *Ban Ban* (?)

Burner: *See* AB.

Bust, or bust your ass: To collide, to crash, to *ding*.

Butterfly: A butterfly-shaped lake just north of the DMZ in North Vietnam.

Call sign: Radio identifier and name for an aircraft or flight of aircraft.

Ca Mau: The southernmost peninsula of South Vietnam at the Mekong Delta

Cam Pho: In South Vietnam just below the DMZ, or 30 NM south of Da Nang.

Cam Ranh Bay: A large U.S. air base about 170 NM northeast of Saigon on the South Vietnam coast.

Canberra: A B-57 medium jet bomber.

Cao Bang: Enemy airfield 100 NM north-northeast of Hanoi, about 10 NM from the Chinese border.

Cap, high cap, MiG cap: Fighter aircraft flying cover or "capping" lower flying aircraft to protect them from hostile planes.

Caribou: The DeHavilland C-7A, a small reciprocating engine U.S. aircraft used to transport troops and cargo.

CBU: Cluster bomb unit; has the same effect as dropping many hand grenades.

Ceiling: The layer of clouds just above the ground under which fighter-bombers can visually work a target; a 200-foot ceiling would be quite dangerous.

Channel 51: A radio navigation aid for U.S. aircraft at Ubon, Thailand.

Channel 97: A radio navigation aid for U.S. aircraft inbound after attacks in North Vietnam.

Chappie: Then Col. Daniel ("Chappie") James, vice commander of Ubon's 8th Tactical Fighter Wing, the Wolf Pack.

Charlie: Short for Victor Charlie in the military phonetic alphabet; a VC or Viet Cong soldier.

Charlie Bravo Flight: Over Laos or South Vietnam. *See* Counter; Frag; Freebie.

Chocks: Blocks placed against the tires of parked aircraft to help keep them from rolling.

Cho Moi: In North Vietnam, about 50 NM north of Hanoi.

Chopper: Nickname for a helicopter.

Claymore: An anti-personnel landmine.

Clear and fifteen: A weather report that indicates clear skies, with fifteen miles of visibility.

Click: A kilometer.

CO: Commanding officer.

Combat pay: Hazardous duty pay; the additional $65 per month received for flying combat in Vietnam.

Commando Nail: A high-altitude radar bomb drop while the aircraft flies straight and level at bomb release.

C-130: The Lockheed-Georgia Hercules, a jet transport plane.

Contrail: Streaks of condensed water vapor created in the air by aircraft flying at high altitudes.

Counter: A combat mission over North Vietnam that "counted" toward the 100 total missions needed by a U.S. flyer for his ticket back to the States.

Credit: For a *counter*, a flyer wouldn't get credit toward his 100 missions for a combat mission flown elsewhere than over North Vietnam; such a mission was a "freebie."

Crispy critters: Enemy soldiers burned by napalm; a macabre phrase perhaps borrowed from the name of a popular American breakfast cereal.

Crosshair, crosshairs: A visual aiming device for delivering ordnance

Crown, Crown Alpha: An airborne C-130 which directs a search-and-rescue effort to recover a downed American flyer.

Crusader: A U.S. Navy jet carrier fighter used in Vietnam, the Vought F-8E.

Cycle: When a flight of aircraft refuels in turn from a tanker while in formation.

Daisy-cutter: A fragmentation bomb armed to explode just above the ground.

Da Nang: A large U.S. coastal air base in South Vietnam some 350 NM north of Saigon and 100 NM south of the DMZ.

DASC: The Direct Air Support Center, which coordinated certain U.S. air strikes over Southeast Asia.

DCO: *See* DO.

Delta: Flat, fertile area where the Black or Red rivers meet the Gulf of Tonkin, or the area in the extreme south of South Vietnam.

Delta One-One: A geographical chart position.

DFC: The Distinguished Flying Cross, a U.S. decoration for heroism or extraordinary achievement during aerial flight.

Dien Bien Phu: A city and fortress in far northwest North Vietnam which was captured by the Vietnamese communists from the French in 1954.

Ding: To collide, to crash, to "bust your ass."

Dingbat: Radio call sign and identifier of a forward air controller.

Divert: To change from a scheduled landing base to an alternate airfield.

DMZ: The Demilitarized Zone at 17° north latitude separating North and South Vietnam, as established by the Geneva Convention of 1954.

DO: Deputy commander for operations, or DCO, who directly supervises all wing air operations for the wing commander.

Dolly: An American flyer's affectionate name for his sweetheart.

Dong Ha: An airfield in South Vietnam, 10 NM south of the DMZ near the coast.

Dong Hoi: Coastal city and airfield in North Vietnam, 30 NM north of the DMZ.

Doppler: Airborne radar navigational device.

Do Son: Enemy airfield 10 NM southeast of Haiphong on the Gulf of Tonkin.

Doumer Bridge: Pronounced DOUGH-mer, the span over the Red River in North Vietnam named after Paul Doumer (1857–1932), a former president of France.

Down, to be down: To be out of commission or not heard from, e.g., "The MiGs were down during our strike."

Down the slide: To dive to release ordnance.

Downtown: Nickname for Hanoi taken from the song of the same name made popular by Petula Clark in the sixties; also "crosstown," "intown," "uptown."

Drogue: A small parachute deployed from an aircraft's tail to slow it during landing.

Droop, or "droop snoot": An F-4, with its mosquito-like nose.

Drop tanks: Aircraft auxiliary fuel tanks that can be dropped when empty.

D.R.V.: Democratic Republic of Vietnam, or communist North Vietnam.

E & E: The escape and evasion of a downed American flyer.

ECM: Electronic countermeasures.

EC-121R: The electronic warfare version of the Air Force's earlier C-121 or C-69, derived from the commercial Lockheed Constellation.

Egress: To depart a target area.

EGT: Exhaust gas temperature of a jet engine.

18.23: A geographical location expressed numerically, hence impersonally or ironically.

8th Wing: The 8th Tactical Fighter Wing based at Ubon Royal Thai Air Force Base, Thailand; under the leadership of Col. Robin Olds, the 8 TFW, or Wolf Pack, shot down more MiGs over North Vietnam than any other unit.

85s: 85-mm (3.35 inches in diameter) antiaircraft artillery.

Eighty-Nine: An F-89 fighter-interceptor, the Northrop Scorpion.

Eighty-Six: An F-86 fighter, the North American Sabre Jet.

Eject: To be catapulted from an aircraft in an emergency and then parachuted to earth; to *punch out*.

ELINT: Electronic intelligence data gathered by aircraft, or aircraft specifically performing that function.

Engineer: A flight engineer; an enlisted man or noncommissioned officer who monitors and maintains aircraft operation in-flight and otherwise aids the air crew.

EOGB: Electro-optical guided bomb.

FAC: Forward air controller, the airborne director of strikes against ground targets; the FAC spots targets and·then helps attacking aircraft locate them.

Fahnestock clip: Perhaps similar to a clipboard mechanism.

Fan Song: A Soviet-built 5A-2 radar system for detecting enemy aircraft; its search energy is converted to an audible signal which can be heard and recognized by its adversary.

FC-47: Humorous designation for the AC-47 or *Puff*, the pre–WW II transport converted to gunship use over Southeast Asia; an *F* designates a fighter aircraft, a *C* a cargo or transport plane, an *A* an attack aircraft.

Feet wet: To begin to fly over water, such as over the Gulf of Tonkin.

Fence, to cross the fence: To fly across the Mekong River into or out of the combat zone.

F-5: The Tiger, a Northrop fighter which saw limited use in Vietnam.

F-4C, F-4D: The McDonnell Phantom, a two-engine jet fighter.

.50 cal., .50s: .50-caliber machine-gun fire; its projectiles are ½ inch in diameter.

51: Channel 51, the radio navigation aid located at Ubon Royal Thai Air Force Base, Thailand.

57s: 57-mm (2.25 inches in diameter) antiaircraft artillery.

Final: Proper aircraft heading, descent rate, air speed, and altitude during runway approach prior to landing, or to a target prior to weapons release.

Firecan(s): Same as Fan Song, but at different frequencies to direct AAA guns.

Fishbed-C, -D: A Soviet-built jet aircraft, the MiG-21.

Fisher, Col. Bernie: Won the Medal of Honor for action in the A Shau Valley on March 10, 1966.

Fives: F-105s.

Flight: Two or more aircraft flying in formation under the command of a flight leader in the number-one aircraft.

Flight leader, or lead: Commander of a flight of aircraft.

Fluid four: A formation of four aircraft just prior to arriving at a target area; flying at the same altitude about 1,500 feet apart laterally, they may vary 500 feet in fore and aft alignment, thus maximizing their electronic jamming capabilities and permitting them to protect each other's tails from enemy aircraft.

FNG: "Fuckin' new guy," a flyer new to combat.

F-111A: The General Dynamics swingwing jet fighter, or Aardvark.

F-105: The Republic Thunderchief, a jet fighter-bomber; also called a *Thud*.

Fox-four, Foxtrot-four: An F-4 fighter.

Foxtrot: The letter *F* in the Air Force phonetic alphabet.

Frag (n. and v.): The scheduled target and tactics for a specific combat mission; to schedule a certain target and tactics.

Frappin': A euphemism for "fucking."

Freebie: A mission flown in combat, but not over North Vietnam. *See* Counter; Credit.

Freedom Fighter(s): The Northrop F-5, designed to be sold to U.S. allies.

Freq: Radio frequency.

FSH: A fighter pilot war cry, often uttered in exasperation; may mean "Fight! Shit! Hate!" which were supposed to be the only essential activities for a genuine fighter pilot; or may mean "Fuckin' shit hot!" which can indicate high praise, great joy, or even ironic contempt.

Funnel: The end of the air-to-air refueling boom is usually funnel-shaped for better aerodynamic stability.

G: A unit of measure equal to the force of gravity times one.

GCI: Ground controlled intercept; an agency which effects aircraft inflight joinups by radar and voice directions.

GE: General Electric, a manufacturer of jet aircraft engines.

Gear: Landing gear.

Gecko: A prolific, ubiquitous Southeast Asian lizard usually three to five inches long which is found on the walls and ceilings of even the best hotels and restaurants; because of its strange cry, it is also called the "Fuck you!" lizard.

GI: U.S. government issue; an American fighting man; also used as an adjective, as in "GI shoes."

Gia Lam: An enemy airfield just north of Hanoi.

GIB: Acronym for "guy in back"; the pilot or navigator who flies in the backseat of the F-105, F-4, or other tandem, two-seat aircraft.

Gibson, Hoot: Commander of the 433rd Tactical Fighter Squadron, or Satan's Angels, of the 8th Tactical Fighter Wing.

Golden BB: A projectile destined by fate since time began to shoot down an American flyer.

Golfballs: CBUs (?).

Gomer: A Viet Cong or North Vietnamese soldier, perhaps from Scots "gomeral," a simpleton, or fool; probably from the simple hero of the U.S. TV show, "Gomer Pyle."

Green Anchor: An air refueling area.

G-suit: An inflatable garment that automatically counters G-pressures on a pilot's body during violent aircraft maneuvers; most G-suits during the Vietnam war went from waist to ankles.

Guard channel: A radio channel used primarily for emergency calls.

Guard pukes: Pilots of the U.S. Air National Guard called to active duty during the War in Vietnam.

Gun: An aerial cannon used for air-to-air combat or strafing.

Gyrene: Slang for a U.S. Marine.

HA: A unit identifier on an aircraft's tail, in this case F-100s from Phu Cat.

Hack: To perform effectively.

Haiphong: North Vietnam's principal port city, 50 NM east of Hanoi on the Gulf of Tonkin.

Hairy: Problematic, or frightening.

Hammer 41: An aircraft radio call sign and identifier.

Hanoi Hanna: A North Vietnamese radio propagandist similar to Axis Sally and Tokyo Rose of WW II.

Hanoi Hilton: American nickname for Hoa Lo Prison, an infamous POW camp in North Vietnam.

Hassling: Practicing air-to-air combat.

Haul ass: To leave as quickly as possible.

Hazard pay: Hazardous duty pay, or *combat pay*.

Hectare: A metric unit of area, equal to 2.47 acres.

HEI: High explosive incendiary.

High drags: Bombs with special fins or other devices to slow their fall.

Hilton: *See* Hanoi Hilton.

Hit the silk: To eject or otherwise bail out of an aircraft.

Ho, Uncle Ho, Ho Chi Minh: Leader of North Vietnam until his death in September, 1969.

Hoa Binh: An enemy airfield 30 NM southwest of Hanoi.

Hoa Lac: An enemy airfield 20 NM west of Hanoi.

Hobo Fifty-One: The radio call sign and identifier of Col. Bernie Fisher's A-1E when he won the Medal of Honor on March 10, 1966.

Ho Chi Minh Trail: A major supply route about 300 miles long just inside and parallel to the western Laotian border; it starts near Vinh in North Vietnam, enters Laos through the Mu Gia Pass, and ends near Kontum in South Vietnam.

Hog: Affectionate name for an aircraft. *See also* Bird; Blue Boar.

Hoi An: A town 40 miles south of Da Nang.

Home drome: The base where a given aircraft is permanently stationed.

Hootch: A hut or building; fighter pilots both live in and attack hootches.

Hose: To shoot automatic weapons or missiles.

Huey: A UH-1, a small U.S. Bell helicopter known for its great maneuverability.

Hundred: One hundred missions over North Vietnam equaled a completed combat tour for a fighter pilot; after the bombing halt of November, 1968, the usual combat tour was one year.

I Corps: A U.S. military command and control area just south of the DMZ, or 17th parallel; South Vietnam was divided from north to south into four areas designated I, II, III, and IV Corps.

INS: An airborne inertial navigation system.

Intruder: The Martin B-57 Canberra, a light U.S. bomber.

Invert: A ground-based, aircraft-radar monitoring agency.

Iron bombs: Conventional bombs, as opposed to napalm, CBUs, high drags, or other specialized ordnance.

Iron hands: Wild Weasels, F-105 aircraft specially equipped to detect and knock out hostile SAM sites.

JCS: U.S. Joint Chiefs of Staff, the highest ranking officers in the U.S. Armed Forces; at the Pentagon they advise the Secretary of Defense and the President, as well as oversee their respective services; also, a JCS-directed mission.

Jinking: Erratic evasive maneuvering of a fighter aircraft after weapon release.

Jock: A pilot; possibly derives from "jockey" or "jockstraps," since those who wear them are usually athletic, manly, and rugged.

Joinup: An airborne maneuver whereby two aircraft join to fly in formation, or for air-to-air refueling.

Jolly, Jolly Giant, Jolly Green Giant: The Sikorsky HH-3E, a large reconnaissance helicopter used to pick up downed American flyers.

JP-4: Aircraft jet fuel.

Jumpsack: Parachute.

Karst: Irregular limestone regions common to Southeast Asia, with sinks, underground streams, and caverns.

Kep, Kep Hay: Enemy airfield 30 NM northeast of Hanoi on the Northeast Railroad to China.

Khe Sanh: A much fought over area 50 miles inland from Hue in South Vietnam.

Khmer Rouge: Cambodian communist armed forces or political party members.

Kirk: An 8th Tactical Fighter Wing MiG fighter in 1967.

Kontum: A town in South Vietnam at the end of the Ho Chi Minh Trail near the 14th parallel.

Korat: A U.S. airbase in northern Thailand about 100 NM northeast of Bangkok, the home of F-4s, F-105s, and other aircraft.

Ladyfingers: 500-pound iron bombs.

Lang Son: An enemy airfield 60 NM north of Haiphong, about 8 NM from the Chinese border on the Northeast Railroad out of Hanoi.

Laos, Laotian: Troubled nation between Thailand and Vietnam into which the war inevitably spread.

Launch light: Indicates the launch of enemy missiles against an aircraft; warns the pilot to maneuver and pray, at the same time, or in that order.

LBJ: Lyndon Baines Johnson, who was president during the war in Vietnam from late 1963 through 1968.

Lead: Leader, or flight leader, the number-one or command aircraft in a formation.

L-5: The Stinson-Vultee Sentinel, a small airborne ambulance used by the U.S. in WW II and in Korea.

LGB: Laser-guided bomb.

Liberator: The B-24, a WW II heavy bomber.

Lifts: Airlifts.

Line: The flightline, where aircraft are parked between missions.

Lion: An agency at Ubon, Thailand, which monitors and controls aircraft arrivals and departures by radar and radio communications; also aids or arranges emergency air-to-air refueling.

Long Binh: A town about 8 NM north of Saigon, the site of a large U.S. Army base.

Looie, or Luey: Slang for "lieutenant."

Lyndon: Lyndon Baines Johnson, U.S. president from late 1963 through 1968.

Mac: *See* McNamara, Robert S.

McConnell Air Force Base, Kansas: A training base near Wichita for Vietnam-bound F-105 crew members.

Mach: The speed of sound.

McNamara, Robert S.: U.S. Secretary of Defense under Presidents Kennedy and Johnson.

Mama: Affectionate name for a U.S. flyer's wife.

Manfield, Mike: U.S. Senate majority leader (D-Mont.) during the Vietnam War who outspokenly opposed presidential policies on Vietnam.

Mao Tse-tung: Powerful Chinese Communist leader during the Vietnam War.

MAP: U.S. Military Assistance Program to specific foreign countries.

Mark 82: A 500-pound iron bomb.

Mateus: A wine popular with U.S. flyers.

Mayday: Traditional radio distress call.

Mekong River: A major river marking the Thai-Laotian border.

MER: An airborne weapons storage and launching rack.

Merlin: An early reciprocating aircraft engine; a V-12 built by Packard and Rolls Royce used in such aircraft as the P-40 and P-51 from World War II through the Korean War.

MIA: Missing in action, an official government classification for a U.S. service member during wartime.

MiG: A Soviet-built series of jet fighters.

MiG Ridge: A place near Hanoi, the site of many downed enemy aircraft.

Mike-mike: Millimeter; e.g., 20 mike-mike refers to a 20-mm gun.

Milk run: A relatively safe combat mission.

Mils, mills: Incremental settings for an airborne weapons delivery sight.

Mini(s): Miniguns, such as on the AC-47 or AC-130.

Misty: An identifier and radio call sign for a U.S. forward air controller.

MK-84: A 2,000 pound iron bomb.

Mobile: An air base ground control facility for monitoring local air traffic.

Montagnards: Vietnamese tribal fighters who were usually loyal to U.S. forces.

Mu Gia Pass: A pass about 60 NM northwest of Dong Hoi, where the Ho Chi Minh Trail enters southern North Vietnam from Laos.

Nakhon Phanom, or NKP: A U.S. air base on the Mekong River near the Thai-Laotian border often used for first recovery of downed U.S. flyers.

Nam Dinh: An enemy airfield 38 NM southwest of Haiphong.

Nape, napes: Napalm; napthene and palmitate, a thickener used in jelling gasoline for air-to-ground incendiary bombs.

Nickel: The Republic F-105 Thunderchief; or the 555th Tactical Fighter Squadron (the "Triple Nickel").

Ninety-four: The F-94, a U.S. nightfighter and interceptor, the Lockheed Starfire.

Ninety-seven: Channel 97, a U.S. radio navigation aid for aircraft use after striking targets in North Vietnam to return to friendly territory in Thailand or South Vietnam.

Nite Owls, Night Owls: The nickname of the 497th Tactical Fighter Squadron of the 8th Tactical Fighter Wing based at Ubon, Thailand; this elite night-flying squadron wore black flying suits and undertook dangerous, often deadly, missions.

Northeast Railroad: Runs for 85 NM from Hanoi to the Chinese border; another 100 NM up the road is the Chinese town of Nan-ning.

North Point: Probably a pilot-coined name for a point of land on the Gulf of Tonkin.

Nozzles: Devices for spraying defoliants in Ranch Hand operations.

Number one: The best in a scale from 1 to 10; a number-ten pilot would be the worst possible.

OAP: Offset aiming point used in radar bombing.

O'clock: Relative position of another aircraft or object to yours; one dead ahead would be at twelve o'clock, one directly behind would be at six, and so on.

O-Club: Officers' Club.

Old heads: Experienced flyers, in contrast to FNGs ("fuckin' new guys").

Olds, Robin: A much-admired WW II ace (12 kills) who commanded the 8th Tactical Fighter Wing at Ubon, Thailand, in 1966–67; he shot down four more hostile aircraft in Vietnam.

100, one hundred missions: *See* hundred.

101: An F-101 fighter-interceptor, the McDonnell Voodoo.

102: An F-102 interceptor, the Convair Delta Dagger.

104: An F-104 fighter-interceptor, the Lockheed Starfighter.

O-1E: A small, single-engine Cessna aircraft used in forward air control.

Ops, Operations: An operational office that directs, schedules, and monitors air combat missions.

Orange: Agent Orange, a powerful defoliant used by the U.S. over Vietnam from 1965 to 1970.

Outboards: The racks farthest out on an aircraft's wings used to carry ordnance or auxiliary fuel tanks.

Overheat light: Warns of an overheating aircraft engine.

OV-10A: *See* Bronco.

Pack, Package, or Route Package: For air combat purposes, North Vietnam was divided into six operational areas from south to north and designated Route Packages One through Six; Pack Six, the Hanoi area, was an extremely dangerous Package.

Package One: The area of North Vietnam extending 60 NM north of the DMZ.

Parole: A French statesman in the late 1960s.

Pass: To dive or lunge at a hostile aircraft; a dive run over a target; over a heavily defended target, the motto was "one pass–haul ass!" which meant to release all the ordnance in one run.

Pathet Lao: Laotian Communist armed forces or political party members.

PC-1: The aircraft primary hydraulic control system.

PDJ: The Plaines des Jarres or Plain of Jarres in Northern Laos.

Pedro: A small helicopter used to monitor landings of battle-damaged U.S. aircraft.

Penetrator: A sharp metal object on the end of a rescue helicopter's cable that can get through the thick jungle foliage to be grasped by a downed flyer.

Per cent: Usually refers to throttle or acceleration speed; e.g., 80 percent of maximum speed available.

Pete: St. Peter, the gatekeeper of Heaven.

Phat Ban, or Ban Phat (Ban Pha Tang): A village in northeast Laos, 30 NM east of Sam Neua.

Phillips Range: A practice gunnery range near McConnell Air Force Base, Kansas.

Phu Cat: U.S. air base on the coast of South Vietnam about 130 NM south of Da Nang.

Phuc Yen: An enemy airfield 15 NM northwest of Hanoi.

Phu Tho: A town and airfield 40 NM northwest of Hanoi in North Vietnam.

Pickle: To push a button to release ordnance.

Pitch Out: A sharp bank to the right or left to position a fighter for landing.

PIO: Public information officer, a liaison between the military and civilian media; a military news reporter or editor.

Pipper: A visual aiming device for delivering ordnance.

Pissed: To become exceedingly angry.

PJ: A parajumper, or paramedic who leaves a rescue helicopter to assist a downed flyer.

Pod: A chamber containing multiple air-to-ground rockets; a container for electronic countermeasures gear effective against radar-directed fighters and missiles; a multiaircraft formation maximizing electronic pod effectiveness.

POL: Petroleum and fuel storage.

P-1, P-2: Pressure gauges for engines nos. 1 and 2.

Poop up: To give information.

Poo-ying, Poo-yeng: A Thai woman.

Pop up: To climb rapidly.

Port of embarkation: U.S. departure point for overseas duty.

POW: Prisoner of war.

Press: To fly below a pre-planned weapon release altitude.

Pucker string: An apocryphal part of the human anatomy which when figuratively pulled causes one's anus to constrict in fear.

Pueblo: A U.S. naval vessel seized by the North Koreans in 1969.

Puff: Nickname for the AC-47 gunship, from the cartoon and song, "Puff the Magic Dragon."

Puke: Synonym for vomit.

Punch, punch out: To eject from an aircraft.

Purple Heart: A U.S. military award to those wounded in combat.

Purple Route: Similar to *Black Route*.

QSY: A command to change radio channels.

Quang Khe: A city in North Vietnam, 40 NM north of the DMZ on the coast of the Gulf of Tonkin.

Quang Tri: A city and airfield in South Vietnam, 15 NM south of the DMZ and 25 NM northwest of Hue on the coast.

Radar: Radio detection and ranging equipment, used in a fighter to detect other aircraft and for ordnance delivery.

Ramp: An air-base flightline for parked aircraft.

Ranch Hands: Crews of U.S. aircraft delivering defoliation chemicals; Ranch Hands sought to open up jungle areas.

Ranch-IN: A play on the word drive-in referring to an Officers' Club frequented by Ranch Hands, or Air Force defoliation crews.

Recce: Air reconnaissance.

R and R: Rest and Rehabilitation leave; military jargon for a vacation away from one's normal place of duty.

Red River, Red River Valley, the Red: A strategically important river and its valley, running from the northwest to southeast across North Vietnam and through Hanoi.

Red River Rat: A title of personal pride for American combat flyers who crossed the Red River in North Vietnam.

Red Route: Similar to *Black Route*.

Regs: Regulations.

Republic bomb, Republic's Ultra Hog: The Republic F-105 Thunderchief.

Ripple: To release bombs in an almost random pattern.

River Kwai Bridge: A famous WW II bridge in Burma.

Robin, Robin Olds: *See* Olds, Robin.

Roger: Means "Yes, I understand and will comply."

Ron: A cape and village in North Vietnam on the Gulf of Tonkin, 50 NM northwest of Dong Hoi.

Round: A single bullet, artillery shell, or ground-to-ground rocket.

Roundeyes: Caucasian women.

Route 1-A: North Vietnam's north-south coastal highway.

RTB: Return to base.

RTU: A replacement training unit which trains air crew members stateside for Southeast Asia or other operational duty throughout the world.

Rumble seat: The backseat in a tandem, two-seat aircraft.

Russell, Bertrand: Famed English philosopher (1872–1970) and activist for peace and nuclear disarmament who in his last years lent his name to an international war crimes tribunal on American activities in Vietnam; he would not have approved of American defoliation efforts in Southeast Asia.

Russian techs: Soviet technical advisors to forces of communist bloc nations, in this case, North Vietnam and the Viet Cong.

Sabre, Sabre jet: The North American F-86 jet fighter famed in air combat over Korea.

SAC: Strategic Air Command, the U.S. Air Force agency responsible for strategic aircraft and missiles.

Sack: Bed.

Safe zone: A relatively safe helicopter pick-up zone for an American flyer downed in hostile territory.

Saigon: The capital of South Vietnam and location of Tan Son Nhut Air Base.

St. Elmo: Saint Elmo's fire, a phenomenon of stormy weather sometimes seen from aircraft or ships.

SAM: A surface-to-air missile directed at opposing aircraft.

SAM break: Evasive action taken to avoid a SAM.

Samlar: A bicycle cab which holds two people uncomfortably; it has three wheels, and the driver, or samlar, pedals in front.

Sam Neua: A city in northeast Laos about 100 NM southwest of Hanoi and 20 NM from the North Vietnamese border.

Sandy: Radio call sign and identifier of an A1-E propeller-driven aircraft most frequently used to suppress enemy groundfire during a rescue operation for a downed American flyer.

SAR: A search and rescue effort to pick up a downed American flyer.

Saravane: A city in south central Laos.

SA-2: A Soviet-made surface-to-air missile; SA-2s were usually placed in rings around a defended target ("a SAM ring").

Scanner: The boom operator of a tanker aircraft such as the

KC-135 who rides on his stomach in the tail; he faces aft and "scans" or looks through a large window.

Scattered to broken: A weather visibility descriptor of cloud coverage over a given area.

Scragg: To make scraggly, or ragged.

Screwhead: A derogatory term for an idiot; a "fuck head."

750: A 750-pound iron bomb.

Seventh Air Force: Headquartered at Tan Son Nhut Air Base near Saigon, it directed all air operations in Southeast Asia.

Shack: A direct hit on a target, usually radar directed.

Shit-hot: As an adjective, it qualifies something as being the very best; as an expletive, it indicates great pleasure.

Short-timing: Early sexual ejaculation of the male; also, being near the end of one's combat tour.

Shrike: The AGM-45 air-to-ground missile designed to home in automatically and destroy an enemy radar installation or missile site; launched by F-105 Wild Weasels, these ten-feet long missiles were highly effective.

Sidewinder: *See* AIM-9.

Silver Dawn East, West: Air Combat operation areas to the extreme west and east in Vietnam; these identifiers were used early in the air war and were dropped probably in mid-1967.

Singhi: A brand of Thai beer especially popular with Americans.

Sioux City, Iowa: Stateside base of an Air National Guard unit stationed at Phu Cat in South Vietnam.

Site: A SAM site or location.

Six: Six o'clock, or behind an aircraft's tail. *See* O'clock.

Six-pack: A six-passenger pickup truck used to transport air crews.

Skoshi: Pidgin-Japanese word meaning "little."

Skyhawk: A U.S. naval aircraft used over Southeast Asia.

Sky Spot: A high altitude, ground-directed bomb drop usually much safer than dive bombing or strafing at lower altitudes.

Slab: The horizontal tail surface of a supersonic jet aircraft.

Slope, Slopehead: A derogatory term for an Asian.

Smoke: A white phosphorus marker used by a forward air controller to indicate a ground target to an attacking fighter plane.

Snivel, to snivel a counter: To inveigle one's way into North Vietnam when not originally scheduled to fly there; a fast-talking fighter pilot would often try to talk controlling agencies into letting him use extra ordnance in North Vietnam when it was not needed elsewhere; thus he could convert a mission which did not count toward ending his tour (a "freebie") toward one which would. *See* Counter; Hundred.

Soft load: An aircraft armed with rockets, cannon, or napalm, rather than with bombs.

Son Tay: A town and POW camp 20 NM west-northwest of Hanoi, the site of the abortive attempt to rescue American POWs on November 20, 1970.

Spare: A ready-to-launch aircraft used to substitute for a scheduled aircraft which is unable to take off, usually because of aircraft or equipment malfunctions.

Sparrow: The AIM-7, a U.S. radar-guided air-to-air missile.

Spectre: An AC-130 Hercules turboprop gunship.

Spin: A deep, spiraling dive, usually uncontrollable.

Split-S: An S-shaped, downward, rolling dive.

Squawked my parrot: To set an airborne emergency signal transmitter on automatic and continuous transmission.

Stab aug: An aircraft's stabilization augmentation system.

Stand down: A period of non-flying because of poor weather, required maintenance, or the like.

Steer: A compass heading to a destination.

Sun Valley: Pilot-coined name for a geographical location, perhaps in eastern Laos.

Super Sabre: A North American F-100 fighter also used as a fast-moving FAC.

Switchblades: Air crews of the F-111A Aardvark, with its variable wings.

TAC departures: Tactical aircraft departing on a combat mission.

Tach: A tachometer, an instrument for reading engine RPMs.

Takhli: A U.S. air base in Thailand 90 NM north of Bangkok.

Tally Ho: An operational area in North Vietnam just north of the DMZ in Route Package One; also, a radio communication indicating that an aircraft has another aircraft or object in sight.

Tan Son Nhut: A large air base just north of Saigon and headquarters of the U.S. Seventh Air Force, which directed the air war over Southeast Asia.

Tay Ninh: A "mountain," 3,234 feet high, 70 NM northwest of Saigon on the Laotian border.

TBC: The toss bomb computer used in the F-105.

Tchepone: A heavily fortified Laotian town on the Ho Chi Minh Trail, 30 NM west of Khe Sanh, or 90 NM west of Hue, which claimed numerous American aircraft.

TDY: A temporary duty assignment.

Tee Luck: English corruption of a Thai word meaning mistress or girlfriend.

Tet: The holiday season of the lunar new year in late January; also, perhaps, a celebration or party.

TFS: Tactical Fighter Squadron; several squadrons make up a Wing.

TFW: Tactical Fighter Wing, composed of several squadrons. *See* Wing.

Thai Binh: A city 20 NM southwest of Haiphong in North Vietnam.

Thai Nguyen: An enemy airfield 35 NM north of Hanoi.

Thanh Hoa: A strategically important large city in North Vietnam 75 NM south of Hanoi.

Thieu, Nguyen Van: President of the Republic of Vietnam (South Vietnam) from 1967 until its defeat by North Vietnam in 1975.

.38: A .38-caliber pistol, official issue to U.S. flyers, usually worn in a shoulder holster.

37s: 37-mm (1.46 inches in diameter) antiaircraft artillery.

Three-sixty: A 360° compass turn, which delays arrival over a target and puts an aircraft back on its original heading.

Thud: A pilot's affectionate name for the F-105.

Thud Ridge: West of Hanoi, a ridge upon which many F-105s crashed.

Thunderchief: Republic's F-105 jet fighter.

Tiger: The Northrop F-5 jet fighter.

Tiger Hound: A combat air operational area in Laos.

TOC: Pronounced "tee-oh-see," the tactical operations center of a fighter wing.

Tonkin: The Gulf of Tonkin on the east coast off North Vietnam, and off South Vietnam just south to Hue or Da Nang.

Tour: A completed combat tour of duty in Southeast Asia for a U.S. flyer; prior to November, 1968, it was 100 missions over North Vietnam; after that date it was normally one year.

Tracers: Incendiary projectiles.

Trail: One behind the other in a straight line, as in "aircraft in trail" or "bombs in trail."

Trash haulers: C-130 cargo aircraft and their crews; the importance of what they carried was frequently called into question by fun-loving fighter pilots.

Triple-A: Antiaircraft artillery.

Tuy Hoa: An American air base in South Vietnam about 70 NM north of Cam Ranh Bay.

Tweat, tweet: A T-37 jet trainer, whose pilots were frequently the objects of jokes by fighter pilots.

20 millimeter: Machine guns with projectiles having a diameter of approximately 0.8 inch.

Two AD: Second Air Division.

Ubon Ratchathani, or simply Ubon: An American air base in southeast Thailand about 250 NM east-northeast of Bangkok, home of the 8th Tactical Fighter Wing, the Wolf Pack.

Up: Operationally active and a threat to American aircraft; e.g., "The SAMs or MiGs were up."

VC: Viet Cong, military supporters of the National Liberation Front; South Vietnamese militant Communists.

Vector: A compass heading to fly.

Victor Charlie: VC in the military phonetic alphabet. *See* VC.

Viet Tri: A hamlet 25 NM northwest of Hanoi with a strategically important bridge across the Red River.

Vinh: An important North Vietnamese coastal city about 150 NM south of Hanoi.

VIP: A very important person.

Viz: Visibility.

Voodoo: A McDonnell F-101 fighter-interceptor.

Vulcan: A high speed, 20-mm Gatling-type airborne cannon.

Wampum: CBUs (?).

Weasel, or Wild Weasel: *See* Iron Hand.

Weird Harold: An imaginary North Vietnamese aircraft ground observer.

Westmoreland: William C. Westmoreland, U.S. army general and overall commander of the war in Southeast Asia from 1964 to 1968.

Willie Pete or Willy Pete: White phosphorus 27-mm rockets used primarily by spotter planes, or FACs, to mark targets for fighter aircraft.

Wing: Consists of several squadrons of approximately 25 aircraft each, plus the men and equipment to support them; the smallest U.S. Air Force unit capable of completely independent air operations.

Wolf Pack: *See* 8th Wing.

Wright, Orville: American aviation pioneer (1871–1948), who together with his brother Wilbur is usually credited with the first U.S. powered flight.

Xuan Son: A small village about 40 miles north of the DMZ in North Vietnam.

Yankee Air Pirate: North Vietnamese English nickname for American flyers in news releases to the world press; the label was later adopted and used with pride by American fighter pilots.

Yazoo: Slang term meaning buttocks.

YGBSM: "You gotta be shittin' me!"; a popular fighter pilot expression of extreme incredulity.

Yen Bai: An enemy airfield 65 NM northwest of Hanoi.

Zapped: To get hit by enemy antiaircraft, missile, or ground fire.

Zort: To shoot or destroy.

ZPU: Enemy automatic small arms fire.

'Zuke: Itazuke Air Force Base, Japan.

Sources and References

Air Force Magazine, May, 1986; April, 1987.

Anders, Greg, ed. "17th Wild Weasel Songbook." 117 songs (unpubl.). Provided by Paul Orf.

Bentley, Logan, ed. "Stovepipe Serenade: A Collection of Flying Songs." 1956 ed. Ardmore Air Force Base, Oklahoma. 62 pp., 115 songs (unpubl.). This edition was prepared after the 1954 limited edition of 75 copies was exhausted; its songs are from World War II through the Korean War, and it has beautiful original illustrations. Provided by Mrs. Charles B. Marshall, Jr.

Durham, James P. ("Bull"). *Songs of S.E.A.* Dur-Don Enterprises, 1970.

"A Fighter Pilot's Hymnal." Bien Hoa, South Vietnam: 3rd Tactical Fighter Wing, 90th Tactical Fighter Squadron. 174 pp., 325 songs (unpubl.). Provided by Garry R. Peters.

Fish, Lydia, contributor. Assorted tapes.

Fordham, Henry, contributor. Tapes and assorted songsheets from the 8th Tactical Fighter Wing, Ubon, Thailand, 1968–69.

Getz, C. W. ("Bill"), ed. *The Wild Blue Yonder: Songs of the Air Force.* San Mateo, Calif.: Redwood Press, 1981. More than 650 songs from World War I through the Vietnam War, with commentary.

Grathwol, John, contributor. Tape with assorted songs from Phu Cat Air Base, South Vietnam, 1968–69.

Hesterum, Vernon D. ("Bud"), contributor. Assorted songsheets.

Jonas, Dick. *FSH Volume I.* Mesilla Park, N.Mex.: Goldust Records, 1969. LP record. 10 original songs. His songs are now available on cassette tapes from Erosonic, Phoenix, Ariz.

————. *FSH Volume II, YGBSM.* Mesilla Park, N.Mex.: Goldust Records, 1971. LP record. 12 original songs.

Lax, Roger, and Frederick Smith. *The Great Song Thesaurus.* New York: Oxford University Press. 1984.

McLean, Alvin, contributor. Assorted songsheets.

McNeil, W. K. "Foreword." In *Folksongs of the American Fighter Pilot in Southeast Asia, 1967–68,* ed. Joseph F. Tuso. Bloomington, Ind.: Folklore Forum Society, 1971.

Pratt, John Clark. *Vietnam Voices: Perspectives on the War Years, 1941–1982.* New York: Penguin, 1984.

Sandburg, Carl. *The American Songbag.* New York: Harcourt Brace, 1927.

Sochurek, Howard. "Air Rescue behind Enemy Lines." *National Geographic* 134, no. 3 (September, 1968): 345–69.

"35th Tactical Fighter Wing Songbook." Phan Rang Air Base, South Vietnam, 1969 (unpubl.). Provided by John Carroll.

Tuso, Joseph F., ed. *Folksongs of the American Fighter Pilot in Southeast Asia, 1967–68. Folklore Forum,* Bibliographic and Special Series no. 7. Bloomington, Ind.: Folklore Forum Society, 1971. 39 pp., 33 songs, all contained in the present volume.

Wallrich, William. *Air Force Songs: Songs and Ballads of the United States Air Force, World War I through Korea.* New York: Duell, Sloan, and Pearce, 1957. 232 pp. with commentary. Provided by Bernard R. Marsh.

"Yankee Air Pirate." Takhli Royal Thai Air Force Base, Thailand: 355th Tactical Fighter Wing. 83 songs (unpubl.). Provided by Bill Craig.

Singing the Vietnam Blues was composed into type on a Compugraphic digital phototypesetter in nine and one-half point Novarese with two and one-half points of spacing between the lines. Permanent Headline was selected for display. The book was designed by Jim Billingsley, typeset by Metricomp, Inc., printed offset by Thomson-Shore, Inc., and bound by John H. Dekker and Sons, Inc. The paper on which this book is printed carries acid-free characteristics for an effective life of at least three hundred years.

TEXAS A&M UNIVERSITY PRESS : COLLEGE STATION